A CHANCE TO DARE:

THE DON BRAGG STORY

by

Don Bragg

with

Patricia Doherty

"A Chance to Dare: The Don Bragg Story" ISBN 1-58939-342-2.

Published 2002 by Virtualbookworm.com Publishing Inc., P.O. Box 9949, College Station, TX , 77842, US. ©2002 Don Bragg and Patricia Doherty. All rights reserved. No part of this publication may be reproduced, stored in a retrieval system, or transmitted in any form or by any means, electronic, mechanical, recording or otherwise, without the prior written permission of Don Bragg and Patricia Doherty.

Manufactured in the United States of America

To my family, especially Theresa,
and to all the kindred spirits along the way.

Acknowledgments

Reconstructing the innumerable details contained in a lifetime, as well as getting it into book form, would have been an impossible task without the help and support of some great people -- Theresa Bragg, Renée Bragg, Al Cantello, Joe Courter, Josh Culbreath, Ira Davis, Sr., Barbara Doherty, Ed.D., Tony Doherty, Gérard Dumas, G. Larry James, Charles L. Jenkins, Ed.D., Gene Kilroy, Don Lewis, Roy Ruth, Special Olympics of Northern California, and all the others who put up with me while I got the story written.

Special thanks are also due Joe Tringali for his painstaking preparation of the photographs.

PART ONE

GENESIS

A test, a trial, a continuous ordeal,
more than often
has an enticing appeal.
Through the span of time
and its complexities,
man continuously challenges
his capabilities.
Through the ever-testing life
that scares,
leading us repetitiously through our nightmares,
what truly makes us stand erect?
'Tis man's pursuit
that gains him respect.

-- "Hunter" by Don Bragg

Chapter One

In the Beginning...

I stood in the Olympic stadium in Rome at the head of the runway, waiting for the wind to die down a little, studying the slender bar resting on the uprights just forty yards away. This would be my final assault on it. If I succeeded, I'd rise to the heights of legendary heroes. Failure would bring instant anonymity.

And still the wind blew, sultry and ragged in my face.

The arena had stilled, but it was impossible to shut out the powerful atmosphere around me, with statues of gladiators and centurions evoking images of battles long past. But all that day under the blistering Roman sun, I'd known that I too was a warrior. So I stood motionless, grasping the staff that had become my weapon, as much as the sword or trident of the gladiator. Fragmented scenes of my quest for unique achievement began to flicker through my mind, like images captured by a camera. I was full of a sense of destiny -- and then I laughed. If Smitty could only see me now!

———————

Situation normal: there I'd be, lying in a puddle, with Smitty sitting on my head, whaling away on me for some dumb thing I'd done. The thing was, Smitty'd get it out of his system in a minute or two. Then we'd take off with the rest of the gang to go mess around behind Weinberg's Furniture Store. I didn't take the chastisement personally: Smitty was a wiry black kid who'd always been the leader of our little gang, and his rules were simple. If you ticked him off, you'd get a shot to the head. If you challenged him, you'd better deliver. I guess that's why I spent so much time flying through the air or crashing into the ground in those days.

My hometown, Penns Grove, was in the wooded marshes near the Delaware River lowlands, west of New Jersey's Pine Barrens. It was a great place to grow up if you wanted to live like Huck Finn, and I sure did. I was the oldest of three: my brother Georgie was two years younger, and our baby sister Diane, or Dietzie, as everybody called her, was two years younger than Georgie. We spent most of our time outdoors, running around and exploring, living wild.

The Braggs were one of the few white families who lived near the mainly black neighborhood of the Cabbage Patch. Year-round there was the stink of cabbage from the nearby fields, and it drove my mom crazy. Us kids didn't care, any more than we cared about the black and white thing. Nobody had time to worry about who was what color: we were all too busy playing every kid game under the sun. There was one miserable constant in all the games, though: the Bragg brothers always came in last. Boy, did I want to be first in something.

Smitty, like the rest of the kids we ran around with, was a little older, faster, and stronger than Georgie and me, street-smart and savvy, too. Whatever those kids did, they had every angle figured, including their probable trajectory if their dads found out. In their way, they embodied the Spartan ethic. For instance, stealing was okay, as long as they didn't get caught. But if they did get caught, they took their medicine stoically. I respected that.

The toughest kids in town, though, were the Gypsies: squatters who lived in a big trailer in what we called the First Woods. I don't remember ever seeing them in school, and they didn't even stay in town all year. We'd go by the woods one day, and the trailer would be gone. A few months later, back it'd be, with the kids hanging around outside, looking like they'd slit your throat as soon as look at you. Their skin was dark, like the people from India, and they seemed pretty mysterious to us. Everybody in our gang gave them a wide berth.

My mom didn't even like the guys in our gang. She always used to say, "You shouldn't be playing with those black kids. They'll get you in trouble." But they were my buddies, the guys I had the most fun with. So of course I just ignored Mom and her nutty rules, especially since they never seemed to apply to Georgie.

I loved my mom, but it drove me crazy the way she babied my brother. He was almost my age, but he could get away with anything. Me, if I screwed up, I'd get kicked in the butt.

One time when we were pretty little, we were up in our room, wrestling around, like brothers do. We got the bright idea to start bouncing on the bed, always fun, and a good way to push Mom's buttons. She was downstairs sweeping the house, and kept yelling up the stairs for us to cut it out. But we were just having too much fun to stop. Finally, Georgie had me by the nose, and when I tried to talk, I sounded like Daffy Duck. We both thought that was so hilarious that our next bounce almost took us to the ceiling, but on the way down we collided with the headboard and plummeted onto the floor. There was an almighty crash, and we heard a kind of strangled quack from the kitchen. The quacking continued, but we could make out the words, "Plaster all over my clean floor!" From the way Mom was honking as she pounded up the stairs, we knew retribution was at hand. She came busting into our room with fire in her eyes, waving a broom.

That was Georgie's cue to dive under me and start yelling. He never got hit: that was my job. He just yelled bloody murder every time the broom landed on me, for dramatic effect. The licking didn't hurt that much: Mom always used the bristles on us. But there was this metal collar on the broom that caught me on the leg and drew blood. It wasn't that bad, but I just sat there on the floor, bawling my eyes out, wailing that my mom had cut my leg off. That got her all weepy, and she ran out of the room crying, "You kids are killing me," the usual mother bullshit. And Georgie never got hit a lick, even though he'd been bouncing as hard as me. All in all, it was great afternoon of family togetherness.

———————

Maybe that's what I liked about my friends: the rules were crystal clear. Everybody dared everybody else to do whatever crazy thing they thought up. If you took the dare and failed, the gang'd get in your face and give you a hard time. If you wouldn't take the dare, though, you were chicken, the worst label to have branded on your butt. At least Georgie and I were game for any stunt the fellows thought up, even though we always got hung out to dry. But I never could stop trying.

That's one quality I know I inherited from my father. He wasn't a quitter. Did I respect my dad? Oh man! He was dedicated, disciplined, a good provider, a hard worker. He never would admit there was something he couldn't do.

His mom had died when his little sister Helen was born, and his dad, my Pop-Pop Bragg, put the kids into Catholic orphanages. They cracked his knuckles for writing left-handed, and for breaking any other of their incomprehensible rules.

The only bright spot for him was the school band. They had a tuba, and since Dad was the only kid who could carry it, he got to play it. He also looked forward to relatives taking him whenever they needed help on their farms. Even back then he was one hell of a worker. He had to milk fifty cows before breakfast, then he'd get on to the heavy chores.

He'd started as a carpenter with Dupont, and eventually got promoted to a job where he covered all of Dupont's pipes with fiberglass. What arms that guy had, knotted with muscle, crisscrossed with veins that bulged like heavy cordage. He didn't hesitate to put those arms to work, either. I can't remember him ever holding down just one job at a time. Even after a full day at Dupont, he'd habitually go off to give a hand adding on a room, repairing a wall, any job for that extra dollar. And sometimes a dollar was all he'd get paid for hours of work.

Now and then he'd get a job down at the Jersey shore, and Georgie and I would go along. We'd sleep on a couch and get away from the awful heat in Penns Grove. It was a fantastic treat for us. We found out later that Dad usually swapped getting paid for the privilege of giving us a little vacation.

Not that he wasn't a fearsome disciplinarian. I remember once Georgie got me in trouble. (But what am I saying? *Once* Georgie got me in trouble? That was his specialty!) Anyway, one night we were having dinner and Dad was talking. But when he wasn't looking, Georgie'd make a face at me. He started with just a twitch, but got bolder real fast. I didn't want to watch him. I knew I'd be the one to catch it when the lid blew off, but I couldn't help it. Dad was looking down at his plate, and I was chewing, mainly peas and stewed tomatoes. Georgie opened his mouth real slow, and stuck his tongue all the way out. I just stared at him: the suspense was killing me. Then he started to roll his eyes and waggle the tongue at me, fast, like some kind of cross-eyed, half-wit serpent. The laugh exploded out of me, spraying the table with half-chewed peas and tomatoes.

Dad didn't have to think about what to do. His arm shot out and bonked me on the side of the face. I sailed off the chair and lay on the floor, holding my cheek and groaning. Dad was giving me a pretty fierce look, but over his shoulder I could see that waggling snake tongue coming at me again. I doubled up, convulsed, still holding my face and moaning in between howls of laughter. Dad got up and stood over me, staring down. I expected to be whacked again, but I didn't try to crawl under the table for cover. I just lay there, cackling like a berserk chicken.

Dad turned to Mom and said solemnly, "Jean, I'm telling you, there's something wrong with this boy." And Georgie sat there looking like a choir boy in church, the little turd.

Despite the occasional walloping, there was never any doubt that Dad was on your side. For instance, I'd always wanted a dog, and when my Uncle Chick said he had a puppy for me, I was in heaven. He said the pup was the runt, but I didn't care. I named him Raggs and I knew he'd be the best dog in the world. But when I finally got the brown and white puppy, his floppy ears were all chewed up, and flies were swarming around his head. Dad took one look at that pathetic pup and grabbed him. He took Raggsie out back and put some axle grease on those mangled ears. That kept the flies off, and finally his ears began to heal. In a way it wasn't such a special thing, it was just Dad being Dad.

I was pretty useless in school, what they called a slow learner. I didn't know what was wrong with me: I kept wanting to read right to left. Once my teacher convinced me I was reading ass-backwards, I tried to concentrate and force myself to start at the left of the page, at the left of the line, every line. I'd sweat with the effort. It was such a relief when it was time for math, the one subject I loved and did well in. Sure I loved it. It gave me a breather from all the damned reading. It only lasted so long, though, and then it was back to left of the page, left of the line, every line.

I looked forward to days when Mom would say, "Donnie, I got something I need you to do. Just forget about school today and come help me." Then maybe I'd go to the store with her and help bring home the groceries. Grocery day loomed large at our house. Sometimes Dad's paycheck didn't stretch so good towards the end of the month, and we'd have to scrounge to get something to eat.

I also liked it when Mom would get a yen to hit the racetrack. Dad would have the car most of the time, and the only way to get to the Garden State Racetrack was to hitch. Mom would bring a big peach basket, turn it over, and sit on it by the side of the road while I did thumb duty, trying to flag down a ride. I kind of liked clowning around, making horns at drivers that wouldn't stop, dancing around. It made Mom laugh sometimes, but then she'd say, "Settle down, Donnie. I don't want to miss the first race."

Antiquing day gave me another chance to ditch school. My mom didn't have a regular job, but she had a passion for antiques. It started as a hobby, but eventually grew into a little business and became her way of helping out.

Mom had big books and catalogs she'd read, and as her expertise and confidence grew, she started going round to farm estate sales and antique stores picking up bargains. I usually went with her to help carry the ladder-back chairs or spinning wheels she'd find. I also learned a lot about antiques, even how to check for marks of authenticity. Soon I could tell whether a pitcher was original-issue Lenox or a set of spoons were Sheffield. That's when I became Mom's spy.

While the owners would be carrying on about how they got stuck with all of poor Aunt Millie's junk, I'd come sidling up to Mom and whisper, "The china dogs are Staffordshire," then slink away. Sometimes Mom could make out like a bandit. And in the process, I even got to like the weird old stuff.

———————

One part of school I didn't mind was getting my first taste of organized sports, especially football. Thing was, I wanted to play quarterback with all my soul, and I couldn't hack it. There was too much to keep track of: the plays, the positions, who was where. So I warmed the bench as the second-string quarterback until I started playing end, which was more like it. I was blocking and catching passes, and doing pretty well at it, though I wasn't spectacular.

School sports had a downside for me, though. During any game I felt this terrifying sense of impending doom every time I played. Basically it was a pride and ego thing. I'd think, "I'd better catch this ball or they're gonna laugh at me."

Kids weren't shy about getting in your face and yelling, "How'd the hell did you miss that pass? It was right in your hands, you dope! What's the matter with you, dumbbell? You blind or something?" That threat of embarrassment and ridicule was the ever-present downside, and getting slaps on the back when I succeeded never quite outweighed the fear.

Chapter Two

Awakening

Saturday was the high point of the week: matinee day at the movies. One red-letter day when I was about eight, the feature starred Johnny Weissmuller as Tarzan. Tarzan leapt off the screen and won me over completely. I'd seen the Tarzan comic books, but they were flat slices of nothing compared to seeing him on the screen. Weissmuller was the first Tarzan I saw, and he was never deposed as King of the Jungle. When we came out of that first movie, us kids were all practicing the Tarzan yell and jumping around. We were just like kids today: "Lookit that guy swinging around in the trees! Lookit that cute chimpanzee. Look! He's gonna ride that elephant. Isn't that neat?"

Besides, Tarzan was a just person, honorable, courageous, a moral guy; and as kids growing up, that was important to us. But I especially loved the physicality of him swinging tree to tree, catching vines, swinging along for miles with the wind blowing in his hair.

Tarzan was a no-nonsense guy, too. He'd never say, "Well, if it's not too cold and the crocodiles have finished eating, maybe we should take a dip." No, he'd say, "Tarzan swim!" And he'd do it. That guy could swim like hell, too, and crocodiles didn't faze him in the least.

It was like the whole Tarzan fantasy was exploding inside me. I'd climbed all kinds of trees as a kid, but now I began to try to get higher, pulling together the courage to try for the highest branches. It was an awful battle, because I'd always had a problem being in any kind of high place, and some of the trees were immense. I remember looking down once and getting dizzy, and feeling the ground rushing up at me like I'd already started to fall. I'd grabbed hold of the branch with my arms and legs, maybe even my teeth, and it was a long time before I could let go. Part of me wanted to get my stupid butt out of that tree and never climb another.

But I wanted to be Tarzan.

I thought about my dilemma. I felt pretty safe if I held on to a branch or vine. And as long as I looked anywhere but down, I avoided that awful dizziness. Okay, I told myself. So don't look down and keep something handy to grab. Hey! I'd figured out how to deal with being afraid. Fear wasn't just some big scary thing that would grab me when I was powerless. It was one more adversary to take on, and I could beat it.

After a few months of watching this guy swinging on vines in the jungle, I decided I had to have a Tarzan swing of my own. It wasn't some kind of weird fixation, but I couldn't get enough of seeing Tarzan swinging around those beautiful trees.

There were big oaks right up by our house that were perfect, but first I had to get a long enough rope. Our house was next to Fineroski's grocery store, and all their cartons and crates arrived tied up with that heavy, hairy twine everybody used back then. So I scavenged pieces of that and tied them to a couple of lengths of old clothesline I dug out of somebody's trash. I coiled it up, threw it over my shoulder, and climbed up to a branch about thirty feet up. That was the scary part, sitting up there figuring out how to tie it to get a good long swing without crashing into anything. Then I shinnied down and dragged the end up to the jump-off point, a crotch on another tree.

I was getting ready to go, when Dad came puffing up the tree after me and gave the rope a tug. "You got six pieces all tied together," he said, with the scowl that usually meant, "No!"

I leaned back hard against my rope. "But Dad, it takes my weight. See?"

He wasn't convinced. "I'd better test it."

Without missing a beat, he grabbed the rope and flung himself off that branch into space, with a bellow that brought everybody running out of the house. They were just in time to see the rope take his full weight and break, dumping him on the ground right in front of them. Mom was sure he'd broken his back, and since Dad was yelping with pain, that's what I thought too. Right away, though, he started scrabbling to his feet, with Mom lifting his shoulders and Georgie and Dietzie hauling away on his arms and me yelling, "You okay, Dad?" My heart started beating again once I knew he was all right, and I called down, "So, Dad! Can I go ahead and swing?"

He kind of swatted one hand at me over his shoulder. "Swing, already," he said, staggering into the house.

I retied the rope and got the end back up to the take-off spot. This was it. I took a deep breath, grabbed the rope above the double knot in the end, and pushed off. I was flying, just like Tarzan. And though the experience was brand new, there was an odd familiarity to it, which I attributed to my hours at the movies.

When the branch sagged under my weight toward the bottom of the swing, I felt a little queasy. But as the arc of my swing came to an end, the branch gave a little kick upwards, and I soared to safety. Luckily, I remembered to throw my left leg around so I'd swing back face first. That way I could see where I was going, and use my feet to fend off inconveniences like castration. Besides, I knew that after Dad's close call, I'd better not get bashed up. If Mom saw one drop of blood, Tarzan would have a real short career.

Once the gang saw me swinging, they all had to try it. From then on, the trees around our house were infested with kids, climbing trees and swinging on improvised ropes, dropping to the ground, and scampering back up the trees like lemurs, ready to try again. Every time there'd be a new Tarzan movie, we'd put up a more challenging swing, and when we'd mastered that, we'd devise yet another. I kept pretty busy collecting the sisal ropes from Fineroski's, but there was always a good supply.

I was also perfecting my own swinging technique. Before long I advanced from simple free swinging to going from one tree crotch to another. I tied up ropes as safety lines to break the momentum of the outward-driving arc. It was a couple of years before I came up with a simpler solution.

The granddaddy of the swings was the last I put up. I tied one end of the rope high in our oak tree, then threw the other end to Georgie up on Fineroski's roof, with the rope stretched out nearly horizontal. This one really separated out the chickens from the rest, and each of my pals scraped up the courage to try it. The only one who had a problem with it was old man Fineroski.

"You crazy kids are going to kill yourselves. What do I say to your mothers, and me with no insurance? Why don't you go home and play nice?"

We'd climb off his roof, but five minutes later we'd be back.

When we were growing up, Georgie was my best friend: he was like my shadow. Yet we two brothers were so different, and I didn't get it. Georgie laughed off everything; I took everything to heart. Nothing seemed to get to him, like life was a total breeze. My feelings were in an uproar a lot of the time.

I controlled my anger, though: I had to. When kids pushed me and called me names, I would have loved to haul off and sock them good. Yet I was too keenly aware that I probably couldn't finish a fight I started. So most of the time I backed down or took the pushing and name-calling, biding my time. I believe most of this anger got channeled into a lunatic willingness to compete in the vain hope that one day I'd come out on top.

The sense of being hurt or betrayed was harder to control, and I frequently burst into tears to my intense mortification. It took me a long time to realize I had to keep a lid on all my feelings.

Control. Rules. I hated even the sounds of the words. And talk about weird! Sometimes it seemed like Mom sat up all night, dreaming up the next day's batch of bizarre regulations. She'd say, "You're going out? Take off those good clothes." But next day, it'd be, "You're going out? Not looking like that, you're not. Put on some nice clothes." So far as I could see, both Mom and her rules were nuts.

Maybe that's another reason I wanted to emulate Tarzan. He could be running around in a loincloth, and nobody told him to change. Or if they did, he could swing off to the next tree and ignore them.

The only rule I really glommed on to growing up was something I heard the doctor say to Dad while he was checking out Dad's chronic stomach problems. "George," he said. "I don't want you trying to hold in those belches. Let 'em out like a man, or they'll be the death of you." Here at last was one rule I could get behind. The logic of it was simple, elegant, and thoroughly male.

About the time I started to be aware of the gulf that could sometimes manifest itself between my brother and me, I began to dream. Or should say I began to remember them. Waking up meant that delicious state of floating from sleep to full consciousness. But I'd always have this nagging feeling that something important had been going on in my head, and that I'd recognize it if I could only remember.

Things became clearer when I was in the woods all alone, swinging, swooping, flying. That's when it hit me why that very first swing seemed familiar. I'd had dreams of doing this. Not exactly swinging, but flying free in the sky, with the wind on me in warm sunlight. Maybe that's why I always felt safe gliding through the air supported by a makeshift rope and unimpressive muscles.

My next experience with dreams was less enjoyable. I sat up in bed one winter morning, all sweaty and panting like I'd been running. This didn't make any sense, because I could see snow falling heavily outside our window, and the room was chilly. Then I remembered my dream. I ran downstairs in my bare feet and found my mom. She was making breakfast, kind of humming.

"Mom, I had this awful dream about Chickie. His whole left side was all torn up." I just blurted it out in one breath and waited.

"Sounds like you had a nightmare. People have them all the time, Donnie. Just forget about it."

I didn't hang around for breakfast. I'd had nightmares where I'd have wild animals chasing me and I'd be running in slow motion, or I'd open a door and find a snake ready to bite me. The dream about Chickie wasn't the same thing at all. I dressed and tore through the snow to my cousin's house, trying to think what I'd say when I got there. Probably Chickie'd answer the door, and I'd tell him about the dream. We'd both have a good laugh, and Aunt Dolly would feed us some pancakes. Then we'd go sledding. Just like every day.

Chickie didn't answer the door, though. Aunt Dolly did, and her mouth looked tight and white around the edges.

"Can Chickie come outside to sled?"

"Chickie got hit by a cab just this morning when he was sledding," she said. "He broke his left leg and his left arm, and there's an awful cut over his left eye. He's lucky he didn't get himself killed."

As she spoke, it was like the dream was flashing by again. The landscape of the shadowy realm of dreams was becoming more defined. I wasn't sure if dreams like this were normal, but my curiosity was definitely aroused. I tried to talk to my friends about it. They didn't mind swapping hair-raising nightmare stories, but they couldn't grasp the idea that the dreams meant something. When I tried to draw some conclusions from my experiences, they'd look at me funny and go play somewhere else.

Something important had happened to me, but I couldn't tell anybody about it. Those kinds of thoughts weren't acceptable to my friends, and I felt myself pull back from them a little. I felt shyer, more awkward, and I found myself watching every word I'd say. I'd already become aware of some degree of alienation from my brother, and now here was something else to make me feel isolated. Yet undeniably, there was a new dimension to my life. I had accessed a place where exciting things happened. I didn't entirely comprehend it, but whole new arenas for adventure were opening in my mind.

That winter I spent a lot of time watching the snow and thinking. It wasn't that odd an activity. Actually, outside of sledding, there wasn't much else that you could do in winter.

Georgie and I did have one absorbing pastime: dreaming up schemes to make some real money. The kids with traps went muskratting, but Georgie and I were still saving our pennies for our first traps. We tried to be patient as we waited for spring. Once it was warm, there'd always be ways to pry cash from tight-clenched fingers.

In those hot Jersey summers, everybody'd go swimming down at the local gravel pit. There were pits all over: places where they'd hauled away most of the gravel, leaving a mammoth depression that would fill with water. We'd stay out there for hours, usually until we'd get crazy with thirst and had to run to somebody's house for a drink. One day I saw dollar signs. We could make lemonade at home and sell it at an obscene price, say ten cents a glass. With a corner on the market, we'd be rich in no time.

It didn't quite work out that way. Georgie, Dietzie, and I made about three gallons of lemonade. We poured it into two huge pitchers, fixed waxed paper over the tops with rubber bands, and figured we were home free. All we had to do was get our product to the gravel pit. So here come the big-time entrepreneurs on the bike. We didn't have a bike basket, so Georgie sat on my handle bars carrying the pitchers. With our rickety card table balanced on one knee and Georgie sitting up front, I couldn't see much. Sometimes the table would start to career off into a gully, so I'd have to grab it with both hands. This shot my steering all to hell. Georgie, on the receiving end of the tree limbs and thorn bushes I ran us into, was also getting drenched with lemonade. Between my jerky steering and running into trees, we only got about a gallon of it to our destination. Little Dietzie did her best to drum up customers, but the lemonade was a little on the sour side. After selling a few puckery glassfuls, we ran out of customers.

And then there was Cowtown. That was a famous South Jersey farmers' market held every Tuesday, where Mom would always go to sell her antiques. We'd go along to help out, but the interminable bartering bored Georgie and me both out of our living skulls. We'd sneak away from Mom's stall to visit the only real reason for Cowtown: the livestock auction. There, every week, a new bunch of horses would whinny their way into our hearts. Georgie and I would wriggle through the crowd, right up to the fence, and pick out our favorites.

We'd collar Dad as soon as he came home. "Buy us some horses, huh, Dad? Please!"

And Dad would throw his arms wide apart. "Horses need a barn. Do you see a barn anywhere?"

We'd shake our heads sadly.

"And feed! That's expensive." Dad was warming to the subject by this time. "Ever hear the expression, *eats like a horse*? Takes money to feed a horse," he'd say, and we'd forget about horses -- for a week or two.

Chapter Three

Discoveries

We'd been in World War II for a while now, so like everybody else we saved bacon grease and tin foil. My dad's job at Dupont was important enough for the war effort that he didn't have to go into the Army, but Uncle Bill McCoy did.

I was real proud when he came home with a Bronze Star and a Silver Star for taking out a German machine gun nest. It was really something: here was a real-live hero like the warriors in the old stories, and he was part of my own family. But I was still glad my dad hadn't gone away to fight.

Even though Dad had been making good wages with extra shift work at Dupont, money still was pretty tight right after the war. We tried our hand scavenging bottles and papers for the junkman, but during the war the town had been picked pretty clean, and we didn't make zip. Only one thing would make a difference: muskrat traps. A lot of guys had lines of traps out in the marshes, and we knew you could make good money at it. South Jersey was one of the largest muskrat producing areas in the world because of the geography, all swampy, with cattails for the muskrats to get fat on.

Of course we thought Dad had no idea of what we were stewing about, but one day he surprised all us kids with muskrat traps. Not the Cadillac safety version, but they were new and shiny, the most wonderful things I'd ever seen. We ran right out to set them. We were in the muskrat business.

Next morning, we took off before the sun was up to check the traps. We were shaking with delight when we saw this fat old muskrat lying in the trap. We snatched it and tore home, waving our prize. Dad was already leaving for work as we came out of the swamp. We yelled, "We got one, Dad, we got one!"

Dad gave us a big thumbs up and said, "All right! I'll see you when I get home."

Right after school we went out to visit our deceased trophy. We stroked his fur and assured each other that this pelt would fetch top dollar. As soon as we heard Dad's car pulling up, we swarmed over and hauled him out of the car.

"Look, Dad. We got a muskrat, right?" and we were standing around, all proud of this.

Dad looked at our prize. He stood there nodding for a minute before he said, "Well, that sure is a big one, but it's not a muskrat. No, this is what we call a sewer rat!"

Georgie and I used to go out together to check our route line of about fifty traps. The swamps we trapped in were in a tidal area, so we had to wait for a low tide to get at the traps. Naturally, half the low tides occurred at night. Georgie had no use for running around the swamps at night in the middle of winter, so I'd tend the traps alone. Sometimes when I'd come back and find him sawing wood I'd yell, "Air raid!" just to see him jump out of bed looking spooked.

I didn't much care for the swamps at night. They were full of blowing mists and noises I couldn't account for. When you were alone and couldn't see more than a yard in any direction, they were eerie and terrifying. I'd be getting twitchy by the time I got back home, but even there I wasn't safe. One night, I'd closed the door and had just put a foot on the stairs when a horrible clanking thunderclap exploded right behind me, like the gates of hell were opening at my elbow. Georgie was pleased to inform me that I covered the fifteen steps upstairs in two frantic bounds. Lazy slug-abed Georgie awake at two AM? Of course: it was pay-back time. He'd strung a bunch of pot lids and kettles on the end of some twine and dangled his collection over the banister. All he had to do was lie in bed, chuckling. As soon as he heard my foot on the lowest step, he cut the twine and timed my subsequent ascent to our bed. The fact that Georgie lived to maturity is a tribute to my self-control and angelic disposition.

It was an unspoken rule that you didn't mess with anybody else's traps, but one morning late in the season we found our traps all banged up and empty. We were walking home in a rotten mood when we saw the Gypsy kids coming through the marsh grass just ahead of us.

Damn! They had to be the ones who'd torn up our traps. Georgie looked at me, and I looked at Georgie. Neither of us was crazy enough to even consider taking on those Gypsies. Not only had we heard they fought with knives, we knew for a fact that they could put curses on you that would turn your privates to mush. So we came to the unspoken conclusion that, just this once, we'd let the whole matter slide.

As soon as it got warm, I was back swinging on the tree by

Fineroski's. It was fun, but I decided it was time to go into the woods and put up a good long rope swing. One morning I was out in the woods in a tremendous oak tree. I was getting the knots just right, when I saw these three Gypsy kids climbing up toward me. My heart skipped a dozen beats. I had nothing but my ropes and a few sticks with me. If they were carrying their knives, I was a goner.

But they didn't have knifing me in mind. They just wanted to see what in hell I was doing, roosting up in that tree. Before too long, they weren't the Gypsy kids any more, just kids who wanted to have some fun. We got the rope tied up and spent the morning swinging and having a ball.

I was better on the swings than my new friends. I could make smoother arcs and could hold on longer. But nobody could hold a candle to those kids on the ground. Merle and Earl were about Georgie's and my age, and Boise was a year or so younger. My brother and I were the only kids in town who'd play with them. We'd fly all over town on our bikes, the five of us. Merle would ride with me, Boise with Georgie. Earl was the lone eagle and rode stubbornly and magnificently alone.

One broiling-hot day we decided to go swimming out at Layton's Lake. It was a three-mile bike trip, but the swimming was fantastic, worth every sweaty minute of pedaling. So off we went. Merle was riding double with me, sitting on a towel folded over the fender. The only road to the lake went by three houses where black families lived, but we didn't know them at all. When we passed the first house, kids started throwing stuff at us, so I just started pedaling faster. Not Earl. He pulled up and yelled, "Who the hell you think you are, you dirty sons of bitches? We'll be back, and you'd better not be here when we do!"

Naturally the kids came for us, and we took off, laughing, and hooting, our bike wheels spitting out a hail of little stones. Boy, did we show them.

On the trip home after our swim we weren't so lucky. The black kids were all lined up by the road, obviously waiting for us. The minute we came in view, they began arming themselves with missiles to hurl our way. Even worse, their number had expanded exponentially during our swim. We coasted to a stop, realizing we'd painted ourselves into a corner. I envisioned growing to a ripe old age right there, frozen to my damned bike, with Merle perched like a gargoyle on the fender.

Earl spat at the ground. "I'm coming, you sons of bitches," he yelled, and took off like a singed cat. I wasn't about to be left behind, so I lit out after him, Georgie and Boise right on my tail. Merle had his feet under mine, and we were double pedaling, choking on the dust Earl's bike was kicking up. I'd swear we hit thirty miles an hour.

Then we were running the gauntlet. I'm not talking about sticks, or a few stones. We were getting all kinds of crap lobbed at us: pieces of concrete the size of frying pans, beer bottles, chunks of metal pipe, real tough stuff. When we got through it I was glad to be alive. But big-mouth Earl had to speak another piece. "Hey, you bastards. Didn't I say we'd be back?" There was a stadium-sized roar from behind us. I ducked down into my shirt and started pedaling like hell, but old Earl just came cruising along easy, with a happy grin on his face. Like I said, the Gypsies were like people from another solar system.

Sometimes we'd go swimming at the closest gravel pit at night. We had this kind of rhyming jive talk we'd use with Earl and them. We'd jump in the water and yell stuff like, "Sara Bootie, Jawbone duty," at the top of our lungs. And eventually all the other kids picked up our patter. Unfortunately, there were a few houses near that gravel pit, and our bloodcurdling shrieks would get to some fusspot sooner or later. When the inevitable cops showed up, Earl would lead us to cover. I could hide with the best of them, but I couldn't melt into stone the way those three Gypsy kids did. So we'd go along, having a great time, then Boomp! The next day, their trailer would be gone.

It was August in 1945, and I was down with one helluva case of flu. My temperature had been hitting a hundred and four degrees for days, when I woke up with a vivid dream fresh in my mind. It was so clear: a stranger was sitting on my chest, and I could barely breathe. He was wearing a funny uniform, and had olive skin and his eyes tilted up at the sides. He seemed to be getting heavier, and I had to fight and claw to get him off me. First thing, when Mom came in with some juice, I told her all about the dream. She didn't exactly listen, but sort of sat there while I talked.

"You have a fever, Donnie," she explained. "People have nightmares when they have fevers." She helped me drink my juice, and that was that.

I slept most of the day, but I woke up when my father came into my room after work.

"Here, you read the comics and maybe you'll feel better," he said, slapping a newspaper down on the bed beside me.

I took one look at the front page and yelled for Mom. She ran in all concerned, like she thought I was going to barf on her clean blanket. The headline said that the war was over, and underneath was a picture of a Japanese general in a funny uniform. I pointed to it. "That's him! The man in my dream." I couldn't get over it, but neither of my parents took what I said seriously. I was just a kid with a fever doing some creative babbling. But I knew what I'd seen. And I had to ask myself, what in hell is happening to me?

———————

It was about that time Dad started his wrestling career. He was fixing a bar at Butch Slater's restaurant, when Butch took a look at my dad's mammoth arms and shoulders and reached the only possible conclusion. "George," he said, "I'm gonna get you into professional wrestling." For me, the revelation was electrifying. My dad, a real professional wrestler! I thought I'd bust a gut with pride, and couldn't wait to tell the guys.

So for a while there, Dad'd wrestle all the circuses and carnivals and fairs, anywhere they could set up an outdoor ring. One night there was a match at the carnival up at the YMCA field, so we all got to go. It was just twilight when we crowded into the bleachers, and I could hardly see the ring. Then they turned on the field lights. All the hair on my arms stood on end: the ring looked like the center of the universe.

Before long, Dad's opponent swaggered into the ring like a tomcat on the prowl: Hennie Hochnell. Though he was powerfully built, he was an inch shorter than my dad. I was sure Dad could take him.

Once the match got under way, though, I almost wished I hadn't come. I cringed every time Hennie socked Dad. He'd had stomach trouble for years, and I was sure Hennie knew it. He just didn't give a damn, and kept jabbing Dad in the belly. The only good part was that Hennie's low blows finally got the crowd on Dad's side, and they cheered him.

By the very end, Dad was hanging onto the ropes, clutching his gut, and I was slouched down in my seat, bawling. I was only a little kid, and I didn't realize both fighters were just trying to give a good show. So there I was, climbing out of the bleachers feeling devastated. Then my friends started coming up to me. I was ready to deck the first one who called my dad a bad name. Did I get a surprise!

"Your dad's got big muscles, doesn't he? He's pretty strong, huh?"

That made me feel a million per cent better. Somehow Dad had given a better account of himself than I'd thought. It was too complicated to sort out right then, so I blew my nose and went off with the gang to check out the rest of the carnival.

———————

Not long after Dad's fight at the YMCA field, the gang was messing around, looking for something new to do. Inevitably, we wandered over behind Weinberg's Furniture Store. Smitty noticed a heap of bamboo rug poles, the kind they used to roll new rugs around. We'd just started fiddling around with the poles when somebody said, "Let's take one of these poles and jump over that ditch." Nobody'd ever tried that, so they looked around for a guinea pig. "You first, Bragg."

So here I was, this skinny, gangly, spidery kind of kid, standing there with that rug pole, wondering what in hell I'd gotten myself into.

My technique was original. I grabbed the pole way up at one end and kind of held it in front of me, with my two fists way up around my nose. The free end of the pole kept waving around all over the place, like a witching rod having a fit.

It took a while, but when I finally got the pole to behave itself, I started running. The ditch was only six or eight feet across, but it looked like the Grand Canyon. I chugged up to the edge, planted the pole, and started to pull myself up. I could feel from the way my muscles responded that it wasn't that different from swinging on a rope. Before I could feel good about that, however, the pole started sinking into the muck at the bottom of the ditch. I had visions of me stuck up on the end of it, hollering for help like somebody's kid sister. Then the pole struck rock, and I had something to push off against. I used every muscle in my body to launch myself. Then I felt my feet land on level ground, not on the treacherous incline or in the ditch itself. I'd made it.

I turned to watch Smitty take his turn. He looked as awkward as I'd felt a minute before. He planted, swung, released, and fell with a splat into the ooze at the bottom of the ditch. He hadn't made it. Wait a sec! He hadn't made it, and I *had*. The guys were shouting, "Way to go, Bragg," and more important, they were razzing Smitty for a change.

I joined in with gusto. "Hey Smitty, whatcha doin' down there? Find any frogs?" He kind of glared at me and told me to shut my face, but he couldn't rain on my parade. A feeling of pride shot through me like electricity. I'd never experienced anything quite like it before, but I was sure enjoying it.

I didn't want to let this new sensation go. I noticed the clothesline strung across our back yard. It was about five feet off the ground, so I said, "Hey Smitty! Let's jump that line." I remember every detail of walking those few feet as we crossed over to our yard. I was sweaty, but a little breeze was kicking up, cooling me off. It was late afternoon, and the trees were making long dark shadows across the grass. When I swung up this time, it felt good. It felt better when I landed unscathed on the other side. Smitty didn't want to be outdone, so he backed way off and charged the line, yelling. I don't want to say he missed, but we all noticed his voice was pitched much higher for the next few days. Of course everybody had to razz Smitty some more, but my mind was elsewhere. I'd found something they couldn't do. Maybe I had the potential to be athletic. This new notion sparked my fire for a long time.

Chapter Four

Growing Up, Stepping Out

Though I wanted a paying job, it was hard for me to stay indoors for long stretches at a time. At age twelve, I found the perfect job making donuts for this Greek guy, George Medios. Although I had to fry them in the store, I'd load them up and take them out to Cowtown and sell them at a stall, so I didn't feel confined at all. There was even time to run over and help Mom with her antiques.

Life was pretty good back then. I was still shy around most people, but I'd acquired some confidence. I was doing my Tarzan thing, and getting better at it. After my crazy pole vault over the ditch, I felt pretty cocky, practically grown up. One day I told Mom I was going to the seven o'clock show up at the movies.

"I don't want you running all over town."

"Mom, it's two blocks away."

"Just the same, I don't want you walking over there."

"I'll ride my bicycle."

"No, somebody'll steal it or tear it apart." She had a point, but I had Raggsie.

"Raggs'll watch it for me." He would too. He'd trot over when we'd go to a show, and he'd lie down beside my bike. Nobody ever touched it, though plenty of other bikes had their chains jerked apart or were swiped outright.

"It's too dark out at nine o'clock when the show gets out."

"I've played out in the dark every summer since I was five."

Her unrelenting illogic thundered on. "That's different: it's cold now."

"I'm twelve; why can't I go? It's the last chance I'll get to see *Sabu the Jungle Boy*." Hell, I was almost a man.

"You can't go, because I'd worry."

It seemed pretty clear that rules were only there to protect the weak or lame-brained. I was damned if I'd be weak, and I didn't need these cockeyed rules.

One day in June I came in from playing to hear some world-shaking news. Our landlord was putting up a Serve-You Electrical Appliance store right where we lived. Since he planned to bulldoze our house, we'd have to move. When I heard this, I was ecstatic. Great! We could live in the woods with the Gypsies and build a house in the biggest oak tree, just like Tarzan. I was ready to pack my loincloth right then, when Mom said, "Do you remember the lot your Uncle Bill bought when he came home from the war? He's gonna let us use it."

I smelled a rat. "What do we need with a big empty lot?"

Then Mom told me the awful truth. She'd talked the landlord into selling us our house for one dollar. All we had to do was move the house to Uncle Bill's lot on Virginia Avenue, about a mile away, and it would be ours.

I didn't hear much after that because I started bellyaching like any twelve-year-old. "I don't have any friends out there. I'm not gonna have any fun."

I remember when she told Dad, he looked startled for a second, then he just said, "Good for you," and went for his tape measure.

The landlord was in a hurry, so as soon as Dad measured the lot he had a backhoe come in and dig the cellar. We put four eight-foot piers of second-hand railroad ties in the cellar as a makeshift foundation. Then Dad hired some professional movers to jack the house up on rollers and move it to the new lot. After they lowered the house onto the piers, Dad put in back steps, attached the water and plumbing, and we were set for the time being.

Next came the fun part. The house was a foot or so off the ground, so Dad had to build the cellar walls up to meet it. First he dug a ditch around the perimeter of the cellar, then filled it with concrete. The cement block walls rested on that. Since he was working double shifts at Dupont the whole time, it took him about six months to finish the job. He was exhausted, but just kept at it without any bitching.

My job was to mix up the mortar with a hoe, then bring him buckets of the mixture as well as the cement blocks. It was hard work for both of us, and for me, mind-numbingly boring.

One day we were slogging along, and some friends came by to see if I could play football. I expected a resounding "No!" from Dad, because I was saving him a lot of legwork. He just stood there for a minute, then he wiped his forehead a couple of times and said, "If it's football, you go on ahead. I can manage by myself." As we were leaving, he stuck his head around a pile of cement blocks and yelled, "But if I find you hanging around the sweet shop in town, I'll kick your ass all the way to Deepwater.

Don swings through the original Tarzanville while Theresa, his future wife, waits on a branch twenty feet from the ground. 1954.

I needn't have worried about being alone at the new house. Not only did I keep seeing my buddies from school, right after we moved I met Alphonse Scioli, who lived close by.

We didn't have any trees up by the new house, but there were all kinds of woods fairly close. When I told Fonzi my plan of putting up swings in the woods, he thought it was the best idea anybody'd ever had. So the three of us, Georgie, Fonzi, and I, would go hiking and exploring until we located a stand of trees that was perfect for Tarzan swings.

Once we started to hang the ropes, I decided it was time to advance to the next stage. We began to install platforms up in the trees so we'd have better places to land. It was then that I discovered the secret of a stable landing, so I dispensed with the safety lines I'd strung in the trees by Fineroski's. It was beautifully simple. All you had to do was pivot as you landed and lean back, letting the rope support your weight until you felt balanced.

Getting rid of the safety ropes added to the feeling of freedom up in the oak canopy. I loved being in the treetops. The breeze that comes to a treetop, it's cleaner, fresher -- there's a different smell. Birds would light on the branch right next to me like I was just part of the tree. Heady stuff for a twelve-year-old.

Word spread about my newest projects, and I always had plenty of company. After I got three platforms in place, we started playing tag in the trees. The game turned hilarious when our friend Dinger was It. He was a fantastic baseball player, but you've never seen anything funnier than Dinger on the end of a rope. We'd be swooping on our ropes all around him while he'd kind of lumber around, crashing into trees, missing us by twenty miles. God, it was fun!

For the first time I had plenty of room for swings, and I finally decided to try to set up ropes so I could swing continuously from tree to tree, just like Tarzan did in the movies. Talk about a fake job! There's no way to do that, unless you preset each rope with the precision of an engineer. I tried a couple of times to swing onto a straight-hanging rope, but I only swayed back and forth like a wound-down pendulum.

So Tarzan didn't really go swinging through the jungle, unless he had his crew of chimpanzees up there setting his ropes ahead of him. Somehow I doubted that. It had to have been trick shots. I was a little disillusioned about that, but the ideal of Tarzan was firmly fixed in my soul. So I kept on setting up swings and platforms, and to hell with the set-up stunts we saw Tarzan performing in the movies.

We kept running our lines of muskrat traps, of course, but once we moved out of town, we tapped into another source of income. The war was over, and scavenging newspapers, bottles, and rags had become lucrative again. We'd haul our loot down Pittman Street to the junkman, and come home with our pockets jingling. Sometimes, though, some of the older black guys would try to take our stuff. One time we were struggling with three of them when a black kid suddenly jumped into the fray on our side, shouting, "Hey you! Don't you be bothering those boys!" He wasn't real big either, just a feisty little sucker a couple of years older than we were.

Our assailants backed off, highly indignant. "Why? What you care if we mess with these skinny white boys?"

Evidently seeing us two scrawny Braggs getting beat up by the three bigger kids offended the newcomer's sense of fair play. "You goin' to the junkman? Okay, I'll go with you so they won't bother you."

His name was James Royal. I'd never met him before, but we became good friends. We'd be back and forth to each other's houses a lot, talking, eating supper, hanging out. Mainly we'd go to his house and listen to a kind of music that was brand new to me. I guess it was just old-time rhythm and blues, but it went to my heart. I fell in love with it, and used to go around singing my version of R&B at the top of my lungs. James played a record of Sister Rosetta Tharpe singing "You Aint Nuthin' but a Houn' Dog" for me three years before Elvis came out with his hit version. But Elvis had nothing on Sister Rosetta. She was my kind of singer.

One time James took Georgie and me to his church for a service, and the results were pretty disastrous. He and his family belonged to what we called the Holy Rollers. Once they got going, they scared the hell out of us, jumping around and shouting. We were only little white Presbyterians, for Pete's sake! But James Royal stayed one of my great friends growing up.

I remember some talk about the Olympics in 1948, but it didn't pique my interest. I was all wrapped up in my Tarzanville, muskratting, horses: kid stuff. The only kind of remark that would have made my ears perk up would have been something like, "Aardvarks will explode if they fart and sneeze simultaneously." They don't, but that was the kind of preposterous notion that captured my interest. What can I say? I was thirteen.

Our eighth-grade graduation exercises were going to be held at the high school, so every day for a week, my whole class crossed the high school athletic field to get to their gym. One day the pole vaulters were out in force, and a bunch of us stopped to rubberneck. Noticing my classmates' admiration for the pole vaulters, I had to comment loudly that I'd vaulted over a ditch and a clothesline with a pole, and that there was nothing to it.

There was dead silence for a second. Then the kids started in. "Sure, Donnie, like we believe you!"

One vaulter looked me over, then handed me a pole. It was bamboo, but the similarity to the pole I'd used before stopped there. This one was old and splintery, and real fat, heavier and longer than what I'd used in Weinberg's back lot. But there was no backing down, with everybody watching. I got myself lined up, hefted the pole skyward, and ran toward the bar, feeling a dozen pairs of critical eyes glued on my every step. Nothing worked right. My street shoes sank into the cinder track, and my legs were heavy as the seven foot bar loomed ahead. I smacked the pole down and started to swing up, but the motion felt sluggish. I teetered, almost upright for a second, before falling over backwards. I thudded onto the ground on my back, the wind knocked out of me. It felt like my spine was trying to climb out of my belly button, but my classmates' laughter hurt worse. I rolled over on one side, away from them, and felt sick. Then I saw a pair of track shoes with spikes, as somebody squatted next to me.

"You all right, kid?"

I managed to sit up as the guy kept talking. "You came at it all wrong. You were gripping the pole at close to eleven feet: no wonder you fell on your butt." He pointed at my spikeless shoes. "If you're not wearing spikes, you need a lot more running room. Why don't you try it again?"

I looked up at him and shook my head. I was done vaulting. He just squatted there looking at me for a second, then glanced over at my classmates who were hee-hawing all over the place at my expense.

"Don't let those jerks bother you. I don't see them trying at all."

That got my attention. He pulled me to my feet and handed the pole back to me. "Actually, you were doing a lot of things right. Come on, one more time, and get those legs going faster."

I marked off about thirty yards and positioned my hands lower down on the pole. I started running, digging in with every bit of strength in my legs. When I set the pole this time, it felt good, not like some unwieldy, alien thing. I pushed off and went feet first over the bar and into the sawdust pit on the ground. I landed straight up without a wobble, completely in control.

My classmates crowded around. They didn't say too much, but the looks of stunned amazement were more eloquent than any words. The best part was that the vaulter, whose name, as I found out later, was Ron

Cochran, came over too. He made a point of asking my name, and promised he'd give it to the track coach. He punched me on the shoulder and walked away, but not before calling back his final benediction. "Don't forget to give your name to Coach Ellis when you start here in September."

I watched him crossing the field, and then I looked up at the crossbar with the blinding sun behind it. Something clicked into place. It was as if a sleeping dragon was stirring, down deep inside me. The funny thing was, I owed its awakening to the compassion of a stranger.

———————

The summer before high school was especially satisfying: I'd finally found a niche, a place where I could excel. I couldn't wait to practice. Out in the woods, I chopped down a couple of saplings and stripped the branches off. I drove in nails to support the crossbar, starting at four feet so Dietzie could join in the fun. When I'd set up this contraption in the back yard with an ancient bamboo fishing pole for the crossbar, I had a pretty fair practice setup.

All three of us Bragg kids spent a lot of time that summer sailing over the bamboo crossbar. I was pretty good, and the two younger Braggs had at least as much talent as their older brother.

It was my dad, though, who really put the icing on the cake. One day he took me to the Inquirer Track Meet in Philadelphia to see Bob Richards jump. I couldn't believe the way Richards did it. All the way up in the stands you could feel his focus and commitment, but he still made it look so effortless. After the meet, Dad dragged me over to meet Bob and asked for an autograph. "For my son here. He's vaulting seven feet already."

I babbled something about wanting to jump as high as he did, and Bob said, "You can do it, you know. You can do anything you want, whatever you set your mind to."

I never forgot those simple, eloquent words, and I was also impressed that he'd take the time to impart them to a green kid.

PART TWO

GETTING HIGH

May our souls sail
Forever, always
On life's ship
Like stowaways

-- "Eternal" by Don Bragg

Chapter Five

Close Calls

L ittle Penns Grove High had a great athletic staff. For the first time in my life, I was receiving instruction from sports professionals, and I ate it up. Jim Devonshire, who'd been a star running back at University of West Virginia, headed the football program. Rudy Baric coached JV football as well as varsity basketball. Rudy was great: if he hadn't sustained a devastating war injury, he surely would have gone on to the pro ranks in basketball.

I was skinny but fast, so Rudy had me playing end. Despite immediately breaking my nose in scrimmage, I fell in love with the game. Hell, snagging a pass was as thrilling as accomplishing a clean jump.

Coach Baric liked to shove the biggest guys on the JV team into a dummy defense so the varsity could run plays. So just a week after I broke my nose, I got pulled out with a bunch of other guys. They ran a wide end sweep, and I went after the guy with the ball. Next thing I know somebody hit me a chop to my knees and drove me straight up in the air. Coming down, I saw stars, and felt this excruciating pain shooting through my left leg. The guy that hit me was Mario Chiacchio, Mott, we called him, not too tall, but powerful. I remember Coach Devonshire came charging up. He grabbed Mott by the shirt and heaved him on the ground. "Don't you ever clip a player like that! You could ruin him for life."

He damned near did.

They took me to the doctor, who figured some cartilage had gotten torn. There wasn't much he could do, so he gave what passed for good advice back then: "Just put heat on the knee, and it'll be all right."

Ten days later I got off the crutches, but I still couldn't walk. I'd go up steps, and the leg felt like it was going out on me. Much as I loved the game, I had to quit the football team. With a broken nose and a torn-up knee to my credit in one week, I thought I'd better stop before I lost any more moving parts.

I missed the team, but I didn't miss the mile and a half walk home after practice. For whatever reason, my legs always pained me once I started training, and I hated that walk. It just plain hurt, every night, every step, with my legs crying for mercy. So in a way the football injury was almost a relief, and not just because the physical demands were grueling. Practice had been consuming every bit of free time I had.

With football out of the picture for the time being, I could tend my muskrat traps. I could also swing in my Tarzanville to my heart's content. During those years, I'd be up at dawn and out in the woods. I had a fool-proof alarm clock: I'd dream myself awake. The dreams of foreboding had been replaced by fantastic nighttime adventures. I spent my sleeping hours swinging or muskratting in rousing dreams of such intensity that they woke me up. It made sense. It was like something inside me was saying, "This is what you want to be doing, so why are you wasting time sleeping? Get up!"

I also started hanging out with another kid from out near Virginia Avenue, Billy Brockenbaugh. Billy vaulted too, and introduced me to the notion of working out with bar bells, a pretty novel idea back then. After school, if we weren't sailing around on the ends of ropes, we'd go over to his back yard and mess around with weights. And gradually, my leg began to improve. I like to think the swinging did it, not the heat compresses my mom chased me around with.

By April, and the start of track season, I was in good enough shape to officially inaugurate my career as a pole vaulter. With the New Jersey winters, we only had track April through June, since most high schools lacked indoor facilities.

There wasn't a lot of sophistication in the coaching we received. Track coach Bill Ellis was a cross-country man, so he'd get all eight beginning vaulters warmed up with a little running, a little stretching, and that was about it. Not that he ignored us. He'd bring me these pole-vaulting books to read, or he'd watch me vault and make suggestions. "Would it help if you pulled this way?" or "Why don't you try kicking a little higher?" He was a good man, and did everything he could to support me.

So between the books and Coach Ellis quietly urging me on, I worked out my crazy style of jumping. It was simple: I jumped upside down. I held the pole so when I was upright I was holding it at my side, and pushed off like you'd push off a stuck canoe with the paddle. I went over the bar feet first, but with my back to the bar. Coach Ellis looked at my form and shook his head, but he kept his peace. He knew it looked screwy, but hell, if it worked . . .

I discovered that what helped me the most was constant repetition, and I developed an appetite for it. It wasn't like football. In football practice, everybody lined up and went through the same dance, whether it was calisthenics or wind sprints at night, with Jim Devonshire barking at your heels. The players were chained to the same unvarying regimen. In pole vaulting, I had my freedom in solitary practice. I also took a sense of power from knowing I could push myself as hard as Coach Devonshire dogged the football team. Harder, maybe. Freshman year I'd started clearing the bar at seven feet and ended up jumping nine foot nine, a freshman record in Salem County.

But as freshman year came to a close I had even more interesting irons in the fire. We'd finally realized that Dad expected Georgie and me to do more than daydream if we really wanted horses. That spring, we must have collected a piece of wood from every new house being built in town, so by summer we'd amassed enough lumber for a modest, shack-like barn, and we looked expectantly at Dad.

He had one last objection. "What about feed?"

We showed him the money we'd saved from muskratting and our trips to the junk man. "And we'll get jobs after school, if that isn't enough. Honest!"

So one glorious Tuesday all three of us kids went with Dad to Cowtown. I knew auctions were a matter of luck, who else was bidding, and so on, so I tried not to get my heart set on any one horse. My eyes wouldn't behave, though, and kept coming back to this sweet dappled-grey mare. So when Dad put the halter rope into my hands, I really wasn't surprised to see the grey mare on the other end. Her name was Belle, and she was fast and wild and beautiful, and I don't know how I'd managed before I got her.

Dietzie was too little for a full-sized horse, so Dad got her a stud pony. The pony wasn't fast, but he had mighty aspirations in other areas. One time we were all riding in the Penns Grove Fourth of July Parade. I was going along, waving to the crowd like Roy Rogers, when I heard all this snorting behind me. I turned around and saw Dietzie standing up in her stirrups and hauling on the reins, while the amorous squirt had his front hooves up on Belle, determined to mount her. I shoved him off, nearly falling on my can, and the crowd howled. My Roy Rogers thing was down the tubes, but man, did the Bragg family ever make a lasting impression on Penns Grove!

Mostly we kept the horses in feed, but a couple of times we ran short. That's when I'd start to sweat. Regular jobs were hard to come by, and ragpicking didn't bring in that much. When the horses started eating their stalls I knew I had to do something, fast.

So I said, "What about old man West's farm? We could borrow a few ears of corn, and he'd never miss them." Georgie got this devious grin on his face, so I knew he was with me. As soon as it was dark, we grabbed a couple of burlap bags and headed out to Westie's. Crafty as foxes, we lay low until the house seemed settled for the night, then we crept across the last field like shadows, heading for the corn crib.

The crib towered over us, piled over eight feet high with fresh corn, with a few more feet of free space under the roof. The whole structure was made of wooden slats, with about an inch between to let air circulate through the corn and keep the mildew down. Scrambling up the slats was easy. When we got up to just below the roof we could see that everything kind of sagged and gaped, and a slat or two was broken. We eased two boards farther apart, wormed our way through the gap, and dropped onto the corn.

We'd only just begun to fill our sacks when a couple of Westie's dogs started barking. Floodlights crackled on all over the farm, and we dove flat onto the corn and lay like corpses. Peering over the edge, we could see Westie and his sons prowling around, brandishing shotguns. The dogs were with them, and they were headed our way. We shrank back behind the corn, and pretty soon we could hear snuffling as the dogs nosed around the base of the crib.

I expected that feeding hungry horses was about to become the least of my problems, but Westie's son Deadbird yelled, "It's just them rats in the corn, Pa."

I thought of the two big Bragg rats hiding in the corn, and I started to grin. Then something moved in the corn right in front of us. I nearly screamed, but bit my lip in time. There sure were rats in the corn, and the big granddaddy rat was coming up to us to say howdy. Georgie looked like he wanted to yell and bolt, too, but we managed to keep perfectly still. Brother Rat crept closer, so we seized the only available defense. We began spitting at him. He kind of sat up and looked at us, his whiskers going like antennae, but he was clearly unimpressed. I wanted to hawk up a nice juicy lung oyster, and nail him with that. But then we'd be having an interesting discussion with guys toting shotguns. So we just lay there spraying spit around, like a couple of sissy cats. I could have kissed Deadbird's ugly beak when I heard him call in the dogs.

When the lights finally went off, Georgie and I lobbed ears of corn at the rat, and he ambled off to tend to other business. The two Bragg varmints were both kind of shaky, and only threw a few ears in our sacks before hot-footing the hell out of there. The horses had a good meal that night, so that was all right. But I never tried anything like that again.

———————

Dad could see that Dietzie, Georgie, and I were enthralled by the horses. Riding also kept us outdoors and out of trouble, so he decided to make a little money with it. He began acquiring more horses and eventually started a riding academy, renting out horses by the hour. The next step was natural: why not have a rodeo? If we made the chutes, stalls, and bleachers ourselves it wouldn't cost too much.

When the livestock arrived, I decided I had to give bull riding a try. With their long floppy ears, the Brahma bulls reminded me of big bunnies, and I convinced myself that riding one would be a stroll in the park. I should have found some manure to shovel instead. Another guy decided to take a test drive ahead of me, and I climbed up on the chute to watch, impatient for my turn. I didn't have to wait long, because the guy was airborne after one jump. The bull was waiting for him when he hit the ground. I watched, frozen in horror, as the big-humped beast gleefully shoved a horn into the man's groin as he lay half-stunned in the dirt.

There was blood all over the place when they carried him off. I heard somebody say cheerfully, "Well, at least he's got one left." I might have been slow on the uptake at school, but this data went right to where I lived. My legs clamped together, and I had to pry them apart to climb down onto the creature. I knew I'd underestimated this animal.

He was no bunny. He was two miles wide; he had flanks of corrugated iron; and fiery brimstone poured from his nostrils. I was ready to forget the whole thing, but determined men had already tied my hand into a rope around the bull. The rope was so tight, I couldn't move my hand. I told them so, but they just grinned. "Hell, son, we can't have you losing the cinch." Right about then, losing the damned rope sounded just fine. But it was too late to back out. I wrapped my legs around my new friend and yelled in a shaky voice, stammering with terror, "Okay, turn him loose."

Now the rope didn't seem half tight enough. After the first explosive leap out of the chute, this horned fiend promptly stood on his head. When my ears passed between his horns, I decided things could only go downhill from there. I jumped clear and lit out for the fence, the Brahma in hot pursuit.

My hind end had one word for me: Incoming!

Boy, did I tuck in my butt. This was probably the first foot race in history where a runner's behind crossed the finish line ahead of his knees. I reached that beautiful ten-foot fence, grabbed hold with both hands, and, with irreproachable form, swung over it.

Dad watched his firstborn head for the horizon in a cloud of dust, and was quoted as saying proudly, "Yup, my boy's a vaulter. Did you see the way he cleared that fence?"

———————

It was in sophomore year when I began to feel an increased strengthening of my arms. Not that I got huge biceps: I still looked pretty scrawny. It was a kind of wiry tendon-ligament strength, inherited from Dad, potentiated by my hours in Tarzanville. As this new strength became apparent, it translated into more security and height in my vaults. About that time I started to arm-wrestle, and I was surprisingly good at it. I was beating guys I thought were much stronger than me, and I couldn't believe it. It was sort of a guy thing, who's got the strongest arm. Maybe I shouldn't say a guy thing, but it's just that I didn't remember any girls arm-wrestling back then.

Sophomore year I experienced a true rite of passage. Georgie and I had been playing pool at the Y, when this guy started flicking the balls all over the table. One thing led to another, and we ended up outside trading punches. I more than held my own, and the guy even steered clear of me at school after that. All of a sudden I realized I'd won a fight. And it felt damned good.

My vaulting continued to improve, but I had to wonder why I wasn't going higher. I began practicing longer hours, past the time allotted. It was standard procedure to lock up the vaulting standards when we were done, but Coach Ellis let me keep out a pair to continue working. When I was done, I'd chain them to a tree, with a little padlock keeping them secure till the next day. I appreciated Coach's support, but even more significant for me was the backing I received from Dad.

We never had any cozy father-son chats that I remember. Dad just didn't talk too much. But if I -- if any of us -- had a problem, especially if it was keeping us from something we loved to do, he was right there to help. Maybe it was because he'd never had a chance to do sports himself, and he wanted me to have more than a damned tuba to lug around.

When I was trying to jump higher than ten feet, I'd come home all banged up because the high school pole vaulting pits were lined with tight-packed saw dust, hard as rocky ground.

Typically, Dad didn't discuss it with me. He just came home one day with this ancient wooden station wagon he'd bought. It ran well, but the wood in the upper sections was rotting. At first we thought Dad had been taken by a sharpster, but he had a plan. He took off the back, from the front seat to the rear bumper, leaving a two-foot high partition along the sides and back. Next, he replaced and varnished all the remaining wood. That left us with a comfortable front seat partnered to a railed section in the rear similar to the back of a pick-up, but low-slung and sleek.

A kind of funny thing happened because of that car. A picture of the converted wagon got in the papers, and eventually a rep from one of the auto companies came by, making sketches and asking questions. A few years later they started marketing the El Rancho and the El Camino.

But whether that was coincidence or not, the wagon surely fulfilled its purpose. It conveyed pillow-soft sawdust to cushion the vaulting pits at track meets. It worked this way. When everybody'd jumped ten feet and they raised the bar, we'd march in with our sacks of sawdust and pour them into the pit. The additional layers not only made the landings bearable, but relaxed me, since I no longer tensed in anticipation of the bone-jarring impact into the hard-packed pit. But I was still dissatisfied with my overall vaulting progress. I wanted to float higher and higher as the crossbar moved toward the top of the standards, and I just couldn't make it happen.

Summer was a welcome respite from the grind of school, and I looked forward to a couple of carefree months before starting Junior year. It didn't work out that way.

One humid Tuesday afternoon, the whole family was out at Cowtown. Mom was selling her antiques, and Dad was with her, sipping his ever-present glass of milk. Mom was laughing at something he'd just said when Dad dropped the milk, clutched his gut, and keeled over on the ground. All he'd say was that his stomach hurt terribly. Everybody was yelling and running around, but Mom stayed real cool. She had Georgie and me help Dad into the car then she drove him over to Our Lady of Lourdes Hospital in Camden, New Jersey. They took one look at Dad and said, "Take him home; he's only got indigestion." That's when Mom went into her banshee act.

"I am not taking him home. He let me bring him to this hospital, and that proves he's dying. You call my doctor! We're not leaving here till he sees my husband."

By the time the doctor got there, my dad didn't look too good, all pale and strained in the face. This doctor quickly diagnosed the problem as a perforated ulcer and told the nurse to prep Dad for surgery. It was almost four hours since the ulcer had burst, and the poison going through his system all that time! If my mom hadn't insisted that the doctor come in, my dad would have died. Dad dying: it was like somebody took my world and gave it a good shake. What would happen if we lost Dad?

Before they wheeled him into the operating room this bald man wearing a white collar on top of what looked like a long black cloak swooped into Dad's room. The nurse told us the priest was going to give

Dad the Last Rites, and she shooed us out. We kind of hung around outside the door, though, and boy, did I get an earful.

Now we went to the Presbyterian church sometimes, but Dad was raised Catholic. Mom had been married before, and had gotten divorced. The priests didn't like that, so they threw Dad out of their church. Excommunicated, the word was. So now they've got hoses running in and out of my dad, and he's full of drugs, and this priest is saying in a loud voice, "I can't give you absolution unless you renounce your wife and family because you've been living in sin. Do you renounce them?"

And Dad made this real weak, "Yes."

What the hell kind of religion was this? I asked my mom what was going on, and she said, "Honey, your dad's afraid he's dying, and he wants to be blessed because he's been living in mortal sin. They won't bless him unless he says what they want. Don't hold it against him."

How could I hold it against my dad, all drugged up with tubes up his nose? The priest was the one giving me a problem. A little later he came marching out of my dad's room. He didn't even look at us. And Mom was there crying and all.

Dad was one tough dude, though. Not only did he make it through that surgery, he came through the next operation three months later. That one took out most of his stomach, but he gradually worked his way back to normal. He didn't leave the family like the priest wanted, either.

We weren't brought up real religious, but I know right from wrong, and what that priest tried to make my dad do was wrong. I think right then I got a little twist against religion that never left me.

Chapter Six

Changing Goals

School had really started to get to me: all I seemed to be doing was marking time until track season. I sweated blood to keep up with my classes, and frantically memorized everybody's recitations in case I got called on. My grades were so bad they told me I had to pull a B in algebra to continue to stay on the track team. In addition to coaching track, Coach Ellis also taught algebra, and he was the one who gave me the big exam. We were coming up on the Tri-County and State Championships, the important part of the track and field season. So the whole time I was taking the test, Coach was sitting up at his desk watching me and kind of twitching. He wondered how I was doing, of course, but he never tried to help me along. He wouldn't: Coach Ellis was a strongly moral guy.

Math was my best subject, so I passed the test with an A. The principal was furious. She came running in after class saying, "You obviously gave him an A because he's a track star."

Coach Ellis looked disgusted. "Then test him yourself," he said.

So I had to take another algebra test, a real toughie, and I still pulled a strong B. I thought the principal was going to froth at the mouth. She was convinced I'd done it with mirrors, but she'd watched me take the test and knew I couldn't have cheated. I think it just about killed her.

During the 1952 track season I was jumping around 11'9", and started getting some attention in the local news, including write-ups in the Wilmington, Delaware, paper. I was still using the peculiar style I'd developed. Coach Ellis caught some flack when one headline read, "Unorthodox pole vaulter breaks record." But since my wacko form was getting results, he continued to leave it alone.

I was still using the old stinky bamboo pole, too. We did have a choice: fat aluminum poles you couldn't grip or bamboo battering rams. The aluminum poles, however, weren't finessed. They were crude, way too thick, with a diameter of about two inches, the size of a rolling pin. Not only were they hard to hold on to, they had practically no give. And though the aluminum poles were touted as being lighter, they weren't all that light. We ended up using the awkward knotty bamboo pole even though the joints bashed all hell out of our hands. It was frustrating, because I knew I could go higher, but I couldn't make it happen. There might as well have been a brick ceiling between me and that twelve-foot mark.

Winning meets was thrilling, but it had a sour side. For the first time I got the impression that some of my classmates were jealous, a little envious of me. When I started breaking some Tri-County records, they didn't acknowledge it, but talked all around my accomplishment, as if it hadn't happened. In that way track was very different from football, where the whole school seemed proud of the entire team for the most marginal victory. I still hung out with a couple of the vaulters, Billy Brockenbaugh from the neighborhood, and a white kid, Tommy Belitza. Tommy was a tremendously talented vaulter, but junior year he opted for baseball, in the same time slot as track. I was feeling isolated, but not lonely. I guess I considered myself good company.

That summer we started going out to Centerton Lake Park, where there was a nice lake below a little dam. There were trees growing out of the dam, with jutting branches thrust out over the lake below. I climbed one of those trees, steadied myself, and looked down. The water looked shimmery and far away. I still had that sickening, dizzy sensation and fear of falling, but I fought it as I stared down at the lake. I wanted to face the demon and hurl myself into the still water in a perfect dive. I edged farther out on the limb, found a balance point, released my death grip on the branch, and held both arms out in front of me. I looked down again, measuring the angle my body would take. The fellows started to yell up at me not to dive, that there were sticks in the water.

I grabbed hold again. I knew there could be a difference between being chicken and being careful. My friend Bobby McGinty had recently tried a dive off the eight-foot cliff at the gravel pit, something we'd all done a million times. But that had been a drought year, and the water level was lower than usual. Because nobody'd checked the depth, Bobby spent the rest of his life in a wheel chair, the result of a broken neck.

I climbed carefully down from the tree, to the relief of my friends, and immediately jumped in the water. After a couple of dives, I found out what I needed to know: the water was just about deep enough, and there were no hidden hazards.

I hauled out of the water and started back up the tree. I'd have to turn just as I hit the water so my shoulder, not my neck, would absorb the impact, but I knew I could do it. Back up on my perch, I balanced for a bare second, then dove, the air icy on my wet skin. I'd never experienced anything like it. I dragged the demon down with me into the pool and left it there. It would never return to me in its former strength, and I knew it.

In the fall I started playing football again, and this time out I played really well. I had a talent for glomming onto passes and hanging onto them like grim death, so I was back at end. I got a kick out of succeeding, and was happy when I qualified as an All-State candidate.

It was through playing football and basketball that year that I was finally inducted into the warrior brotherhood. It was close to the same feeling of belonging I'd experienced in Smitty's little gang. Now, however, I was an equal among fellow warriors. We hung out together, we stuck up for each other.

It was this close rapport that finally compelled me to face down my own emotions. When we went into the locker room, everybody'd dump their books on a wide window sill and pick them up after practice. I always tried to get my homework done before last period, and I'd tuck it into my book for safekeeping. There was no problem with this until somebody started knocking the books off the sill. A couple of times my homework got messed up, which really pissed me off. So I started keeping my eyes open. One day I checked to see how the books were doing, and they were fine. Elio Chiacchio, Mott's brother, came in a minute later, and I checked again. The books were all over the floor. So I said, "Elio, why in hell did you throw everybody's books all over?"

Elio came at me with a bellow, and we both started swinging. The rest of the team had to break us up. Of course Elio forgot about the fight the minute it was over, but I tore into the boy's room. I locked myself in the stall and began to cry. How could my teammate that I blocked for and protected on the field go after me like I was some stranger?

When I calmed down it was like I was able to get outside myself and look at my situation. I was a mess, huddled in the john, sobbing, blowing my nose, at the mercy of my feelings. It struck me that during my tearful outburst, emotion controlled me as surely as somebody holding me in a headlock. I didn't like the feeling of vulnerability, of being laid wide open against my will. For the first time I became determined to see that didn't happen again.

The Korean war was going on all during high school, but I barely noticed. I was too preoccupied with living and surviving my own little war. I had my parents' goal of college hanging over my head, and it felt like a threat. I wondered how I'd survive it. Early on in my high school career, the principal had told my mom, "Jean, I wouldn't even think about sending him to college. Academically he just can't hack it."

I agreed with the woman. I was an idiot. I had the mechanics of reading down pat, but retaining what I'd read was a battle. I'd read a book and try to get something out of it, but two minutes later I'd be sitting there wondering what in hell I'd read. It was as if I was looking at the words through a sheet of clear ice. I could see them: I just couldn't get at them.

Another thing: I knew I wanted to learn, but what I thought was important was never what the teachers had in mind. Maybe I'm rationalizing my failure, but honestly, using the right tense or remembering dates for battles just didn't matter to me. Communication mattered. Like I'd read a story about, say, Christopher Columbus. And I'd think: boy, it sure was hard to get everything together, the money, the ships, the commitment from the queen. And I'd think about how hard it was for the men, eating rats, ready to throw Columbus overboard, and then somebody yells, "Land ho!"

Those were the things that stuck in my mind. But I never remembered how many people were on each boat or the names of the Rinta, the Niner, and the Santa Anita, or what ever the hell it was. It was just my bad luck that kind of stuff was all the teacher was interested in. Like I said, I was an idiot.

Vaulting, however was better than ever. The school never had a humongous athletics budget, but they managed to find me a new pole. It was a beauty, aluminum alloy, with nickel and copper added to give it flexibility and strength. Slender and easier to grip than its predecessors, it gave a little when you slammed it into the box. So there wasn't the same nerve-jarring impact you'd get with the fat bamboo pole. Using it was a revelation, and I began to attain the heights that had been out of my reach before. So I broke through that brick ceiling senior year.

In addition, I received an unexpected bonus from Tarzanville. About the time I got the new pole, my upper body began to develop an impressive muscularity that translated to an ease in vaulting I'd never imagined possible. It occurred to me that I might be the best high school vaulter in the country, and it felt pretty good. Then I read in *Track and Field News* that Ronnie Morris in California was jumping higher. So I wasn't top dog, and that pissed me off. I thought, if I could just meet this guy heads up!

One day I was by myself after track, working at just above thirteen feet, when Coach Devonshire came off the field with the baseball team. He stopped by the vaulting pad and asked me, "How high is that, Bragg?"

"Thirteen feet."

"What are the best vaulters in the country jumping?"

I bumped the bar up to fifteen feet, and Coach's eyebrows shot up. "Could you ever jump that?"

I though a minute. "Yeah, I can."

He got this funny look on his face, half solemn, half excited. "If you can jump that, you could probably make an Olympic team someday."

The Olympics? The idea kind of sparked. In '52 everybody was excited about the coming Olympics, and you're dreaming, hey, wouldn't it be something to win a gold medal at the Olympics? When I was jumping nine foot, ten foot, it'd occurred to me: how could I make the Olympics where they're jumping fourteen-six, almost five feet higher than my best jump? With this new pole, a couple more feet was conceivable. Damn right, I could do it. An Olympic medal might well be within striking distance. Not yet a goal, but not out of the question any more.

I couldn't wait to tell Dad about this, but that night he and Mom had a row. The ulcer surgery had enabled Dad to have a drink or two without severe abdominal pain, but that night he really overdid it. The sounds of battle must have reached all the way to Wilmington. This only occurred now and then, so I didn't think much about Dad's drinking. But it was to affect me mightily within a few years.

———————

It didn't take me long to get my vaults over thirteen feet, and I couldn't wait to meet Ronnie Morris, still the leading high school vaulter. I kind of envied him being out in California where they had such terrific facilities and could practice almost year round.

One of the high points in track and field had to be the Penn Relays, with a third of the contestants picked from high schools in the Philadelphia area. The Penn Relays and the Drake Relays in Kansas were the two places where top-ranking high school athletes could strut their stuff in direct competition with the best athletes in the country. I made the cut for the School Boy Invitational pole vault at the Relays, and I was tickled pink.

When we got there, everybody was talking about the junior at mighty Overbrook High who was breaking all of Ira Davis's old basketball records. Of course we had to go over to see this new kid on the block compete in the high jump and mile relay. He was amazing to watch. He looked about seven feet tall, and he went around the track like a giant gazelle. I'd never seen anything like it, so I made a point of remembering his name: Wilt Chamberlain.

In my own event I managed to jump thirteen foot six and a half inches, my best mark so far, and I felt pretty good about it. There was just one problem. My number one nemesis from California, Ronnie

Morris, had jumped thirteen foot ten at some West Coast meet, and he wasn't about to go away. Damn! I wanted to go head to head with this guy so bad I could taste it.

———————

After the Penn Relays, I had to do some serious thinking about my future. I was one of the best high school pole vaulters in the country, and I was proud of that achievement. Nonetheless, I felt I'd come to the end of a very good run. Of course Coach Devonshire was determined to get me into college. He said, "If that boy doesn't get a scholarship in track, I can get him a full ride for football at West Virginia. He can catch a football with the best of 'em." Somebody else said I could surely get a partial scholarship from Temple.

Me? I had mountain-sized doubts.

I didn't see how in hell I could handle four years of collegiate academics when high school had been such a grind. In fact, I knew I couldn't, but it was a gut-wrenching decision. It wasn't the idea of academic failure that bothered me. Not succeeding in an area imposed by others, even though it was for my good and well-being, mattered not at all. It was knowing I'd never succeed as an athlete that tore me up inside. Without college, I'd be giving up serious athletic competition, certainly any Olympic aspirations. I told myself I could always compete for the Shanahan Catholic Club where you didn't have to be a collegian, but I knew deep down that my career as a premier pole vaulter would be over.

Late that spring I told my folks that I just didn't see the point of struggling with school for another four years. It was no big deal. I could just go get a job like everybody else. Dad couldn't conceive of my having scholarships worth a lot of money and not taking advantage of them. There'd even been offers from Penn State and Villanova. But I'd made up my mind.

A few days later Mom and Dad said that since I'd be needing a job, I should talk to my Uncle Chick about working out at his pig farm. "Be a chance to learn the pig business from the ground up." That didn't sound too bad: at least I'd be outdoors. So that's where I went the next Saturday to try my hand with the pigs.

Uncle Chick seemed kind of preoccupied and busy, and didn't train me or anything. He just sort of said "Hey, Donnie!" and handed me this pair of high boots. "You can start by feeding the pigs."

I'd fed dogs and horses, and I figured I knew how to feed animals. But pigs are a breed apart, and no good pigman would just put corn in a trough and expect them to eat it. No, he's gotta get a ton or two of garbage fermenting, then jump into the mess and stir it up good.

Uncle Chick went off to do something else and left me alone with the pigs. I took a deep breath and climbed into a vat of muck with an unbelievable stench. This would be my new life, shoveling swill to the swine. It wasn't too bad as long as I breathed through my mouth, but after a while I could have sworn I was tasting the slop. I tried to stop breathing all together.

About that time, I noticed my left foot was feeling mighty damp. Damned if there wasn't a hole right in the boot sole, and the sensation of rising moisture was the sewage inching up my leg. I wondered if I could get a different pair of boots, but nobody was around, and besides, the damage was already done. All I could do was keep slopping.

Then I noticed something lumpy on my shovel. It looked like a dead possum. I swallowed hard and tossed it to the pigs. It was just protein, after all. The next lump was a double: one dead rat plus two legs attached to a hairless tail. That's when I started gagging, but the pigs squealed with delight at the succulent hors d'oeuvres.

It seemed like swilling the hogs took about three hundred years, but finally Uncle Chick comes out, grinning, telling me what a fine worker I was. I expected a break, but he dragged me off to another pen. I went hobbling after him, squelching and stinking, my leaky boot dragging with its load of God only knew what.

"See these pigs?" he said. "You herd half of 'em into this pen over here. Then get the rest into the smaller one over there. Got it?"

I got it, but the pigs didn't. Maybe I still smelled too clean for them, because wherever I went, they scattered, squealing and kicking up muck. I wasn't about to be outdone by a few pigs, so I tried to wrestle them into submission. Trouble was, the damned things were round and smooth, like immense pumpkins, and the only place you could grab 'em was by the tail. And boy, did they have a defense against that. Grab a porker by the tail, and he can break wind and drop a load in your hand before you can spit. By the time I had the damned pigs sorted out, I stank worse than the slop yard. And no wonder. I had pig shit way down inside my shirt and dripping off my eyebrows. I stared at the sky in despair. Why wasn't it nighttime yet?

Then I heard this voice booming at me. "The pigs need their bedding laid down," said the evil man I used to call Uncle Chick. "Scatter that heap of straw nice and thick so they'll be warm tonight. And Donnie," he said, poking me in the ribs, "you're doing great."

So now I had to make up cozy beds for the bloody oinkers. Well, I could manage that, as long as Uncle Chick didn't expect me to tuck them in and kiss them goodnight. I got busy with my pitchfork, and started scattering that straw. The sooner I was finished, the sooner I could go home. I was just about done when I heard a horrible wailing shriek. Right there on the end of my pitchfork, impaled on the tines, was a rat, screaming in pain. I bashed him against a fence post and put him out of his misery, but I couldn't put me out of mine. I just stood there, my guts in an uproar, hanging on to that pitchfork, grieving over a damned sewer rat. I thought I was really losing it.

Uncle Chick came over about then and began pounding me on the back. "Donnie, you've been great. I can see you have a real future in pig farming. Now go home and get some sleep. We've got an even bigger day planned for you tomorrow."

I don't remember for sure how I got home. They say there's always light at the end of the tunnel, but it was pitch black in the one I was crawling through. There was no light at all because some big-assed pig was in there with me, blocking the exit, backing up so he could take a dump on my head.

When I did get home, I was filthy and bone-tired, but I went and found Mom and Dad first thing. I had something to say.

"Hi, guys. Guess what? I'm going to college."

———

A couple of days after high school graduation I packed my bag and went over to Penn State to check the place out. As soon as Dad dropped me off I felt overwhelmed. The campus was huge, and over six hours from home. Coach Warner took me under his wing right away and started introducing me around. At the frat house where I was staying, he called over an immense black guy. "Rosie," he said, "meet Don Bragg. Don, Rosie Grier. Big Rosie's a shot-putter." Rosie was friendly, and so were the other guys I met, and the prospect of Penn State suddenly seemed less daunting.

I hadn't come to Penn State just to look around, though. The big carrot Coach Warner stuck under my nose was a chance go along with the Penn State team to compete at the National Amateur Athletic Union Championships in Dayton. Ronnie Morris was going to be there. I was finally going to get a shot at him in direct competition.

Ronnie turned out to be a tough little guy, about five foot ten, and an intense competitor. I realized this was one vaulter who'd never hand you a victory: you'd have to take it from him. When we met, nobody swung any punches, but there was an immediate competitive tension between us. I knew we were never going to be good friends.

Happily for me, I was the one who kicked butt that day, jumping 13'9" to Morris's 13'5". I was short of his 13'10" record, but the victory was still plenty satisfying. Bob Richards and George Mattos were competing, too, and just being in the same stadium with these men I idolized was the biggest thrill of my life up to then. Though I was just a high school kid, I was one of six vaulters who placed third in competition with the best American vaulters in track. Of course, comparing these marks with what they're hitting today with fiberglass poles makes us all look like wimps. It's hard to remember that the metal poles we were using, though durable, were even less flexible than bamboo poles. If Ronnie and I'd had fiberglass back then, we could have hit the moon.

I also learned an important lesson at Dayton: the disadvantages of having too many advantages. Ronnie made a fuss about the runway being too slow, too soft, the wind too strong, the pit not up to snuff. Hell, it was one of the best pits I'd ever competed on. Maybe my big advantage was having to practice in a pasture full of cowshit.

I had pretty well decided to attend Penn State, but that went out the window when my dad picked me up. I was waiting for him outside the frat house, right beside trash cans brimming with beer and liquor bottles. I got in the car, and my father was glowering with disapproval. He pointed to the empty bottles. "Looks like all they do here at Penn State is booze it up."

I brushed away his concern, "Aw, Dad, you know I don't drink."

"That's right, and we're gonna keep it that way. We'll go check out Villanova."

I didn't understand what had turned my dad into a temperance zealot until I found out Villanova's coach, James "Jumbo" Elliot, had been buzzing in his ear while I looked over Penn State. Jumbo'd given Dad a intense sales pitch, harping on how far away Penn State was, not just from home, but from all the big East Coast indoor track meets. The winning point had been Jumbo's eloquence in describing the advantages of working out during the winter on Villanova's indoor board track. That sounded pretty good to me, too, so I was more than a little interested in what the Philadelphia school would be like.

In a way it was more frightening than Penn State. I realized that I would be surrounded by people from an entirely different social circle, Irish WASPS, who wouldn't take kindly to my working-class rough edges. On the other hand Villanova was only an hour or so away from home: family, friends, Raggs, and the life I loved. I confided my concerns about keeping up academically to Jumbo, and he brushed them away with a few words. "There's all kinds of help available if you really make an effort," he said, and that convinced me. With the backing of Dad and Jumbo Elliot, I agreed to enter Villanova University in the fall.

PART THREE

AGE OF ENLIGHTENMENT

But when the time came upon them
There was created a fraternity of men
To follow one another

        -- from "The Leap" by Don Bragg

Chapter Seven

Hotshots

When I entered Villanova in 1953, I envisioned having some pretty lonely years ahead of me. Things started looking up, however, when I noticed a familiar-looking black guy on my way to orientation. We said hi, and then I asked him, "Aren't you Charlie Jenkins, the runner from Boston?"

He shoots back, "Yeah, so I am. I just drove down from Baahston in the caah."

"Don't give me that 'caah' shit," I said. That broke the ice. Athletes tended to gravitate towards each other anyway, and Charlie and I were both in track, both on track scholarships, so we had things in common. Charlie, who'd broken the high school quarter-mile record, had been one of the leading high school athletes in the country. He also had the kind of mental alertness that produced instant zingers, and I liked that. I also loved to razz him over that accent of his, and even though he took it like a good sport, he'd always get me back. He was kind of a cocky guy who wouldn't take anything from anybody, although he usually tried mind over muscle first. He also had the habit of churning up mischief, then pushing somebody else, me for instance, into the middle of it. Then he'd sit there, all innocent, and watch the fun.

We went through a lot together freshman year. The first thing Charlie and I wanted to do was to go admire the indoor board track Jumbo Elliot had been bragging on: the indoor board track that would keep us toasty-warm during winter practice sessions. That was one of the things that convinced both of us to sign up at VU. Down at the gym we saw trainer Jake Nevins. He was a little leprechaun of a guy, maybe five foot, puffing cigar smoke at us as we asked if we could please see the indoor board track. He looked us over and said in this gruff voice, "What are you guys, freshmen?" And he throws his cigar ashes all over us. "It's right outside."

"No, you don't understand. We want to see the *indoor* board track."

So he says, with a little sing-song inflection where the brogue used to be, "The indoor board track is outside on the football field." We just stared at him. He took us by our elbows and walked us to the door of the gym. He pointed with his cigar. "The indoor board track, gentlemen."

Charlie and I looked at each other and ran outside. The indoor board track that Jumbo had dangled before our gullible eyes was indeed a board track, the type normally used indoors. Yet there it sat, completely exposed to the elements, next to the wind-whipped football field. We were both ready to sit down and cry.

Another trial Charlie and I endured together was the wearing of the beanie. All freshmen had to wear the damned things, which made us feel we should be skipping along like Jack and Jill, clapping our hands or some such shit. Jenk and I were crossing campus one morning when we saw some upperclassmen stop this one guy. They snarled at him, "We've never seen you around school before, so you must be a freshman. Where's your beanie?"

The guy said, "You're right, I'm new here, but I'm transferring from the community college as a junior." Satisfied, the upperclassmen let him go.

As soon as they were out of sight I whipped off my beanie. "Jenk, no way am I wearing this damn goofball hat," I said, and threw it under the bushes.

Jenk said, "If you're not wearing it, I'm sure as hell not wearing it." And another beanie goes into the bushes. Next upperclassman we see stops us and says, "Hey, aren't you freshmen?"

Jenk and I managed to look guileless and a little hurt. "Us? We're just transferring in from the community college." So the despised Villanova beanie made Jenk and me partners in crime, and solidified what was to be a life-long friendship.

But my mind never was as fast as his. One day we were in the room and started tussling. He pushed me, I pushed back, and all of a sudden he reached down, grabbed my leg, and threw me. I landed on my hands, almost doing a handstand. Leaping to my feet, I was ready to do some damage myself. "Oh ho, so you want to get serious!"

Jenk glanced at his watch and held up one hand urgently. "Good grief," he said. "We're gonna be late for our next class."

"You're right!" So I started looking for my books.

After that, Jenk always seemed to be chuckling to himself. I finally remembered our unfinished wrestling match and went looking for him. He was in his room studying, and he immediately knew what I had on my mind. He let out a howl of laughter. "Five days! It didn't come to you until five days after the fact that I conned you out of beating the shit out of me." He gave me a wicked grin. "Not that you could have," he finished, and returned to his book.

Of course nobody had much time to socialize. Jumbo Elliot was not only a hard-talking salesman for Villanova, he'd been a successful quarter-miler himself and was a superb running coach. I was no runner. Every time I set foot on the track Jumbo would start laughing. The hundred-forty-pound runners he was used to would scamper by like light-footed deer with this little pitter-pat. Then I'd go by: the Clydesdale. Bang, bang, bang on the wooden track. Jumbo called me "Horse," and concentrated on giving me a better running style.

"Don't flap; try to carry your hands like this. You're leaning too far forward; lean back a little," he'd say.

If Jumbo made me a better runner, he couldn't help much with my vaulting. But did I ever luck out. One day I was practicing while Malvern Prep School was working out on our field. A guy came over and watched me for awhile. "What are you doing?" he finally asked.

"Pole vaulting. What does it look like?"

"You'll have an easier time if you'd pivot before you release. You'll pick up another six inches. And your hands are wrong. Slide the left hand to within a few inches of the other. It'll put you in a higher position."

I tried pivoting. It was a departure from my technique, but I could tell it would work. Then I looked up and there was Jumbo barreling across the field. He squared off with the stranger.

"Who the hell are you?"

"I'm James Tuppeney. I coach at Malvern." It turned out that Mr. Tuppeny had vaulted at La Salle, and also had experience in hurdles.

"Vaulting and hurdles, huh?" I could see the wheels turning behind Jumbo's crafty eyes. It just happened that Villanova had a few vaulters and hurdlers but no coach for their specialties. He cocked his head at the other man. "How would you like to coach here at VU?"

"Hey, I'd love to, but I have a contract with Malvern."

Jumbo put an arm around the guy's shoulder. "That's nothing that can't be handled." A few weeks later James Tuppeney started at VU as an assistant coach. Like I said, Jumbo was quite a salesman.

Jim Tuppeney took me in hand immediately. One of his first chores was to put me straight about markers. "If your steps are even slightly skewed, you can't connect the power of your run to the vault. Look, you take off with your left foot. Make sure that left foot hits the marker as you come down the runway, and the vault will take care of itself."

I soon learned how to adjust the marker for wind and the speed of the runway. I also realized why Jim described the footwork of clueless vaulters as chicken steps. They'd come blazing down the runway, then do these little stutter-type steps as they tried to get their feet in place for the vault. They never jumped worth shit.

———————

Unlike athletes in California, who could train outdoors nearly year round, we on the East Coast were disadvantaged, weather-wise. It wasn't unusual to see Jenkins running time trials in a blizzard, bundled up in long johns, mittens, and a hooded shirt. I had no time to laugh at him, since I was down there too with a pick axe, breaking the pit sawdust into chunks rather than boulders so my landings wouldn't be terminal. And my grandkids ask me why my back doesn't work any more!

What the East Coast did have was a fantastic series of indoor meets. I was revved up for my first one at the Boston Gardens, but I nearly came to grief. It was a Villanova tradition that uniforms and equipment would be issued to upperclassmen before the freshmen were outfitted with whatever was left. Thus I ended up with a very large pair of shorts, though I lucked out and received sweatpants that fit fine. At least I thought I was lucky, since the sweats held up the baggier shorts.

Now at the bigger meets they'd call out the jumping order: which vaulter was jumping, who was on deck, who was in the hole. Well, I was nervous, and kind of stage-struck. It was my first indoor meet, and all the events are run close together, not spread out over a stadium. So I was looking around at everything, completely distracted. I was shocked when they announced that Don Bragg was now jumping. I swiftly jerked down my sweatpants. A blast of cold air warned me that something was very wrong. A fat guy sitting ringside began pointing at me, hollering, "Hey, look at the guy with no pants."

Looking down, I saw my jock and a hell of a lot of skin. I yanked up the sweats and tore off the track. I collapsed on a bench in the locker area, holding my head and groaning. An older athlete who was just changing asked me what was wrong. When I told him, he dismissed the problem.

"Forget that fat guy. He can't perform, so he shoots off his mouth instead. Nobody else gives a damn about your shorts. Get out there and show 'em what you're made of."

I returned to the track, and, sure enough, the fat guy started pointing at me and jeering. As I walked by him I said in a clear but pleasant voice, "Hi, Fatty!"

That was the last I heard from my fat friend, and my confidence surged. I finished in third place, pretty good for an eighteen-year-old in an open invitational event. Afterwards, I went to Jumbo and asked about the guy who'd given me such good advice.

"Him? That's Bones Dillard. He's quite a guy." I realized he was talking about Harrison Dillard, who, during the 1948 Olympic Trials, had tripped over a hurdle, disqualifying himself. Not missing a beat, he ran over and qualified in the hundred meters, and went on to win the gold. Four years later he took the gold at Helsinki, but this time in the hurdles. Jumbo was right about Dillard. He was a good guy and a real gentleman.

One great track venue I loved was Madison Square Garden in New York City. There were always three or four meets a year with good crowds and the added excitement of performing in the Big Apple. But when the National Championships were held there the atmosphere in the packed Garden turned electric. The band played during the entire evening, and only stopped as each event was introduced. Madison Square Garden was the original glittering three-ring circus of the track and field world, and it was an honor to compete there.

During the Nationals all the athletes got plenty of publicity and excellent press coverage. We also received tons of attention. One gentleman from Philadelphia, Russ Baum, had the marvelous custom of inviting the winners out to Mamma Leone's, a restaurant light-years from the reach of athletes' wallets. We reveled in the sumptuous ambiance of the place, to say nothing of the unending procession of Mamma's delectable Roman specialties and the tables laden with cheese and fruit. Or Russ would take us to legendary watering holes like the Stork Club or the Latin Quarter. After my rigorous training the week before competition, it was great to let loose for an evening. We didn't need any further motivation to win at the Nationals other than those provided by Russ's generosity.

When you arrived at the Garden you'd pick up your number for the meet. Some of the officials would be chewing the fat, and not paying too much attention to what they were handing out. Occasionally, Art Bragg, a sprinter from Morgan State, and I would realize we had each other's numbers. It became a Madison Square Garden tradition for me to hear that I was running in the fifty meters, or that Art Bragg was at the head of the runway in the pole vault. After we got to know each other, we'd pick up our numbers and say, "Hey, cuz, you have my number again!" Then we'd sneak a look at the officials. They'd be scratching their heads over the "cuz" reference since Art was black and I was white. That always broke us up.

I was feeling pretty good about myself when we started out for my first Knights of Columbus meet in Boston. I was no longer inexperienced. I knew the ropes, from meet procedures to practical things like the best method for stowing vaulting poles on trains. That was simple: we just handed them in through the back door of the last car. It worked beautifully on all the trains, even on our little Paoli local, the train into Philly. So we were stunned to find an unexpected dogleg in the Philly-Boston train's corridor just inside the back door. The metal pole had a little give, but we couldn't snake it around the obstacle. Jumbo was stumped too. "What in hell do we do now?" he demanded. "There's no other train to Boston for hours!"

I led the way to the front car which boasted a fine straight corridor. Trouble was, we'd have to dismantle the engine to get at it. But we had to do something, fast. I climbed inside and hauled the pole toward me as Jumbo and Mr. Tuppeny pushed from outside. It was tough going, especially where the back of the engine curved and sloped inward. The space was cramped, especially at the top, near the diamond-shaped electric pantograph which pulled the current from the overhead wire. As we crammed the pole into the inadequate space, it wedged against the back of the engine, bowing slightly. Jumbo said, "Whatever you do, don't let it -- "

And the world exploded into a reverberating roar in one blinding flash.

I think what Coach had been trying to say was, "Don't let the pole whip upward and hit the pantograph, or you'll be sorry."

Of course that's just what happened. I saw Jumbo and Mr. T. thrown back out of sight, so I knew I was on my own. The pole was still vibrating frenetically, and I thought maybe I should do something constructive, like pull it off the live contact. I'm glad I hesitated, because a crewman behind me yelled, "Don't move a muscle!"

He had reason for his concern. My nice shiny pole was having a melt-down on one end. I couldn't tell what happened to the other end since it was sticking out a brand new hole in the roof. Everybody thought the humongous bolt of electricity should have electrocuted me, but they didn't know about my dad. During my first trip to the frozen northland my hand had frozen to a pole, so he'd made a thick canvas cover for it. He'd given it to me that very morning after stenciling on it: *Don "Tarzan" Bragg -- World's Record 15'9" or Bust!* The crewmen looked at the cover in disbelief. They said that the canvas alone wouldn't have turned the charge I'd received, and that Somebody was looking out for me.

They pulled me out of the car and rushed me upstairs to the doctor. When I got there, I had to sit on a bench forever while people in white charged around with frenzied looks in their eyes. I stopped a nurse and told her I was really in a hurry, and couldn't I just see the doc for a second?

"You'll have to be patient, young man. We're expecting an emergency case. Some poor boy was hit by a million volts of electricity just now. We probably can't save him, but we'll do our best."

"That's funny," I said. "The same thing just happened to me."

The nurse gave me a peculiar look and galloped off, yelling for the doctor.

With the exception of a pulse rate of 160, I was fine. As soon as the doctor turned me loose, I went hunting for Jumbo and Mr. Tupenny. I finally tracked them down in the bar, solemn, silent, throwing down shots of whisky. They were holding an impromptu memorial service, they explained, since they were sure I was dead. Hell, they weren't too sure they were still among the living themselves. Gently, I pried them away from their grieving and told them we still had a train to catch.

Unfortunately, it took awhile to arrive. My little adventure had short-circuited everything in the station and blown the power out completely. It was an hour later that we were Boston-bound. I'm sure the station crews were glad to finally see the back of us.

———

So on to Boston. What I mainly remember about the meet was walking around with a fixed smile saying, "I'm just fine." I was, too, especially after I jumped fourteen-six. I broke the freshman record that night, with a pole that Boston College's Bruce Hescock lent me.

I took a lot of razzing about my little stunt, though. Mike Agostini, a VU sprinter who hailed from Trinidad, commented as he trotted by, "Hey Don. You jumped pretty good tonight. Maybe you should jam your pole into electric outlets more often."

Without thinking, I bellowed across the arena at his departing back, "Hey Mike! Kiss my sparkling ass!" It got real quiet there for a minute, and Jumbo came running over to tell me to watch my mouth. I apologized profusely. "Sorry, Coach, I didn't mean to shock you." He gave me a dirty look, but let the matter drop. You don't chew out somebody who's narrowly missed a horrible demise *and* just broken a record.

Chapter Eight

Getting Attention

At the time, my buddy Jenk was the anchor of the VU relay team, and our big rival was Morgan State, coached by the great Edward P. Hurt. A guy named Josh Culbreath, one of Morgan State's premier runners, usually anchored their relays, so he and Jenk were often going head to head. Their races usually went this way: Josh would be ahead by several yards, and Charlie'd be trying to catch him. When Josh really started to fly, he'd hunch up his shoulders, and I'd yell, "Look out, Quasimoto! Here comes Jenk." And afterwards I'd say, "Josh, you almost pulled it off."

Josh would say, "Yeah, I thought I had him this time."

Josh was fast, but his specialty was the 400 meter hurdles. To appreciate this you have to realize that Josh was also short, so when he ran the hurdles, he was high-jumping as well.

Though Josh was to be another lifelong friend, it took me a while to figure him out. At first he came on all serious, and I didn't catch on that he was really busting balls. Like he'd come up, huffing and puffing after Jenk had just beat him, and gasp, perfectly deadpan, "Jenkins really isn't that fast, you know." He had an innate dignity, but he liked guys like me when it was time to send in the clowns. He dearly loved to get me in hot water. He'd go over to some behemoth and point me out to him. "See that guy? You don't want to mess with him. He'll really kick your ass."

"Oh, really?"

I'd look up and see this one-man defensive line headed my way to determine whose ass was going to get place-kicked. Josh would be right at his heels with this earnest straight face of his. I think he enjoyed watching my craziness as long as he wasn't sucked into it.

This was all exciting for me, and I threw myself into training with more enthusiasm. One essential element was lacking at VU, however: Tarzanville. When I talked longingly about swinging from Tarzan ropes, the guys in the dorm thought I was nuts. My father, knowing the conditioning effect of the rope exercise on a vaulter's arms, was the only one who knew I was crazy like a fox.

Not ready to do without rope work, I decided to improvise. I tied a rope to the fire escape of Alumni Hall, where I lived. The idea was I'd climb down the rope on my way to class and shinny back up afterwards. No exercise in the world like a good rope workout, I told myself.

It was unique, all right, climbing up that rope three, four times a day. It was specially fun in the cold, with rain pouring down on me and my armload of books, most of which I dropped. I tried it for two weeks, then gave up. The next thing you know, Dad's up at VU with a rope and a bunch of connectors. We slung the rope over a rafter in Alumni Hall's old gym, just one floor down from my room. Once I was swinging again I felt I was doing everything I could to excel at my sport.

My studies were another matter. Like many of my classmates, I experienced collegiate shock. Unlike high school teachers, the profs at VU weren't into being policeman. At first you're all triumphant, like you'd gotten away with something. After the first pop quiz I mended my ways in a hurry.

I could read okay, but focusing on the ideas? Man, it was hard. The stakes were high, so I kept struggling, though not nearly hard enough. Economics was what brought me down. I couldn't make head or tail of it. What was worse, there were two or three brains, nerds we called 'em, and they screwed up the curve for us jocks. The nerds served a purpose, though. There was a river of information flowing from those unsuspecting souls as the jocks around them bent over to cough or pick up a pencil and a few right answers on the way. This would flow in ever-narrowing tributaries throughout the class, to the benefit of everybody except a dumbass from Penns Grove who didn't cheat. Of course I crashed and burned. The other jocks merely laughed.

"What's wrong with you? We told you to copy the answers!"

Jumbo didn't have any sympathy for me either, and asked me why I hadn't requested a tutor. He also told me that if I didn't pack Economics, I'd have to pack up and hit the pike.

A tutor? When in hell was I supposed to work with a tutor? Classes, practice, studying, and meets every weekend ate up all my time, leaving me a bare six hours a night for sleep. I didn't know how I was going to make it.

Then somebody told me, "Every prof has a favorite place to stress the important stuff: on the blackboard, in his lectures, or in the reading he assigns. Figure out which one, and key in on that. Then you'll do okay."

That appealed to me. The studies were battles in my war against extinction. I was the warrior, the teacher my adversary. Stealthily, I watched and planned my attack -- blackboard, notes, or book -- and dug in as hard as I could.

It was easier when I was intrigued by the subject matter of a class. I was interested in religion, so I signed up for a religion class. But reading Thomas Aquinas! It was murder: if they only allow one book in hell, it'll be his *Summa Theologica.* I plowed through that, but I was completely lost. Then somebody told me I should try Descartes and some of his gang. I realized there were all these brilliant guys who proved all kinds of contradictory things. How those old boys could twist things and rationalize! They'd arrive at whatever conclusion they wanted. I had to learn more, so I'd come to class with a laundry list of questions. One day the professor, Father O'Connell, said, "Don, can I see you after class?"

And when we were alone, he said, "Don, you're Catholic, right?"

"No, Father."

"Then what the devil are you doing at Villanova?"

I was surprised he didn't know. "VU gave me a scholarship, Father."

Then this guy starts on how fortunate I was to have a VU scholarship. Come on! I was winning meets for the school. He'd begun to get on my nerves, so I said, "Father, I had lots of scholarships. Hundreds."

He sat there stroking his chin, then asked. "So Don, why are you taking this religion course?"

At last something relevant. "I'm trying to learn about it, but I've got a million questions. I just want to understand religion, that's all."

He rubbed his forehead like he had an itch. "If you just come to class, that's a C. If you come in prepared, you get a B." I'm waiting for him to tell me about my A. But he continued, "If you keep asking all these questions, you're going to flunk. You're disturbing the whole class, you understand."

Then it hit me, wow! Religion isn't something you become engrossed in for the thought process, it's just dogma: you believe this because we say it's right. Or else. And that really got to me. I became increasingly cynical about religion after that. I was really growing up. It was more than finally learning to study and cope: I stopped thinking like a little kid. I owe a lot of that to Father O'Connell.

———

Villanova was just an hour and fifteen minutes from home. Sometimes we could make it in an hour, if we'd catch the Chester ferry just right. It was great to take a breather from the grind and see the folks. But I had a more pressing motive. Villanova's scholarship was incredibly generous, covering tuition, books, a dorm room, and meals in the school cafeteria. But it didn't cover extras like money for laundry or bus fare, though, so Christmas vacation I earned a little walking-around money as a substitute mailman.

I was still pretty shy around girls, but over Christmas I went to a dance at St. James High School in the quonset hut they used as a gym. I was kind of sitting around when I saw this pretty girl, a tiny little thing, but with an incredible figure. I asked Dietzie who she was, and she said, "Oh that's my friend Theresa Fiore." She dragged me over to meet Theresa, who was astonishingly easy to talk to. I liked her a lot and immediately felt comfortable with her. We saw a lot of each other at holiday parties, but being four years younger, Theresa was more Dietzie's friend than mine. But Theresa Fiore became a very pleasant part of coming home.

Though I continued my training, as spring approached I began having problems with my left leg. I was fine on the pole vault's straight runs, but ever since Coach had started me running the quarter mile or the 220 on the board track, I'd begun toeing in. It was a bad habit, but I couldn't seem to correct it when I was on the board track. The track had sharp corners, which was okay for the lighter runners. But being heavier, I really pounded my leg, running in these little shoes I had, low-cut blue-back Kangaroos, with no real arch support.

The pain got so bad that I finally got my butt into the doctor, the first of many visits. They drained a bucket of fluid out of the leg a couple of times, but the relief was minimal. Once the pain became constant, however, they cut the leg open. They found that the muscle had ruptured and had come out of its sheath, bringing a nerve right along with it. The doctors at Bryn Mawr hospital shot me with a bunch of needles, rolled out the gauze, and started to cut a skin graft. I immediately yelled bloody murder.

"Something wrong, Don?"

Their entire battery of needles hadn't done the job. They stuck me again, but the leg never really went numb.

I was lying there, and the shot still hadn't worked too well. I was wondering if I'd get through it when I noticed a little bird sitting out on a branch right outside the window. I focused my mind on this bird, just a little funky old sparrow with rumpled feathers. Wherever that bird is now, I want to thank him for keeping my mind off the doctor's excavations. I think God said, "Bragg's in trouble. Well, he likes animals and things, so let's just put this little bird out in that tree. He'll appreciate that."

My main concern after the surgery was whether or not I'd ever be able to resume vaulting. The leg slowly healed, erasing my fears of a permanent injury, but having to mark time during the outdoor season was murder. It had its compensations, though. I finally had the time to enjoy college.

I'd joined the Villanova choir as a first tenor because I loved to sing. That spring, the choir would visit the girls' colleges in the area to give concerts.

After one such musical interlude at Harkham Junior College, one of the young ladies took me for a walk, ostensibly to show me the campus gazebo. But what she really had in mind was to try out her French-kissing technique. I was no expert on the subject, but I was damned sure you were supposed to spit out your chewing gum first. She didn't, and left me stuck with this weird chewy thing rattling around in my mouth. So much for the gazebo. I high-tailed it home as fast as my legs would go, and doused my mouth with all the mouthwash I had. The other guys caught up to me in the dorm.

"What happened to you? We saw you all cuddly-wuddly out at the gazebo, and the next thing we know you're running across the field like a bat out of hell."

The choir also visited Rosemont for a joint concert at the tea house they had on campus. The singing was great, but the stuffy atmosphere was stifling. I like warmth and spontaneity, and everywhere I looked, there were people all revved up to disapprove of anything interesting that might happen. I decided not to let all that reproachful energy go to waste. Stealthy as a hunting cat, I climbed the tallest tree I could find and made the campus reverberate with Tarzan yells. You'd have thought someone had lobbed a hornet's nest into the crowd, the way people carried on. The campus police showed up, but they were no match for Tarzan. I eluded them with ease and made my triumphant way back to VU. Damn, that had been fun. I realized that the tang of flirting with disaster was what had been missing from college life. I set out immediately to remedy that deficiency.

My first project was sneaking some guys down to the pool so we could dive from the rafters. That became a favorite pastime, but once we were almost nailed. We were perched on the rafters, ready to take the plunge, when the door opened. A priest strode in and stopped right under us. Methodically, his eyes swept the pool area, everywhere but straight up, where the three of us were dangling. We started breathing again once he left, but he'd taken my buddies' last reserves of courage with him. I had to spend another hour coaxing them to jump, dammit. Then when we'd all made it back to the dorm, they began strutting around, bragging how we'd put one over on Father So-and-So.

We were all macho and kind of juvenile, but it was times like these that I still regard as the high points of collegiate life. College was a struggle: studies, vaulting, meets. Yet when you added horsing around as an ingredient, it helped you juggle everything else. When it worked, there was nothing like it.

———————

Summers I kept busy with jobs and training, but it was also good just to spend time with friends and family. I couldn't believe how much Dietzie had grown up during the past year. At fourteen she had an incredible competitive spirit, which I attributed to a life spent keeping up with her big brothers. The best training a competitor can have is going head-to-head with a bunch of siblings every day. And at our house you could do just that.

It was also great fun to go to the local meets, and one weekend I decided to represent the Shanahan Catholic Club in Philly. I took Dietzie with me, and it was lucky for the Bragg family honor that I did. The vaulting pit was like cement, and I didn't have my pick axe handy, so I decided to run the hundred instead.

A few paces into the race I pulled a muscle and had to stop. But Dietzie won the softball throw, took second in the high jump, and vaulted eight foot six, surely an unofficial world's record. She was only fourteen and already looked like a top athletic prospect. I was very proud of her.

After the fall semester started, I had to cut back on my weekends at home. The timing and height of my vaults suffered from even two days away from the board track. Dad asked me what the big deal was. We already had the vaulting pit alongside the house.

"Off-season we practice on the board track with needle spikes, Dad. It's a whole different feel from a dirt track."

That week at practice, Jumbo came up to me and cleared his throat portentously. "I just talked to your father."

"Really? What about?"

"Well, that's none of your business," he said, and strolled away.

I shrugged it off. If Jumbo wanted to be mysterious, that was fine with me. But when I walked up Virginia Avenue Friday night, everything made sense. Protruding out of the front yard, almost onto the road, was a wooden board track leading to the vaulting pit. Working nights, Dad had constructed the runway for me, just to be sure I'd have what I needed when I came home. He'd missed out on a lot of opportunities growing up, but his kids wouldn't if he could help it. Once more I counted myself lucky to have George T. Bragg for my father. The Olympics were the next year. Wouldn't it be something if I could bring him home a gold medal?

———————

Unfortunately my biggest battles weren't on the field, but at a desk, struggling to focus. No matter who you were, they didn't cut athletes any slack at VU, which was a good thing.

Now I say it was a good thing. You'd get an assignment Friday afternoon and leave right after school for a meet. Some little old priest would come out to bless the team and see us off. "Be good boys and study hard!" Once he added inexplicably, "And beat the stuffin' out of those Jesuits." Jesuits? I'd thought we were playing Georgetown! But winning the meet was always easier than trying to study on the train with all the talking and other distractions. I'd come home dead beat Monday morning, retaining zip. But I didn't quit. Not only did I pass Economics, my name even started appearing on the Dean's List. First time that happened, I really felt good.

Don (left), Bill Cosby, and Josh Culbreath compare war stories at Franklin Field during the Penn Relays in 2000.

I continued to work at the vaulting with the added incentive of an Olympic gold medal. It was a real possibility. I was one of the best vaulters in the country, and I believed I could win the gold if I stayed dedicated.

Sophomore year I also noticed a new face at the meets. The vaulting pits were next to the high jump area, and I noticed this one high jumper meet after meet. We said, "How ya doin'?" a few times, then one day at

Franklin Field, Josh grabbed us both. "Hey Don, do you know Bill Cosby?" Cos always had a little grin on his face like something was funny, and you'd wonder if it might be you.

With a little experience under my belt, it was easier to enjoy the meets, even traveling by train. Jenk, high jumper Phil Reavis, Ed Colleymore, our 200 meters specialist, and I would be kicking back, singing these great songs. Once I was wailing along with them, "Cherry pie, cherry, cherry pie," but I noticed I wasn't following the same rhythm as they were. Reavis finally said, "Are you trying to sing, or what?"

I got all huffy. "I am a member of the Villanova Choir."

One of these characters piped up in this wimpy little voice, "My, my! Aren't we special!" This ended the singing, since we were all splitting our sides.

As the year progressed, I started getting a big helping of publicity. Word had gotten to *Sports Illustrated* that there was a crazy guy at Villanova who thought he was Tarzan, swinging through the jungle. They sent a man down to do a story about me. My family got a kick out of it, but the guys at school razzed me and started calling me Tarzan.

And not only the guys at school.

I was jumping in the National Collegiate Championships at the Los Angeles Coliseum, and in the middle of the meet I needed to retape my pole. When I went over to get some tape, I found a photo of Johnny Weissmuller and Cheetah in my bag. Over the chimp's head was written, "Don Bragg." They had him saying to Weissmuller, "You Tarzan, me monkey." I looked up and saw Ronnie Morris and his vaulting partner grinning at me. I asked around, and guys said they'd seen them messing with my bag. Okay, fine. If they wanted to stick it to me right on the field of competition, so be it. It hit me that I'd become enough of a threat that the competition would take pains to unnerve me. All their pathetic monkeyshines managed to do, however, was to create an indomitable determination in me to become the best vaulter in the world.

With the Olympic Trials only about a year away I focused all my energy into jumping well at the National Collegiate Championships in Boulder, Colorado. It was hard to keep my mind on business, though. Charlie Jenkins had other plans for me.

When Jenk went to run time trials, the track looked and felt like it had been plowed. It had been: by the dainty hooves of the football team, who were about as light on their feet as pregnant bison. I saw Jenk talking with a couple of the players, and then a minute later, he walked by me with a satisfied grin on his face. I should have run for cover. Next thing I know, here comes team captain De Luca.

"So you want to arm-wrestle, huh?"

It seems Charlie had thrown down the gauntlet when he said, "You wanna use our track? Okay, send your biggest guy over to arm-wrestle for the right to use it. But watch out! Don Bragg will whup his behind."

So here's De Luca, big as a house and mad at me. We set up the large traveling trunk in the supply room and got down to our contest. As soon as we started pulling, I knew I'd win if I could hang on. It took a while, but I outlasted him.

Jenkins and the rest of the track team were all over me, pounding me on the back. I was glad they were happy, because I still wasn't sure what the beef was about.

It was the same story in Boulder. The night before the championships, I was already half-asleep when Jenkins, along with Phil Reavis and Ed Colleymore, came flying into my room looking indignant as hell. "There's a guy playing the piano in the Commons. He's bragging he can beat any of our guys at arm-wrestling. Are you gonna let him get away with that?"

"You guys out of your mind?" I said. "Final trials are tomorrow."

Jenk wasn't impressed. "You're gonna let some piano player dump on us?"

"If it bothers you, wrestle him yourself." I pulled the pillow over my head. Jenkins pulled it off.

"He's singing, too."

I figured it would be easier to wrestle this guy than get rid of the three gooney birds flapping around the room, so I pulled on some sweats and staggered off to the Commons. With the three of them talking trash all the way, I was getting a little hot too by the time I got there. After all, a piano player! I hurled myself into the Commons and stopped dead. A large man was playing the piano, but jumped up when we came in. He was a very large man indeed.

"Hi, Rosie," I said, swallowing hard.

Rosie Grier, the normally affable Penn State football star, was standing there resembling an aggravated volcano. What Jenkins hadn't told me was this: Rosie'd been playing the piano and singing along, trying to relax before throwing the shot in the next day's meet. Some guys in the upstairs hall had bellowed down from the balcony for him to quit making such a racket. When Rosie stood up to contest their opinion of his playing, they disappeared. Jenkins immediately decided the situation had my name on it, and volunteered my services as sacrificial lamb.

I gulped again and waded in. "Hey, Rosie. I hear you're up for some arm-wrestling."

"Think you can take me, pole vaulter?" he snorted derisively, flexing his platter-size hands.

News of the impending battle must have spread quickly because the rec room was jammed by the time Rosie and I took our positions at the pool table. Rosie put his ham of an arm on one end and somebody said: Go!

He took me half way down immediately, and I noticed a roar of approval from our audience, including Jenks, Reavis, and Colleymore. What the hell was this? For a second I was keenly aware that I was the only white guy in the room. I recovered in time to put on the brakes and hold Rosie at the halfway point. Ten seconds later I started pulling back up. Once my hand was straight, I shifted slightly to come over the top, and I started to drive him down.

Rosie let go. "We're nuts to do this the night before a meet," he said, and began to shake out his hand.

"Absolutely," I said, with a grateful heart. "Let's get some sleep."

Jenk and the others were slapping me on the back, evidently jubilant that I'd held my own. But I was a little paranoid after that, wondering what other mischief Mr. Jenkins might be cooking up for me.

As it turned out, the next day's agenda included more than vaulting. The erroneous word that I'd beaten Rosie Grier in an arm-wrestling showdown spread like bear grease in a skillet. My heart sank when the California track contingent demanded that I take on their best man, Gwen Smith. All of a sudden, the honor of the entire East Coast was at stake. During a break in the meet, we ran over to the first aid tent and had our match. Gwen was on the small side, but had immense strength in his arms. I never saw daylight between his forearm and his biceps, but eventually I pulled his arm down, and his entire body followed, up and over onto the table.

The Californians were dismayed at my victory, but immediately asked if I could walk on my hands. I said I could, and a minute later I'm out in the middle of the field walking on my hands like I had the devil after me. I made it to the fifty-yard line, but Gwen passed my mark by ten yards. No wonder he won. I heard later he could do multiple one-handed pull-ups.

I couldn't believe I'd done something so stupid as arm-wrestling and hand-walking right before my event. I came in something like eighth, but I still pride myself in my victories in the unofficial events.

I also wondered why the California guys had singled me out. As I pondered the events, I thought I discerned the fine hand of Charles Jenkins. This was confirmed when I heard him say, "I guess that'll teach the Californians not to dump on us East Coast guys." I'd been crazy to even think of participating in such sophomoric shenanigans. I couldn't move my arm for three days after my little escapade, but the pain was a small price to pay for my unique Rocky Mountain high.

Chapter Nine

Hanging On

We'd barely gotten back on campus that fall when Jumbo hit us with an unpleasant ultimatum. He caught a bunch of us -- Ron Delany, Jenk, me -- playing football before practice, and he lowered the boom. Anybody, *anybody* caught with a pigskin in his hands would lose his scholarship.

I'd thought he just didn't want us deflected from our specialties, but I was wrong. Almost immediately, Coach started putting me in events other than vaulting during dual or triangular meets. When my 9.8" hundred-yard dash on a cinder track took third place, he was pretty pleased. I was too, until I realized where Jumbo was going with it: he was considering switching me to the decathlon. The problem was, because of my size my poles often buckled under me. Coach tried to soothe me, reminding me that I'd been working with the javelin and the shot, and that I was running well. Switching to the decathlon wouldn't be that much of a stretch. I told him emphatically that I was a pole vaulter. Jumbo replied, "Right, but only if you keep your weight down."

The poles could take 195 pounds, but no more. After experimenting with things like wheat germ and Knox gelatine, I settled on a one meal a day regimen: salad, juice, lean meat, and occasionally a little ice milk. My daily 1200-calories barely covered the tremendous energy I needed to keep up with studies, practice, attending meets, plus doing mundane stuff like laundry. I managed it, though. No sacrifice was too great if it would put an Olympic gold medal around my neck.

A few years earlier I would have folded, but two years under Jumbo's tutelage had toughened me immensely. I'd learned that to compete effectively, I had to conform to certain rules of technique and behavior, including total submission to the will of Jumbo Elliot. Discipline was everything to him, and he tolerated no lapses of obedience.

Not long after he'd put football off limits, he told me to start warming up with the football. Without thinking, I reminded him of his prohibition on football. He went red in the face and screamed that I'd was to do what he said, and do it fast. I was miffed by his dictatorial behavior, but I assumed he had his reasons.

He did. Evidently he'd been bragging to the football coach that I had a powerful arm. When the time came for me to put up or for Jumbo to shut up, I heaved the ball a good eighty yards against their star quarterback. Jumbo made a hundred dollars off the football coach, but he generously shared his winnings. With an evil grin, he tossed me ten bucks. "Go buy yourself a salad," he said. "And by the way, if I catch you playing football again, you lose your scholarship."

Over the years I've come to appreciate Jumbo's iron will which he tempered with humor. His rigorous standards enabled us to dig down to the best we had to give, on and off the field. He was responsible for six or seven athletes of national prominence, with egos to match. Without breaking anyone's spirit, he had to weld us into a team, no small accomplishment. I didn't fully appreciate it then, but man, could we ever use Jumbo's kind of no-nonsense coaching in today's professional sports world.

This third year of college, I began to eagerly anticipate the camaraderie of the athletic meets. It's so hard for seasoned warriors to put down their guard, even for a minute. So you try to hang on to the few guys you've learned to trust completely, the ones who know about dedication, perseverance, hard work, even the rigors of maintaining a sports scholarship: Jenk, Josh, Phil Reavis, Ed Colleymore, Ron Delany. At a meet with La Salle, I met another guy with whom I was to have a close, if not lasting, relationship -- Al Cantello. At about 5'9", he was one helluva javelin thrower, heaving it farther than athletes half a foot taller. He'd already been in the Marines, so he was a little more seasoned than the rest of us. He was a welcome addition to our little group.

I never did become too friendly with other vaulters, even though we shared many singular qualities. Not only are we the best all-round athletes, we also possess a mind-set that revels in physical testing. Who else would volunteer to hang upside down, nearly twenty feet in the air, with only a temperamental length of metal for support?

But it was dangerous to become overly close to competitors. You run the risk of losing your edge. I almost managed it with Bob Richards. He had been my idol since he'd given me such good advice at the Inquirer Meet. But it was only after he retired from competition and became something of a mentor that we became close. And that was closer to a father-son relationship than to friendship between equals.

I always admired Bob. For a while there, I even thought of following his example and entering the ministry. Wouldn't that have been something! But I'm absolutely terrible at leading people around when they should be making up their own minds. Besides, the church had enough problems. It was my duty to spare it the additional ordeal of dealing with me as a clergyman.

--- --- ---

It was ironic that just as I seemed to be coming into my own as a competitor, trouble started brewing at home. My dad's younger sister Helen was back in town, and started pestering Dad to help her with this or that. Trouble was, after he helped her, they'd sometimes end up in a bar, drinking the evening away. Mom had started to complain about Dad's drinking, but I kind of thought she just resented the time he spent away from her. One evening late in the fall I learned different.

Don and Bob Richards at the Montreal Olympic Games in 1976.

Mom called the college in tears. She sobbed that it was payday, and that Dad hadn't come home yet. Somebody had told her he and his sister were down at Batches' Bar, drinking up the mortgage and grocery money. She begged me to come right away and bring Dad home.

I felt a little panicky. I had two tests the next day, and I didn't dare screw them up. I told Mom I couldn't and asked why Georgie couldn't help her.

"You know he's scared of your father. Please come right home, Donnie."

I told her about the tests, and that I had to study all night, but she began to cry hysterically. I couldn't take that. I told her I'd hitch to Chester, then take the ferry over to Jersey.

"For God's sake, hurry, Donnie. I'll meet you at the ferry."

It was a dismal trip, hitching through those desolate little towns, worried sick about Dad. When I got off the ferry it was very late, but Mom wasn't there. I started walking, but when I'd gone about two miles along the ferry road, she showed up. She pulled me into the car, and we lit out for Batches' Bar.

Dad and Helen were still inside, but thoroughly smashed. He looked up at me, raised his glass, and said, "How about a little drink?"

"I don't drink. You know that."

I took his arm, but he pulled away. "I'm stayin' right here with my sister!"

About then Mom started yelling at Helen and slugged her right off the bar stool. I tried to grab Dad, but he caught hold of the bar. He still had his powerful carpenter's hands, and I had to bang them with my fist to make him let go. I threw him over one shoulder and took him out to the car. Mom already had the engine running when I threw him in the back seat. But before I could catch him again he opened the opposite door and crawled out into the street, where a passing car barely missed him. I had to run him down before I could haul him back into the car. He was fighting mad now: if he hadn't been so drunk I couldn't have handled him. He was still a powerful guy.

No sooner did we get him into the house than he charged out the back door. I chased him down again, slung him back over my shoulder, and began to jog around the outside of the house with him. He was mightily pissed off.

"Stop! You're killing my stomach!"

I told him I'd stop as soon as he promised not to leave the house, and he told me to go to hell. Finally he began moaning that his gut didn't feel so hot. He began to retch, and then I felt the vomit running down my back.

He beat on my back with both fists. "Okay, you win. I'll be good and stay home."

I got him cleaned up, gave him a cigarette, and put him to bed, then stood guard for an hour or so, About two A.M. I went into my old room and lay down, but I woke up at dawn when Dad came into the room. I turned back to the wall, away from him.

"Aren't you going up to the college?"

`I sat up and faced him. "No, I can't do it any more. I've been cramming all week for logic and statistics exams I have today. How do you think it feels to work my ass off, then have to come home to this? It's too damn much."

"If I promise not to drink anymore, will you go back?"

I shook my head. "You won't keep your word."

"Hey!" He made me look him in the eye. He looked like my dad again, not the wild man from last night. "Have you ever seen me break it? Let's go."

We got back to VU in time for my ten-thirty exam. I managed to pull a C in statistics and a B in logic, a subject I actually enjoyed. Luck, or Somebody, was keeping an eye out for me again.

Dad battled to stay away from the booze, but he wouldn't have been able to do it without the support of the Fiore family. Theresa, just sixteen or so, went with him to his AA meetings, and did everything she could for him. Her mom and dad looked out for him, too. If it hadn't been for Theresa, I don't think I could've made it through that year.

Even before Christmas, however, trouble erupted from another quarter. I came home one weekend and found Mom crying. "Dietzie's pregnant," she said, and sobbed into her handkerchief.

Since I was away most of the time, I only heard bits and pieces of the rest of the story. Dietzie and the baby's father announced they were in love, and quickly got married. But it was only a matter of months before they divorced. Dietzie had her little Bridget with us for awhile, but moved into her own place soon after. She raised that little girl by herself, driving a bus, raising dogs, muskratting, doing whatever she needed to do for her daughter. I was still terribly proud of Dietzie, but it was painful to think that her promising athletic career was over.

The rest of the season, I took refuge in preparing for February's National Indoor Championships in Madison Square Garden. It wasn't only a question of physical readiness. Since Ronnie Morris had tried to mess with my mind with the Tarzan-Cheetah photo, I'd majored in another aspect of competition. Keep your guard up mentally: you're the fastest gun on the runway now, so expect all comers to try and shoot you down one way or another.

The last night of the Championships we started at six-thirty, but we were still at it at half past eleven. Bob Gutowski and I were the only competitors left standing, with the bar at fifteen feet. We raised the bar in one inch increments. We both made 15'1", but neither of us could go higher. About midnight, we agreed to a jump-off, and they dropped the bar back to 15'1". It was a war of attrition now, and the first competitor to show any chink in his armor would lose.

I was dead beat, and I knew Bob had to be, too. I cleared the bar, then started psyching Bob out. I quickly pulled on my sweats and covered my poles. An official scurried over and told me that the meet wasn't over until Bob jumped. Bob happened to be passing us on his way back down the runway. I said in a voice he was sure to hear, "Nah, he's too tired to make this one: he's got nothing left. I'm the winner."

Carrying my poles, I passed Bob as I walked toward the exit. But as soon as I was out of his sight, I doubled back and watched him miss the bar. I was the National Indoor champion! Of course, I had to jog back to the pole vault pit and pick up my first place card so I could collect my medal. Bob just sat in the sawdust and looked daggers at me. Those infamous California psych artists had just been taught a lesson by Tarzan.

So much heavy stuff was coming down in my life, it was a relief to relax for a while in VU's nutty production of *The Man in the Gray Flannel Toga*. Ron Delany and I, both done up in togas, were supposed to sing this crazy love song. Ron, however, took one look at the football team crowded in the front rows, and decided discretion was the better part of valor. He bugged out, leaving me to sing my duet with nobody.

When the curtain opened, I was terrified, out there by my lonesome. At first my worst fears seemed justified as they screamed at my cute little costume. One of them yelled, "Look at the skinny legs on that sucker!" I kept going, though, and eventually the crowd started clapping to the rhythm of my routine. I brought down the house, and really won points with the football team, since I had the balls to keep going. Delany was the one who had to take all the razzing for the next few weeks.

About this time I began to acquire a national reputation and the attention and respect that went with it. The Severne Brothers had just started marketing Addidas shoes in the U.S. I began talking to the two Brits about a shoe that would give vaulters some cushioning and stability, especially in the heel. The vaulter's Achilles heel needed extra protection from painful bruises. Eventually they came out with a shoe that did just that.

The Arrow shirt people also contacted me about modeling some shirts for them. I had a bit of a name, I wasn't a bad looking guy, and it was an opportunity to obtain some excellent shirts for free. The Olympic Committee got wind of this, however, and scotched the deal with puritanical vigor. They told me the only reason Arrow wanted me was because of my athletic abilities, so doing the ad was out.

Something wasn't right here. Most athletes I knew were barely able to make ends meet, but the AAU or Olympic officials seemed pretty well-heeled. I remember seeing Avery Brundage in a restaurant once. All of us athletes had ordered the cheapest items on the menu to stay within our budget. But here's Brundage, laughing it up as he sent a huge steak back to the kitchen. We watched it go back, salivating. We were ready to fight for the bones of that sucker, and Brundage sent it back because it wasn't good enough. Wow!

It was only with an effort that I was able to clear my mind of these petty details and focus on earning that gold medal in Melbourne. The stakes were especially high for me. Jumbo had introduced me to Dr. Barney Bellieu, who offered friendship as well as his expertise in sports medicine. In addition to his medical practice, Dr. Bellieu was also a writer, and knew his way around the movie studios in Los Angeles. He told me there was an excellent chance that Gordon Scott might be stepping down as Tarzan to pursue other acting roles. They'd need a new King of the Jungle, and he thought it would be worth my while to pursue the role. Talk about a mind-blowing opportunity. A chance to step into the role Johnny Weissmuller had made so famous! It was as if the Fates had decided to give me something I'd never even dared to dream about.

Dr. Bellieu did everything he could to help make my new dream a reality, inviting me to stay at his home during LA meets. He even had Harvey Hyutin, one of the guys who owned the Tarzan film rights, come up and look me over while I was swimming. Harvey was pleasant but non-committal. So were other studio people who discussed my aspirations. Dr. Bellieu told me privately that the best way to solidify my claim to the Tarzan role was to bring back a gold medal from the Olympics.

———————

June rolled around, and with it the National Collegiate Championships at Berkeley. I stepped up my training and conditioning to be at my best.

Most people assume that the hardest part of pole vaulting is attaining height. I wish! I'd love to have a medal for every time I've reached a record-breaking height only to come down on the crossbar. A successful vaulter must learn to calculate a complex parabolic equation comprised of speed, momentum, lift, take-off, timing of the pivot, push-off, and release. This results in an arc that apexes high enough to clear the bar with maximum economy of energy. If the arc is too wide, you lose the momentum needed for height; too narrow, you lose control and risk taking down the bar.

Saving energy is also an essential ingredient. I've seen inexperienced guys clear the bar by six inches on the earlier jumps, just to show off. They'd invariably be worn out and perform badly at the end of the competition. I'd just slither over the top of the bar, which left me with an energy reserve for the all-important higher jumps.

This is the equation that can only be translated into physical action by hours of practice, and even then it sometimes isn't enough. In outdoor competition, you also run into the spoiler: the wind. Coming down a windy runway, you're fighting an invisible wall that changes your timing and knocks you off to one side, making the motions you've performed thousands of times seem stiff and unfamiliar. Even at your back the wind is fickle at best. While it can give wings to a vault, it can also push the vaulter hard against the crossbar. That's why vaulters from Cornelius Warmerdam down to the present fiberglass era have learned to distrust the wind.

In Berkeley for the National Collegiates, I took a little time off to see the sights in San Francisco. Unfortunately, I hadn't taken the famous hills of that city into account. I was with some of the best runners in the world, who barely noticed the grades, and I had trouble keeping up with them.

By the time we got back to Berkeley and the stadium, I was in trouble. My legs felt rubbery from charging up and down the city's mountainous streets.

Jumbo had been looking for me. "Where the hell have you been? The press is ready to leave. Get out there and do a few vaults."

I knew the value of publicity by this time, so I didn't bother to warm up much. As I swung up for the bar, I felt a ripping sensation in the front of my right thigh. I went under the crossbar and into the pit, grabbing my injured leg. So the only photos the press got were of Jumbo helping me hobble off the field.

The right quadriceps was torn, but nobody knew how badly. It was kind of funny. Dave Sime, a sprinter from New Jersey, had ripped a muscle, too, and he was lying beside me on another table. Here we were, two guys from Jersey, pissing and moaning about how two favorites might not make the Olympics.

The problem for me was I'd expected to qualify for the Olympic team at that meet, and now I wasn't going to. Therefore it became imperative for me to jump extremely well in the National AAU Championships the week after the Berkeley fiasco. I managed to jump well, but reinjured the leg. Jumbo tried to get a waiver for me, since I was one of the top three vaulters in the world, but the officials wouldn't hear of it.

Jumbo took me to Dr. Bellieu, who gave me a shot of what I believe was procaine and cortisone. He felt the leg and asked if it hurt. There was a twinge, but no real pain. Dr. Bellieu said he thought that the numbing concoction could pull me through the Trials.

That Saturday, the day of the Olympic Trials, the leg felt a little better, but began hurting once the competition started. By the fourth jump the pain was agonizing, and I thought I was finished. Jumbo took me out behind the stands, and Dr. Bellieu shot the leg full of his magic mixture. It started working immediately, which was lucky since I heard the loud speaker announcement, "Bragg's up, jumping."

I told myself, hold it together for one more jump. At least the leg didn't hurt anymore. I pounded down the runway, slammed down the pole, and swung over the bar at 14'8", clearing it easily. I landed in the pit feeling exultant. I'd won a berth on the Olympic team.

Then I glanced up.

The kid who was supposed to catch the pole grabbed at it but bobbled the catch. My pole slid from his fingers and fell into the uprights. I jumped up, and as I did, the crossbar fell. The official keeping the jump records at the podium shouted at the top of his voice, "That's a miss. You're off the team." I understood his elation. He was a Southern Cal guy, and I'd been kicking the collective ass of California vaulters for several years. This was payback time for California.

Of course Jumbo was instantly in the official's face, screaming that the jump was good, but the guy wouldn't budge. The rule was specific and iron-clad: the bar must stay up or the vault's no good. I was disqualified.

So here comes Ronnie Morris down the runway with the wind at his back. He pushed off, but didn't shove the pole away hard enough against the wind. It came straight through, hit the cross bar and knocked it down. The impartial official sat there looking dejected. "That's a miss," he said in this quiet voice.

The fact that Ronnie was disqualified didn't make me feel any better. I was shattered. I'd been a contender for a gold medal: now I was nothing. I tried to tell myself that I might not have won in Melbourne. Going into a contest as a sure winner can be the kiss of death for an athlete. But despite my puny mind games, I knew everything I'd worked toward for years was down the tubes.

Not that I was the only disappointed athlete. My good friend Aubrey Lewis, also from New Jersey, had been leading the field in his heat of the 400-meter hurdles by at least a full hurdle length. He glanced back to see how the rest of the field was doing and tripped over the hurdle. By the time he untangled himself from it, several other runners passed, and Aubrey was eliminated.

My friends all took my loss in stride. "You'll be back in four years, Don."

Oh, really? I would have given a lot to peek into the rosy crystal ball they seemed to be consulting. I wasn't even sure I'd ever jump again. That night a bunch of us went to a Doris Day movie, *The Man Who Never Was*. I didn't watch much of the picture. I only remember sitting in the dark theater wondering how in hell I was going to survive this immense failure. Then Doris Day was up there singing a little song that cut through the crap and made me feel better. "*Que Será, Será*" -- what's gonna happen is gonna happen. I went to the rest room and washed my face off under the faucet. Yeah, I'd get past all this. I'd make it through the next four years somehow, and I'd be there in Rome. And, by God, nothing was going to keep me from my gold medal.

A few days later, I saw the controversial jump on the Movietone News. The kid failing to catch the pole cleanly, the pole falling into the standards, the crossbar falling. The Movietone announcer even asked, "Did this man make this height? Think he did? Well, he still missed making the Olympic team."

Olympic officialdom had yet more stones to sling, though. Jimmy Graham, a talented pole vaulter from Oklahoma, was scheduled to go to Melbourne, but he sprained his ankle. It was only a sprain and would have healed in the month prior to the Olympics, but the officials said they couldn't take a chance. Alternate Bob Gutowski would vault in his place. Jimmy could go to Melbourne, but he could only watch. I can just hear Jimmy saying, "Oh, goody!" Jimmy had earned the right to compete, but they took it away and gave it to the Californian. Isn't it swell the Olympics are above politics and favoritism?

Even though I'd failed to make the Olympic team -- which effectively destroyed my hopes of playing Tarzan in the movies -- I still waited anxiously for the results of my friends' competitions.

Since English miler Roger Bannister had retired, everybody expected John Landy to capture the gold in the mile, with Chris Chataway probably taking second. So we thought Ron Delany had a good chance for a bronze medal. Ron blew everybody's mind when he cruised to the gold medal, beating both silver medalist Klaus Richtzenhain, and Aussie John Landy, who won the bronze.

Bob Gutowski took the silver medal in the pole vault, Bob Richards the gold, both solid achievements. But I wished I'd been there to battle it out with the two of them. It almost hurt too much to think about.

By contrast, I got a kick out of hearing that my dearest friends had medaled. Josh took the bronze in the 400-meters, and Charlie Jenkins trotted off with the gold in the quarter mile. The fleet-footed team of Jones, Mashburn, Courtney, and Jenkins also won the gold in the 4 X 400-meter relay.

The real letdown came when I got home from VU. My mom had told me that when they heard I'd been eliminated, Dad just went out back of the house and lay in the tall grass for hours, not saying a word, just letting the wind blow over him. He didn't mention my failure, but I knew I'd let him down. Sometimes, in my room at Villanova, I'd just shut the door and cry.

The person who snapped me out of it was Theresa Fiore. She didn't get all sentimental on me, but if I got depressed, she'd suggest we go swimming or to a movie. She was also positive I'd win my gold medal in Rome, and she told me so. Theresa comforted me in a way no one else ever had, and managed to get me through those dark days.

I also found a poem that I put up on my wall at school, and I read it a hundred times a day. It said if fortune was too kind to you at the start of a struggle, you might not build up the strength for the final battle. I nailed a nice big picture of Gutowski up there, too. First thing in the morning and last thing at night, I'd see his great big mug grinning down at me. With the help of these two motivators, I made up my mind to be tougher and more aggressive than ever before and never take my mind off my gold medal that was waiting for me in Rome. A four-year wait that was to last an eternity.

Chapter Ten

Stormy Weather

Senior year was both my best and my worst year at Villanova. At the National Collegiates, Bob Gutowski'd set a new record, even though his pole had fallen under the bar and into the pit. It hadn't knocked the crossbar down, so they didn't disqualify him. The jump didn't entitle him to a world's record since the falling pole passed the plane of the crossbar, but Bob was still the National Collegiate champion. I was sure he'd make All-American, so it was a nice surprise when I was named All-American for the third year in a row. I assume I got the nod because I'd won more meets than Bob, even though he was the current record holder. That felt very good indeed.

One bittersweet milestone occurred that year when I flew to Chicago for the Chicago Daily News Relays. I'd managed to tie Bob Richards a couple of times, but I'd never beaten him. If I was ever going to beat him head-to-head before he retired, it would probably be at this meet.

Bob Richards was a competitor like none other I'd ever faced. He was totally consumed with competition, a superb, tenacious athlete. His roommate at the 1956 Olympics told a story about him. It was pouring rain when everybody woke up, which depressed most of the guys. Not Bob. He was jumping around the room, clapping. "Everybody's saying we can't jump in the rain, so I already have an edge. I'm a winner!" This was the extraordinary athlete I was about to face.

On March 16, 1957, I jumped 15'3½" to Bob's 15'½".

It wasn't that my long-time idol had grown smaller. Rather, I had come of age. I was twenty-three and at the top of my form. Bob was about ten years older, and it honestly showed. It was hard to watch the guy who'd brought home gold medals from the 1952 and 1956 Olympics laboring at fifteen feet. Yeah, I won the meet, but I got no satisfaction in beating Bob. I went over to him afterward, but I couldn't begin to say how I felt. I ended up apologizing for beating him in front of his kids, but he was gracious in defeat.

It wasn't until after I'd consumed a huge steak at the Stockyard Inn that I began to feel good about winning. I'd come a long way from the scrawny kid asking Bob for his autograph at the Philadelphia Inquirer meet. To me it was almost reminiscent of Plato finally surpassing his mentor Socrates. So the only unpleasantness I took away from the Chicago meet was the extra six pounds I'd put on at my victory dinner.

The next week Bob and I met again in Cleveland. I jumped like a shot-putter, and he sailed past me at 15'3½". He got me again that June in Dayton, clearing 15'1½" to my 14'10½". But I beat out Ronnie Morris, which was nice. A few months later, it didn't surprise me when I heard that Bob had retired. Again, I took no joy in it, but I should have. His retirement marked the beginning of a closer relationship between us.

I began another long-standing friendship that year when I met Johnny Weissmuller in the flesh at a *Sports Illustrated* Olympic fund-raising banquet. I was completely overawed and tongue-tied, just being in Johnny's presence. Finally, I blurted out, "Mr. Weissmuller, about the word *Ungawa*."

Don and Johnny Weissmuller arm wrestle at Florida's Swimming Hall of Fame in 1971.

He looked at me for a second and said, dead serious, "It's an ancient African word. I picked it up from the natives who handle the elephants."

I leaned closer ready to receive the wisdom of the ages.

"It means shit, Don," he said solemnly. Then he broke up, and so did the ice. After that, we matched Tarzan yells and gabbed all night. Certainly that was one of the highlights of the year for me.

At the end of that year, Villanova also gave me a nice tribute by naming me the school's outstanding Senior athlete, even though Jenks had won two Olympic medals. It was as if the school was telling me that it appreciated all my hard work, confirming that I'd honored the terms of my scholarship.

VU had been very good to me. It was more than just scholarships, with all tuition and room and board paid in full. They'd made it clear they were concerned for me academically. VU's unwavering emphasis on academics, combined with Jumbo's insistence on discipline, were instrumental in my success as an athlete and as a person.

During my years at Villanova, we'd had the most successful track team that the college had assembled in years: Alex Breckenridge, Ed Colleymore, Ron Delany, Charlie Jenkins, Phil Reavis, Charlie Stead, George Sydnor -- and Don Bragg. One year we won the indoor collegiate championships as well as the IC4A and National American Championships. Our relay teams were also consistently one of the top teams in national competition. Under Jumbo Elliot's coaching, we developed not only a zest for winning, but also the close bonds that potentiated our athletic ability. It taught us the meaning of competition at the highest level.

I remember getting ready at the National meets and feeling the electricity, almost like an aroma of competition, as the testosterone began to build up. It's what happens when a warrior prepares for combat. He has to get into what I call the testosterone zone if he's going to survive. It's no different for the warrior-athlete. Any physical activity boosts testosterone, but competition pushes it through the roof. Men, women, it doesn't make any difference for top competitors. Just watch any one of them and you can see it. I'd look up and notice the T-zone crackling around Ron Delany like some kind of aura as he'd withdraw from the rest of us, collecting himself to go out and compete with total control.

To reach this point, an athlete must approach his sport in the way a Christian approaches the Eucharist. A believing Christian must take the Body and the Blood and become possessed by it. If you are not consumed by it, you have already failed. In just this way, the athlete must internalize his sport, feast upon it, let it take him over, if he or she has any hopes for greatness.

That's another thing I'd have never learned if I hadn't gone to

Villanova.

———————

I wish senior year had been one long inspirational high for me, but it wasn't. Things hadn't been going so well for Dad. He'd kept his promise to me and stayed off the booze after I'd jogged him around our back yard, but only for a few months. By my senior year he was drinking to the point of jeopardizing his job at Dupont. I think that would have killed him. Mom had to go up and talk to his managers. "Twenty-five years he gave you, and you dump him the first time he comes on hard times? What is that?"

Mom saved his butt for the moment, but he'd still get dinged every so often for taking too much time off. I tried to tell myself that he'd started deteriorating after those stomach operations. But I couldn't stop thinking about him lying out back of the house after the Olympic Trials, staring at nothing because I let him down. It wasn't just Dad I'd let down, either: I hadn't been there for my little sister. Maybe if I'd been home more she wouldn't have run out and gotten pregnant.

But I couldn't change anything, past or present. Mom and Dad had moved into a trailer so Georgie and his new wife could take over the mortgage on the old house on Virginia Avenue. Georgie's marriage didn't last, though. A little later I heard that Mom and Dad had separated, too, so the house sat empty. I remember going home several times and staying in that deserted house. I walked through the rooms, remembering all the love, realizing that it had finally crumbled. That was hard.

I'd always found emotional refuge in constant vaulting practice, but there was no solace there for me now. I'd naively assumed I'd win the gold in Melbourne, and could gracefully retire after I graduated. But I didn't, and now I'd have to manage four more years of training if I was going to try again in Rome. I had to be realistic. I was completing my final year at VU. If I was to continue, I'd have to do it without proper training facilities or financial support. Could I do it? I tried to take stock of my situation.

Vaulters take a beating from their sport. Was I really willing to take it for four more years? The biggest problem was the landing. We'd go over feet first, hoping to land with at least one foot, initially. But then you'd roll onto your shoulder, which sometimes took a real pounding. I'm a little envious of the pits they have today: full of foam for the head-first landings they do now. If we were lucky, we had sawdust and a pit raised three feet off the ground to lessen the fifteen foot drop from the crossbar. That was one thing that drove me nuts in European meets: the floor-level pits filled with sand. Sand is not a soft material, boys and girls. I've knocked myself out on sand.

———————

Yet physical pain was not the biggest drawback to vaulting. While I'd learned to perform with poise, I was never free from the terror of public ridicule if I failed. If I could jump fifteen feet, if I could set a record, that was acceptable because the crowd would cheer and go crazy. But that only worked in public. During my hours of solitary practice an acceptable jump just wasn't enough. I had to go higher, then higher still, and merely being safe from ridicule wouldn't do it for me. So even if it meant facing ridicule, I had to keep competing until I'd made that trip to Rome.

I'd committed to continue vaulting through the 1960 Olympics, but the decision was nearly taken out of my hands. I was still battling to keep my weight down, but poles were still buckling under me, and with increasing frequency. I wondered if using a fiberglass pole might be the answer. I'd heard they gave you extra height, and I knew Bob Richards had tried one of them. When Jumbo handed me a fiberglass pole, I was eager to try it. I worked my way up to 15'3", but it felt more unstable than my first attempt in Fineroski's back lot.

That sensation was a result of the way the new poles worked. Fiberglass had a great catapult action that could fling the vaulter to new heights, but to a vaulter trained on metal poles, that flexibility felt like the pole was caving in. It was completely different from the metal poles I'd used, and I knew I'd have to relearn all my vaulting technique if I switched to fiberglass. That would take a good three months of steady training, and I was on the verge of leaving VU.

Then I made a discouraging discovery. If I attempted anything higher than 15'3", the fiberglass splintered with a crack that felt like a gun going off in my armpit. I was just too heavy and gripped the pole too high.

I didn't know what I was going to do. Heart and desire aren't worth much to a vaulter if he doesn't have a pole that will hold up. I'd been considering quitting vaulting, but having the decision thrust on me was like a bucket of ice down my pants. Damn! I was a vaulter, I had to vault, and something had to break for me besides my poles.

So I didn't give up hope. People who developed new poles knew about me, and when they'd come up with a new prototype, they'd send one along. Dupont even talked about making me one out of titanium and molybdenum, but the cost would have been prohibitive. I tried Swedish steel, English aluminum alloy, and American aluminum. I broke twenty-seven poles during this invigorating period.

Then I met Brett Marrett, who owned Gill Sporting Goods. He developed an aluminum alloy pole for me like the kind I'd been using ever since high school, but with a difference. It accommodated 205 pounds rather than just 195. However, the pole had one drawback: it was stiff, so it beat hell out of my shoulder and back. I thought it was just me until another guy borrowed it. The damned thing threw his back out completely, so I figured I was lucky it worked for me at all. I dreamed about a fiberglass pole with enough resin and graphite to hold my weight, because it was only a matter of time until fiberglass poles became standard.

If they'd come out with a finessed fiberglass pole in 1957, it would have ended my career right then, and I would never have been an Olympic champion. My career was on such a knife's edge, that when Brett gave me this new pole, I knew God had to be giving me another chance at victory.

Okay, so I'd confirmed that I had to keep vaulting, but I had to figure out how to make a living. One time at the Nationals we were in Rosie Grier's room, chewing the fat. Rosie was telling us about his great contract to play pro football. I think it was for $6,500. "And," Rosie said, "I get another $6,500 for being a beer rep during the off-season."

We were all impressed. "Wow, that's a helluva deal. There's no way we can do that in track."

Rosie had cocked one eye at me and grinned, "Hey, Bragg. Didn't I say you should've been a football player?" Now I was beginning to fear Rosie'd been right.

PART FOUR

NEW HORIZONS

To come into the world to see
To live the things not known before

-- from "Birth" by Don Bragg

Chapter Eleven

Other Worlds

Bob Gutowski was in fantastic shape and jumping superbly. He took top honors at the National Collegiates, beating my jump of 15'1¾". Bob Richards was first at the AAU meet, but my lackluster 14'10½" second-place effort qualified me for a European tour anyway. Since I'd never been out of the country, I was excited about seeing the British Isles and Scandinavia for the first time. But I was also grateful to be able to put off the inevitable question of how in hell to earn a living and still keep my Olympic dream alive.

When we landed at Heathrow Airport, we were immediately inundated by a swarm of sour-faced officials, shoving entry and customs declarations under our noses. What was worse, they were jabbering at us in some strange unintelligible dialect. Man! I hadn't expected to have to deal with a foreign language in England. Then a platoon of men in matching London Fog raincoats showed up, shooing the customs people away, herding us disorganized Yanks onto buses. I also experienced a rush of relief when I realized I could understand what these guys were saying.

As soon as we were settled, some of the guys said we had to go check out Piccadilly Circus. The attraction, I found out, was the swarm of working girls hanging around the statue of Nelson. When the guys started negotiating the price for their services, I knew I was way out of my league, so I went back to the hotel alone. As the day went on, I noticed one particular hurdler escorting a different young lady upstairs every hour or so, and I was a little envious. What a stud!

This was not to say that I was immune to the charms of the British women. The first night at dinner, our waitress, a black-haired cutie from Wales, seemed to be making an extra fuss over me. I wanted to respond in kind, but I was overcome with shyness every time she approached the table. Josh finally kicked me in the shins.

"Why in hell don't you ask her out? She obviously likes you." I mumbled something about not knowing what to say, and Josh shook his head in disgust. "Am I gonna have to do everything for your sorry butt?"

He waved the young lady over to our table and said, "This gentleman would like very much to see you after work, if that's possible." She hesitated, fluttering long, dark eyelashes, but finally agreed to meet me about seven in front of the hotel.

You'd have thought Josh was the one who'd just scored. "There you go, man. You're all set up, so just get out there and go for it."

At seven o'clock I locked myself in the bathroom, too shy and embarrassed to leave. I thought the guys would never let me live that one down.

I was on my best behavior, but trouble seemed anxious to chase me down, like the time I was attacked by an elevator. A bunch of us were going up to the room, and I was telling a story to hurdler Aubrey Lewis, my buddy from Jersey, when the elevator stopped dead. We pressed all the buttons, but when the door opened we were facing a brick wall. The opening for the fifth floor was only visible through an eighteen-inch gap at the top of the car. However, bars on the car door blocked access to it. After about ten minutes -- Aubrey says ten seconds -- I began to panic, and started beating on the bars. Aubrey kept saying, "Take it easy, they'll get us out of here," but I was in no mood for reason. It was clearly time for Tarzan to leap to the rescue.

I hitched myself up and began to pry those bars apart, while the others huddled in the corner, as far away from me as they could get. I finally had an opening I could clamber through. But when I offered the others a hand up, they said they'd just wait for the hotel people, thanks anyway.

Still, I was pretty proud of my escape until the coach confronted me. "Bragg! Why in hell did you have to go and break their elevator? If you're gonna act like King Kong, just climb up the outside of the building, for Pete's sake."

Our hosts threw us a big party in an enormous room overlooking the White City Stadium, where we'd be competing, and I had my first taste of British stuffiness. A party with nothing but embalmed-looking people staring down their noses at cucumber sandwiches just didn't do it for me. I kept pulling at my stifling collar, wishing I were back in Jersey.

We were introduced to an army of dignitaries, including Prince Charles. He was just a little kid, but he looked as gloomy as everybody else. With difficulty, I stifled an impulse to yell, "Sara Bootie, how ya doin', kid?" It looked to me like he could've done with a few weeks in Tarzanville, swimming at the gravel pit and muskratting at night. What's the point of being a prince if you never have any fun?

There was one girl about my age who seemed as unimpressed with the constipated gathering as I was. We started talking, and soon she suggested we take off for a party with more pizazz. She looked me over. "It's formal, you know. Do you have a tuxedo?"

"Are you kidding?"

She dragged me over to her father, who happened to own the London *Evening News*, one of the event's sponsors, and after a whispered conference, he said, "Send him to my Saville Row tailor."

The next thing I know, I'm all done up in a tux and climbing into a limousine beside Elizabeth. What an adventure! Then I walked in and saw the crowd of elegant, vivacious people chatting and sipping champagne. I stood there swallowing hard, very much aware that I was just a farm boy from the South Jersey swamps.

But unlike the bunch at the official do we'd left earlier, this crowd was having fun, and I felt myself relaxing. Elizabeth introduced me to a young singer named Tommy Steele, and to members of the British theatrical crowd: Diana Dors, Anthony Steele, and Dirk Bogarde. Tommy Steele wished me good luck in the meets, "But not too much good luck, since you'll be taking on our British chaps."

After a while, Elizabeth suggested we go for a spin out in the country. Her car was one of those little English jobs designed for malnourished midgets. The only way I could fit in was to jam both feet under the seat. Besides the numbness in my legs, I don't remember much about the drive, except that Elizabeth and I were talking easily, as if we'd known each other for years. A few blocks from her house she pulled over, and the sense of intimacy increased. I tried to shift closer, but it wasn't easy. I had to haul one foot out from under the seat, but when I got it free, it came whipping out and ended up wrapped around the steering column. I didn't want to seem like an uncoordinated oaf, so I tried to think up a real suave move as an encore. Just then, a tap at the window made us both jump. I cranked the window down and peered over the fogged-up glass. Two bobbies were peering back.

"Good evening, ma'am, sir. Is everything all right?" they asked.

"Absolutely," I said and started to crank the window back up.

"Begging your pardon, sir, but we were asking the lady."

Suddenly demure as hell, Elizabeth said, "Yes, constable. How kind of you to inquire."

Minutes later, Elizabeth and I bade each other a chaste good night, thanks to those two guardians of virtue. It's a wonder any British babies manage to get born at all.

————————

The British Committee had arranged meets for us in London,

Manchester and Scotland, and I was pleasantly surprised at the warmth of the crowds. The great English runner Roger Bannister had retired, and the British teams seemed to lack the depth of ours. Unless we got cocky or obnoxious, that is: then the Brits would come roaring back, rubbing our noses in our own hubris. Mostly though, the British crowds applauded our victories warmly, and I realized we'd dipped into the greatest mother-lode of sportsmanship in the world. The athletes were great to us, too, and even invited us to join them at their favorite pub. I was shocked at the way they put away the beer. "They let you drink beer? Isn't that breaking training?"

The Brits just laughed. "Who in hell's going to stop us, lad?" I laughed too, thinking of the apoplectic fit Avery Brundage would throw if we followed our British cousins' lead.

Even more interesting to me was the fact that many British amateur track athletes played professional soccer. "Sure we play soccer. How else are we supposed to keep body and soul together?"

How indeed! So it wasn't just the evil communist countries who were getting around the Brundage Brigade and their pristine Olympic standards. I began to realize that only American athletes were held to the those impossibly strict rules.

We had one meet in Scotland at a spruced-up dog track, and once again we were well-received. I loved Scotland, where I saw my first ancient monument, Hadrian's Wall. I also fell in love with its glens and craggy mountains. Though it was nothing like Penns Grove, it almost felt like home.

Since I wanted to buy my mom a nice present, I made a special point of looking at the marvelous woolen goods. I found a pretty green sweater I thought she would like, but then realized I'd left my money at the hotel.

Josh heard me bitching and said, "Not to worry. Go talk to that hurdler over there. He'll loan you the cash, then you can pay him back at the hotel."

This didn't make sense. None of us had that kind of money. To my surprise the guy turned out to be the stud I'd seen with women in London. He whipped out a roll of bills and asked how much I needed. I was impressed until he let me in on his secret. He was no ladies man, but rather a business man, sort of. He'd been bringing the girls to all his buddies after negotiating a price for their services, and tacking on a nice commission for himself. Josh and I laughed all the way back to our hotel. So super stud was only an ingenious pimp!

Of course, Coach got wind of his take-out bordello operation, and just before we left for Sweden, shut down this unofficial department of foreign trade.

———————

Josh Culbreath had all of us primed to sample Swedish folkways. "Wait till you see those Swedish women," he said. "In their culture, sex is no big deal. If girls like a guy, they sleep with him. It's a whole different thing."

I reminded Josh I was still terribly shy around girls, but he magnanimously gave me the benefit of his vast experience. "What you do is get a bottle of good brandy and tell 'em, 'I have this incredible cognac up in my room.' That's all you do. They'll come by the hundreds."

By the time we debarked in Malmö, everybody was ready for a little culture shock with those sensible Swedish women. It was like the Viking invasion in reverse, with us cast as the predators.

Our first stop after landing in Malmö was a luncheon sponsored by two local newspapers and the sports organization, Club MAI. After a sumptuous meal I was ready to stretch my legs and see something of the town, but Josh insisted we visit Johanssen Mens' Clothiers first. "This is Scandinavia. You pick out your own prizes, and Johanssen's is the place to do it," he said. "It's the best mens' store in Sweden."

Pick out your own prize? I was beginning to appreciate the Swedish way of doing business.

Right away I headed for the coat department since I wanted a London Fog type coat. A lovely young woman came over and asked how she could help me. After an awkward start I managed to ask if I could see her later. Her name was Marie-Louise, and she stunned me when she accepted my shy invitation. That night I learned first-hand that everything Josh had told me about Swedish women was true.

A few dates later, she took me home to meet her mother -- and her own young son. In Sweden, she explained, any baby born out of wedlock is supported by the state until the age of eighteen. There's no pressure for the parents to marry.

This came as a shock.

In the ingenuous pre-AIDS world, premarital sex was a given. Nobody bothered about protection, either, but if a guy got his girl pregnant, the right thing to do was to marry her and start a family together. At least that's how it worked in Penns Grove. And here's the Swedish state supporting something I didn't consider very moral. Marie-Louise was beautiful and seemed to adore me, so I pushed the dilemma aside. But I knew my idea of family was on a collision course with hers.

As much as I was enjoying the trip, there was something a little different about this tour. The kind of light-hearted adventures I'd enjoyed with these same guys in college occurred only rarely. Now, we were young bulls in our prime, and more interested in Nordic courtship rituals than in playing Joe College pranks.

Our five meets in Sweden were incredibly successful, with huge crowds applauding every athlete's performance. Coach tapped me to run second leg on the sprint relay. Over a short distance, I could pour on the energy on any track, so I was surprised when I couldn't pull away from the Swedish sprinter.

After the meet, Josh clued me in on the fact that I'd been running against the Swedish champion, and I went over to talk to him. However, I had to wait until he finished taking pictures of all the other athletes. He was very open about what he was doing: making a living selling the pictures to newspapers. This not only supported him but also left him plenty of time for practice.

It was one more accepted route around the so-called amateur rules. Swedish sports officials not only turned a blind eye to this, they evidently used their ingenuity to help athletes sidestep the impossibly strict code of amateurism. This would never happen in the States, as if the fact that the athletes needed money to continue in their sport was irrelevant. This bureaucratic attitude was making less and less sense to me.

Swedish society was relaxed in many ways. For instance, Swedish women really went for black athletes, and it was no big thing seeing a black guy with a gorgeous blond on his arm. Nobody seemed to take notice at all. One evening, however, one of the runners -- who happened to be black -- was with a lovely blonde. We hardly even knew each other, but he kept grinning and gesturing at me, pointing to his flaxen-haired date. He was all triumphant like he'd put one over on me or something. I finally realized he was flaunting the fact that he, a black guy, was with a white woman. Well, no shit, but who cared? His behavior started to rile me, but Josh calmed me down.

"Pay him no mind," he said. "He doesn't understand that you're one of us." That was one of the biggest compliments I've received in my entire life.

I was soon distracted from the guy and his blonde, though. There was a flourish of drums, and the band leader announced that a famous performer from America would sing "Red Sails in the Sunset" for us. To our astonishment, Bobbie Barksdale was the one grabbing the microphone. He nearly carried it off. Bobbie had a pretty good voice, and looked fine standing up there in front of everybody. Trouble was, he had no idea of the words to the song. He stood there and sang the title over and over, "Red sails in the sunset, red sails in the sunset," while we laughed till we choked. The Swedes had these fixed smiles on their faces while they eyed one another, looked at us, then looked back at Bob. They clearly thought the American track team had slipped its gears. For the rest of the tour, Bob had to answer to "Red Sails."

Bob also helped keep us entertained during the long rides on the Swedish railroad. He had an able ally in Josh Culbreath. We all knew Josh carried a cognac flask, but we never saw him nipping from it. But when we heard him and Bob start doing a hilariously raunchy Amos and Andy routine, we knew that cognac was behind it.

We negotiated for our prizes throughout Scandinavia, and Tom Courtney became very skilled at it, using the same aggressiveness at the negotiating table that he did on the track. In Oslo he was running against Belgian Roger Moens, the European favorite and current record holder, and Tom expected a prize worthy of the occasion.

The Norwegian officials never knew what hit them.

The papers had been full of the Courtney-Moens race, but the promoters kept hedging when Tom brought up the question of his prize.

Minutes before the race was to start, Tom limped up to the promoters, his face registering a twinge with every dragging step. He asked if they'd reached a decision on his prize. When they continued to waffle, Tom shook his head sadly as he hobbled away. "It's just as well. This leg cramp is killing me, and I don't think I can run."

One of the officials came scuttling after him, and we saw Tom's eyes narrow and his mouth twitch into a tiny smile before he nodded his head. He then made a great show of grimacing dramatically while the trainer supposedly loosened up his cramp. Finally, he took his position, and the race began. The runners were neck and neck until the very end, when Tom shot ahead with an explosion of speed. He crossed the finish line a winner and received a thunderous standing ovation.

Afterwards I asked how he'd managed that incredible spurt at the end. "That was the deal. If I didn't win, I'd get zip." He gave us a knowing grin as he strapped a luxurious Omega watch on his wrist.

I decided to take a leaf from Tom's book once we were back in Sweden. I approached the meet coordinator.

"Sir, about my prize? Um, I'll be competing in twelve meets."

"Yaa, true. Twelve meets."

`"I have a pretty good chance of winning them. Maybe even setting a few stadium records."

"New records would be good. The Swedish people would be most grateful."

"So what about if I asked for a Volvo?"

"Excellent Swedish automobile. Yaa, with stadium records, a Volvo is possible."

It was that easy!

Then the official began totting up some figures. "A very fine automobile. Of course you will pay all duty and customs charges, yaa? About a thousand dollars American."

I swallowed hard. "Tell me about Swedish crystal, please." At least I'd be popular with my relatives when I got home. They'd be getting most of the loot.

From Göteborg we flew back to Norway, visiting Oslo again, plus Bergen and Stavanger. The surprisingly dark-haired Norwegians seemed more reserved than their Swedish counterparts, though they were certainly hospitable.

They held a large meet in Oslo, and the highlight was to be Josh going for a world record in the 400-meter hurdles against the Norwegian champion. Fifteen minutes before his race, Josh was nowhere to be found. We were getting worried, when a gate opened at the end of the field and a motorcycle roared into the stadium. The rider wore a cap and goggles, and sported a long white scarf floating dramatically behind him. He had one other impressive accessory: a ravishing blonde clinging to his waist. We were irate at the intruder. "That son of a bitch has some nerve, driving onto our track like that. Let's go tell him off."

We stopped dead when the guy stripped off his goggles. Norway's "Easy Rider" turned out to be the missing Josh Culbreath. The stadium exploded with laughter and applause as he changed into his running gear in the middle of the field. With all the distractions, however, Josh placed second in his race in a dramatic photo finish. He was philosophical about his loss. With his arm around his date, Josh grinned and said. "I guess you can't have everything." He did break the world's record a few days later, however, which shows all good things come to a man with his priorities straight.

We were happy to be going home when we finally boarded the plane. We didn't take off, however: our plane sat immobile on the tarmac for ages. When the flashing lights of police cars suddenly surrounded the plane, one of the runners headed for the washroom, dumping something in a pillowcase on an empty seat as he hurried by. We watched, fascinated, as irate Norwegian police swarmed into the main cabin. It seemed that a priceless Norwegian vase had been swiped from our hotel, just when we were checking out. One of them noticed the pillowcase and pounced on it. They immediately congratulated themselves on recovering the Viking vase, but before they could search the plane for the culprit, the rest of us began protesting vigorously about the delay in taking off. The police exited the plane, triumphantly bearing their prize, and we started breathing again. Only after we took off, did our runner emerge sheepishly from the john and collapse in his seat, looking like he'd had a conversion experience.

Before I knew it, I was back in Penns Grove wondering what in hell I was going to do next.

Chapter Twelve

Beware of Greeks

I t made sense to try and put my degree in finance to good use. But nothing came together until my mom came home with the news that the record store where she worked was for sale. When I looked into it, I found to my surprise that the owner was Tommy Belitza from my vaulting days at Penns Grove High. I borrowed the money and started my first business venture with high hopes.

I jumped the '58 indoor season, but my top jump was only 14'6", due to my weight and my ongoing problems with the pole. Brett Marrett, who'd made me the pole in the first place, came around after one of the meets and said that my jumps seemed to be off. I told him how much using the pole hurt. He nodded and looked extremely thoughtful. "Shoulder shock. Let me see what I can do about it." I didn't think too much more about it because I ran into another kind of a shock.

A couple of months after I opened my record shop, the local drug store started selling records, then the five and dime. There was no way I could meet their discount prices, and within the year I had to close the business.

Since I hadn't jumped that well during the season, I didn't expect to qualify for a tour. So I was pleasantly surprised when I was invited to join one headed for Greece, the Middle East, and Asia, winding up in Ceylon. What won me the berth was the fact the tour was to start in March when the super-qualified college jumpers were tied up with school. The fact that I wasn't jumping at my very best wasn't even a factor, since the tour wasn't competition-driven. The tour athletes were to give clinics and exhibitions, do interviews on Voice of America, and generally act as good-will ambassadors. But they selected me anyway.

———————

Our main objective in giving clinics was to help other countries build up track teams that would be more competitive in the Olympics. So it was nice that we kicked off the program in Greece, the country that started it all: sort of an athletic payback. Yet I wasn't prepared for the incredible thrill I felt when the plane actually set down in Greece, the cradle of just about everything. I especially looked forward to seeing the land of the Spartans, the warriors who wrote some of their country's greatest history with their own blood.

Tarzan turns Samson while testing the Pillars of Hercules on the Acropolis in Greece in 1958.

When we arrived at our hotel, my first thought was to have a look at our stadium, which was a replica of the original Olympic model. It was very beautiful, but the track was a straightaway with sharp turns, not the gently curved ovals we were used to. In fact it reminded me a lot of VU's indoor board track. Josh had a bad time in the 400-meter hurdles, since his speed created a kind of slingshot effect on the turns that nearly threw him off the track. He managed to win, though, due to his experience and fiercely competitive spirit.

We had another taste of ancient competition when we visited a display of artifacts from the original Olympics. The discus thrower of old stood on a pedestal two feet off the ground. He had to maintain his balance on this two-by-three-foot platform, unlike today's discus throwers who have an eight-foot circle. I hopped up onto the pedestal and had no problems until I tried for some distance with the discus. It took several attempts, but I eventually surpassed the long-distance mark set by a Greek athlete more than two thousand years earlier. I thought I was pretty hot stuff. Then Josh deflated my ego with a reminder that I had a humongous height advantage. It was easy to forget that those scrappy Greek warriors were just over five feet tall.

We stayed in downtown Athens at the Athena Palace, a hotel with a long and elegant past and an accommodating staff that went out of its way to make us comfortable. They seemed worried when I'd leave the hotel with just a bite of breakfast, but I never ate much before a meet. After one day's round of competition and lectures we were all signing autographs, when my stomach began to rumble ominously. I was famished. Josh was still chatting with fans -- he loved people -- so I hopped in our waiting cab and returned to the hotel, where I beat a path to the dining room. Lobster tails were on the menu, so I ordered two, wolfed them down, and ordered two more. The waiters were delighted. At last the ascetic American had an appetite. They urged me to take three more, bringing the total to seven. Now I was satisfied.

A resonant belch rumbled forth just as Josh and four others charged into the dining room. All of them were thoroughly pissed off that I'd left the stadium with their cab. But they didn't want to hear my excuses, because they had food on their minds, lobster tails to be exact. When the waiter started to explain that, due to the hearty appetite of a single diner, lobster tails weren't to be had, I excused myself and headed for the door. I was only halfway there when I heard a chorus of "Bragg!" and I made a hasty exit, pursued by my hungry teammates. From then on, whenever I suggested it was time for dinner the others stuck to me like glue.

After the guys finally had something to eat, they were ready to go night-clubbing. I didn't drink, so I thought I'd take in a movie. A Greek kid of about seventeen had been pestering us to make him our guide ever since we'd arrived, so I took him with me to see John Wayne and Sophia Loren in *The Lost City*. It was kind of a trip to hear fluent Greek coming out of the Duke's mouth and his cowboy twang reduced to subtitles.

The next night I was ready to turn the guys down again, but they began to razz me about preferring the company of young Greek boys. I thought at first that they really liked having me along, but then I realized they were all on the small side physically, and they were counting on big ol' Bragg to play bodyguard.

We ended up in a sleazy tavern, where girls were working the bar with practiced skill. One of them started to hang around me, so I told her, "I have no money, I do not drink," over and over. She was still hovering when the guys started to leave with their dates. They wanted me to join their party. Over my objections they each chipped in for my handmaiden's ten-dollar fee, and I was committed.

The women took us to a shabby rooming house that featured unsavory characters hanging around just outside of the lamplight. You could feel their hard eyes following you. Inside, a muscular bald man guarded a hallway lined with doors. The girl took a candle and brought me to a room with a narrow bed and a wash basin. I wasn't sure what to do next and was nervous as hell: no rule book covered this situation. The girl began talking to me in her gentle Greek voice, and then rules didn't seem to matter at all.

Afterwards, however, I noticed she was kind of whimpering, so I pulled the candle nearer and saw that the bed was badly blood-stained. I was out of there with a leap that would have made Ira Davis proud. The Curse! I'd heard Mom and Dietzie talking about it, and now I'd caught it. Here in the prime of my life, I'd gone and jeopardized a couple of precious parts I really didn't want to have shrivel up and fall off.

The girl had really started crying now. I think she was afraid of what the bruiser in the hall might do to her if I demanded my money back. I kind of patted her on the head and took off down the hall. The bald bouncer blocked my way, but I glared at him and he backed down. I wasn't sure what he'd do to the smaller guys, but at that moment I had more urgent worries.

It was about a mile to the hotel, and I ran the entire way. When I got to the room, I threw my clothes in the trash. Next I filled the bathtub with hot water, seized the bath brush, and spent the next hour scrubbing the affected body parts with strong yellow soap.

I awoke the next morning with searing pain in my nether regions, and found my entire groin area aflame with a scarlet rash. Curtains for Don Bragg, the vaulting stud! I was relieved when I realized the source of the rash was my own frenzied scrubbing, which had removed most of the skin from the area.

This wasn't something I was about to tell the guys, but they wanted to know why I was walking around with my knees two-and-a-half feet apart. I took a lot of ribbing after they pried the story out of me. A night or two later they invited me to come clubbing with them, but I'd learned my lesson too painfully to want to tempt fate again.

I was happy to let George take over as my guide to Athens. He was a funny kid: small and dark, with street-smart eyes that could have belonged to a fifty-year-old. We'd walk through the streets and squares while he'd tell me about his city. One night we stopped at one of the outdoor cafés on a little square, and George had me order a special coffee that arrived in a doll-sized cup. This was the first coffee I'd ever had to chew.

I was sitting there munching my coffee, when a couple of men strolled up, nodded to George, and asked who I was. George told them that I was a pole vaulting champion like George Roubanis, the bronze medalist at the '56 Olympics. One guy looked me over speculatively, staring intently at my arms. George listened to a flood of Greek, then translated. "He says his name is Demetrios, and wants to know if you arm-wrestle." Demetrios looked a little like Charles Bronson, maybe a little bigger, the same sort of scary features. But hell, I was pretty good and could take him easy. We squared off right there at the table, and he put my arm down in a couple of seconds.

I was flabbergasted. Nobody'd ever done that to me, and I had no idea how he'd managed it. By the second match, we'd drawn a crowd of onlookers that watched him take me down again, but this time I'd analyzed his grip and arm motion.

"One more time," I said, smiling sweetly at him.

I won the third and fourth matches, surprising both George and Demetrios. He jumped up and told George there should be one more match, but at the Black Cat Café. "This time for champion."

It was a twenty-minute walk to the café, and when I saw it I knew there might be trouble. It looked like it was under the same management as the sleazy boarding house I'd visited. I went to the bar and started to order a Coke, but George shepherded me into the back room, saying, "Don't worry, no problem," as if he could read my mind.

In the back room were half a dozen tables crowded with guys smoking water pipes. The air was filled with an acrid smoke I later identified as hashish, and for a moment I thought I was either going to pass out or float away. As George pulled out a chair at the central table, I threw a swift glance around the room. There were no exits beside the door we'd just entered. My only defense, if it came to that, would be to grab a chair and make some kind of stand in a corner.

Just then the door swung open and in walked Demetrios. His eyes were vacant and unfocused as he announced, "One time for best in Greece."

As we started, his arm felt like steel, and he stared at me with eyes that didn't really see my face. This was a lot more than I'd bargained for, but I still thought I could take him. I bore down, locking my wrist, anticipating the turn he would give to his. My next job was to sustain his shoulder thrust and hold him upright until it was time for me to make my move and bring him in and down. We were locked like that for five minutes before I felt him weaken. As long as I was on top, I could keep the pressure on him. After a few more minutes under the full force of my arm, he gave way, and I won.

With a low growl Demetrios seized the heavy table and heaved it against the wall. I snatched a chair and backed into the corner. At least they'd know Americans could fight. But the crowd didn't rush me. My opponent came at me, eyes bloodshot and glassy, then grinned. "Now we drink."

After my second Coke with a whiff of rum, I asked, through George, how he'd gotten so strong for this match when he'd been so weak during the previous one. Demetrios rolled up his sleeve, displaying the tracks of heroin needles. He said that he was out of shape and had needed an extra hit after I'd poured it on in our fourth match. He was thirty, looked forty, and seemed saddened when he told me he hadn't been beaten since he was seventeen. "The greatest wrestler in Greece," he said, and had another belt of ouzo to help him forget it wasn't really true any more.

We continued to give clinics and exhibitions throughout Greece, and as the tour wound down, we were invited to a party by King Constantine and Queen Frederika. Coach Olsen -- from Michigan, I think -- was the tour manager, and he started acting paranoid. "You're going to be with royalty, Bragg. No Tarzan yells, no spitting, no nothing, get it?"

Since the luncheon was part of a national celebration, we thought it would be a rigidly formal meal. However, the king and queen were charming people, and quickly put us at our ease. The food was unlike any I'd eaten before, but it was delicious. There were stuffed grape leaves, fried salted smelts, pastries full of savory fillings, countless varieties of olives, and other Greek delicacies. There was a large balcony at one end of the reception room, and as we ate, we watched a military parade saluting the king and queen as it swept by below us.

I was caught up in all the pageantry, and maybe not paying attention to business, so I was as surprised as everybody else when a sonorous belch erupted out of me. There was dead silence, during which Coach's fingers started twitching as if he were about to grab me somewhere painful. Queen Frederika put a gracious lid on his anger. "I see you have already mastered the Middle-Eastern art of complimenting a meal, Mr. Bragg."

Evidently, the louder the belch, the better the meal, and I'd just awarded her chef five stars. I grinned triumphantly at Coach Olsen, who looked like he wanted to drop right through the floor.

I needed something to read on the flight to Istanbul, so later that day

I wandered over to a bookstore that had busts of all the funky old Greek philosophers in their window. I had an urge to read up on Socrates, so I bought copies of Plato's *Meno and the Slave* and *Phaedo*, which I remembered from VU. So when I left Greece, I had a couple of nice souvenirs right in my pocket.

Call it Byzantium, Constantinople, or Istanbul, this Turkish city was completely different from anything we'd seen in Greece. Minarets rose from the shabby remains of the ancient city. Most of the streets were oxcart-wide and had a dangerous feel to them. On the way to dinner one night, we passed a run-down corner where several men huddled around a small fire. I asked the driver if they were vagrants.

"No, Turkish Army men, greatest fighters in the world!" he said with pride. "Loyal, too. In prison they chew up meat for sick comrades."

I needed such a comrade shortly thereafter when our repast of curry and rice taught me the meaning of the words amoebic dysentery. When we reached the stadium for the next day's competition, my highest priority was to locate the toilet. Luckily, it was only fifty feet away, so I survived the meet, but realized we'd be seeing a lot of our new amoebic friend as the tour continued.

Most of the guys noticed the macabre atmosphere that seemed to hang over the city, especially at night, so there was little desire to go night-clubbing. The last evening, however, all of us decided to go to a club famous for the exquisite blonde, blue-eyed European show girls who'd dance with the customers. The place lived up to its reputation. One of the entertainers danced with me several times, and I enjoyed her company. We were in the middle of a dance when she was summoned to a table where a sheik with his entourage was holding forth. Josh and the others began razzing me for losing my girl, so I had to do something. I went to the sheik's table to ask her to dance again, but two bodyguards blocked my way. I didn't want to create a scene so I went back to my buddies at the bar, peaceable as a rabbit.

Josh, however, was in a helpful mood. "Get back in there, Tarzan, and if they give you any crap, we'll heave 'em over the railing."

The bodyguards were still being unreasonable, so the guys charged in and sent the whole delegation sprawling across the tables. We swung down from the balcony and sprinted down the mysterious streets, laughing like hell. We hailed a cab, piled into it, and got our butts back to the hotel, scot-free.

Or so we thought. Later that evening, one of our guides asked if we'd been at that club. We said, "Sure. Is there a problem?"

It seemed we'd mightily miffed our sheik. Evidently he went home and began issuing blood-curdling death threats against the American hooligans. Our anxious guides banished us to our rooms until our flight the next morning. I was the only guy who wasn't sharing a room, so I spent an uncomfortable night by myself, with an armoire shoved against the door to keep out any scimitar-wielding intruders. When Coach knocked on the door, he heard furniture being moved before it opened. I finished up my explanation by saying, "I don't know why I get in so many scrapes."

Coach patted me on the shoulder and said, "Hell, son. You're crazy, that's all."

Chapter Thirteen

Magic Carpet Ride

The next stop on our eastward trek was Beirut, the flower of the Middle East. They put us up at the American University, but we didn't spend much time at the dorms. There was too much to see. The day after our arrival, we took a day trip inland to the ruins of the Roman fortress of Baalbek. As we approached the outlying foothills to the east of the city, the fortifications seemed to appear magically from out of the barren plains surrounding this ancient oasis.

Examining the ruins, we could tell the Romans had been security-conscious. The fort's entrance had been built deep into the rock, well below the first floor, and they'd had lions running loose in the entry chamber to guard it. If the sentries liked your looks, they rounded up the lions, then admitted you. If they didn't, they rang the dinner bell.

On the upper floor, magnificent columns soared at least a hundred feet in the air, reminiscent of the Acropolis, but made of sandstone rather than Grecian marble. Costumed in my underwear, I hopped up on various pedestals, striking poses suitable for a Roman warrior, while Josh snapped photos. Our impromptu shoot was interrupted when I received an urgent reminder of my bout of dysentery. Our guide directed me up several flights of stairs, but I only found a hole in a dingy corner. I yelled back down to the guide that all I could find was a hole, and he yelled back, "Yes. One must squat."

I squatted, and noted in passing that the wall beside me was covered with brown finger prints. Disgusting, I thought, as I reached for the toilet paper. Of course there was none, and a moment later my fingerprints joined the others.

It was getting late, so I hurried back to the car. To do so, I had to pass several camel-riding Arabs, who began to beg for a donation to the Lebanese economy. The tour people told us to ignore beggars, because if you gave to one you risked being inundated with a hundred others. One of these beggars was hard to shake, though. He gestured eloquently that he really wanted some of my pocket change. When I ignored him, he hissed at me, "You cheap son of a bitch."

I turned, expecting a fight since he was sliding off his camel, but fervently hoping he didn't have a knife. Then I realized my Arab looked damn familiar. It was Josh, of course, doubling up with laughter as he struggled out of his robes and turban. "I got you, Tarzan, admit it!" The rest of the camel drivers thought it was a pretty good joke too, and gave us a rousing send-off back to Beirut.

Our competition was held the next day in an old stadium dating back to before Jesus's time. No one had yet vaulted fifteen feet in the Middle East, and I promised I'd try for it if they gave me a raised pit. They did exactly as I'd asked, but the pit was filled with three feet of sand rather than sawdust. On any jump over fourteen feet, I knew the landing would smart like hell, but I gave it a try. After I'd worked my way up to 14'6" in four jumps, I landed so hard I saw stars, all sizes and colors. My crash landing had resounded all through the stadium, so Coach Olsen and the others came running over. When I picked up my pole and started to head off the field, Coach said, "We didn't bring you all the way to Lebanon for you to quit after four jumps. Besides, these people came a long way to see you. At least go over and throw the shot or discus, for Pete's sake."

At the shot-put circle I was greeted like a brother by a huge Lebanese. He won the shot, but I beat him out in the discus throw. Next, he shook my hand, but I was ready for him. He exerted incredible pressure, but I didn't flinch, and he looked at me with new respect. After all, he had about a hundred pounds on me. He cocked one eye at me and asked, "Do you do arm-pulling?" When I said I did, he flashed a smile that lit up the whole stadium. "I win shot, you win discus. One more contest for winner."

So we arm-wrestled in the middle of the hushed arena, with all eyes on us. Forget my measly pole vaults: this was the main event. I thought I could take him after my experience with Demetrios in Athens. Well, all the experience in the world couldn't have stopped this phenomenon. Caught between his size and his mastery of the style, I was a goner right from the start. All I could do was slow down the inevitable. He was a gracious winner, and he took the time to explain the technique. Evidently Lebanese guys practiced constantly, working out with heavy coiled springs even while studying. Arm-wrestling was an art in that part of the world, he explained, almost apologizing for beating me. With a twinkle in his eye, he added, "Tonight we meet for dinner and maybe another contest. You eat much? Good, tonight we have eating contest. Everybody come. Okay?"

I was actually looking forward to the evening, but, like Coach had said, I was crazy. That night we were each served a ten-pound heap of something dusted with cracked wheat and topped with a ladleful of olive oil. It looked like raw meat, all ground up. That's because it *was* raw meat: Lebanese kibbee. The waiter smiled expectantly, awaiting my reaction, while Josh sat there, keeping his head down, shading his eyes with one hand.

"This looks absolutely delicious," I lied, and I took my first bite of the uncooked lamb.

It's funny how you learn things when you travel. I'd always assumed teeth went to work automatically when you put food in your mouth. Not so. At the first bite, it was like they said, "What in hell do you expect us to do with this?" What taste there was reminded me of inner tubes and onions mixed with caulking compound, but I continued to cram it down, matching my opponent forkful for forkful. At last we leaned back, eyeing each other's nearly empty plate.

My opponent stood up. "A tie. Okay?"

With as much regret as I could fake, I agreed to a draw. Just then there was a lot of commotion as the belly dancer ran out to proceed with the show, so I excused myself and headed for the can. I locked the door and returned all that tasty lamb to its rightful home, a smelly hole in the floor. Tears were pouring from my eyes, and I thought my eyeballs would follow the lamb into the toilet.

When I came back to the table my host asked me what was wrong with my eyes. I responded that I was just allergic to something. Immediately he was sympathetic. "Ah yes. Much pollen in Beirut," and then everybody settled down to watch the show. I could hardly believe I'd made it through my trial by sheep without losing any standing with my arm-pulling friend.

As the girls began their belly-dancing routine, the other men told me that the belly dance was created to prepare women for child birth. Uh-huh. Then why weren't these slim-waisted beauties doing their thing at a clinic for expectant mothers? It sounded as nutty as some of the things I'd heard in religion class at Villanova. It was nice to learn that Christians weren't the only ones that could rationalize up a storm when they wanted to.

The star of the show came over and sat at our table, mainly to honor the local dignitaries sitting with us. She had just finished a part in *Land of the Pharaohs,* starring Joan Collins, so she was a celebrity in her own right. Josh ended up sitting next to her, and began explaining the stretching warm-ups that he used in order to prepare for running the hurdles. I upheld the honor of pole vaulters by demonstrating my special exercise, walking on my hands all over the dance floor. You'd have thought neither of us had ever seen a girl before. We were becoming the center of attention, until coach told us to stop enjoying ourselves so much.

The dancer was tremendously interested in my method of exercising and said she wanted to study it at greater length. Like a fool, I suggested we meet at the practice field the next day to exchange conditioning programs, but she stopped me. "Not outdoors, please. In my culture, in my profession, the skin must always be of the whitest, so I do not go outdoors."

We met indoors, all right. When I finally returned to the practice field, Josh told me that Coach had been looking for me for several hours. He collared me about then. "Where in hell have you been all morning?"

Not batting an eyelash, I said, "I was giving a private session and conducting diplomatic relations." I left him standing there scratching his head.

––––––––

We'd had a marvelous time in Beirut, and we were shocked to learn that only days after we left, the U.S. Marines arrived to restore order. Josh swore the Marines' deployment had nothing to do with us, but I wasn't so sure.

Iraq, the land of *The Thief of Bagdad*, was our next stop. But we found none of the good spirits we'd seen in Lebanon. We were treated cordially, but much of our hosts' hearty manner seemed forced.

All of the U.S. athletes were still pursued by amoebas. We were scheduled to perform in yet another ancient stadium, this one dating back to the dawn of civilization. Grant Scruggs, one of the sprinters, had become so weak from dysentery that he tried to beg off from his race. Coach threatened to send him home if he didn't perform, but the threat had no teeth, since that sounded like heaven to Grant. Finally Coach walked him off the field, giving him some kind of a pep talk. It must have been good, because Grant came back and got ready for his hundred-yard dash. He didn't warm up, however, because his legs weren't the only things all ready to run. He tore through his race like one possessed, not even bothering to stop after he'd crossed the finish line a winner. The poor guy went charging into the infield, dropped his shorts, and complied with an urgent request from the interior.

Coach ran up, red-faced and wrathful, but Grant figured *he* was the injured party. "What do you want from me? Didn't I tell you this would happen?"

Josh remarked, "We're all in deep shit now." And that was a good summation of our trip to Iraq.

––––––––

This Middle-Eastern tour was especially important for me because it really started me thinking. Most people in Penns Grove were white. At VU whites were still in the majority. On this trip I was a minuscule white dot in a sea of color, and I began to wonder where in hell the white skins came from.

And another thing -- I kept running into my dad all during the tour. We stopped at an airport in Italy, and I saw somebody checking passports that was a dead ringer for Dad. Same guy popped up in Greece selling Turkish delight, and again as a waiter in Beirut. Same nose, same build, same frizzy hair.

Don's father, George T. Bragg, in 1935, the year of Don's birth.

That motivated me to start tracing my own family's history. It seems my people had originated in Kent back when the Romans had encampments in Britain. Given Dad's aquiline nose and frizzy hair, I didn't have a hard time believing that some legionnaire of old had a hand, so to speak, in the family bloodlines. Along the way I also learned about the struggles and wars some of these countries been through, and eventually I developed an honest appreciation of their various contributions to world culture.

Being driven to study by the dictates of my own heart was light-years away from the fearful pursuit of facts that some teacher might expect us to know for a test. In fits and starts, I began to read voraciously. At the age of twenty-three, my education finally commenced.

Our magic carpet ride next took us to Pakistan, which impressed me as unusually clean. I was surprised to learn many of the fine athletes we met were vegetarians. Though I was interested, I wasn't ready to try it myself, being content to eat what a pride of lions might consume on a good hunting day. We also heard first-hand accounts of the hardships that resulted from the religious and cultural separation from India, and some of them were heart-breaking. All of this made me more eager than ever to visit India.

My first exposure to the poverty in India made me realize how rich my upbringing had been, and how easy it was to become spoiled in America. I'd known that Hindus believed in reincarnation, but I'd never seen people living that belief before.

What was hardest to take was seeing healthy cows wandering the streets, stepping over starving people using prayer beads to ask God to give them food. It looked to me like He'd already answered their prayer, but their religion forbade the killing of a few animals to fill a hundred hungry bellies. I'd been raised Christian, and the Indian religion was a hundred and eighty degrees from anything I'd ever believed. I started looking for a readable book on Hinduism.

Josh was particularly enthralled by Mother India, and when we'd leave some shrine or other, I often had to go find him and drag him out to the car.

We had to bypass Calcutta because of a cholera epidemic, but we went just about everywhere else. But of all the places we visited -- the ruins of the past and the growing cities and universities of the new India -- my favorite was the Taj Mahal. When you hear so much about a famous place, sometimes it's a letdown when you actually see it, but Shah Jahan's tribute to his wife was more magnificent than I'd even imagined.

And that's not counting the cobras.

Out in front of the edifice was a holy man playing a flute, moving the instrument back and forth rhythmically until a cobra emerged from the basket in front of him. The snake swayed as if mesmerized by the music, though in reality it was the movement of the flute that mastered the reptile. We threw coins into a woven tray, and the man responded with an exciting encore. An assistant appeared with a mongoose which was straining on a leash. The piping began again, and the cobra rose once more from the basket. The mongoose watched the snake intently, swaying gently as if he and the cobra were performing an ancient dance. Then the mongoose lunged so fast you didn't see the motion. With the same blinding speed he avoided the cobra's strike and attacked a second time, seizing the back of the snake's neck. The man dropped his flute and separated the two, stuffing the cobra into a lidded basket. We asked why he didn't let the fight continue.

He shrugged as he returned the mongoose to his cage. "The mongoose would kill the snake", he said, pocketing the coins the crowd had thrown. "No snake, no show."

I turned to see Josh's reaction, but he'd disappeared. Then I heard, "Come on Tarzan, let's go." Now I could die happy. For once Josh was the first one out to the car, and I owed it to one little cobra.

There was a cocktail party that evening at the ambassador's home, and we were all looking forward to it. But the New Delhi diplomatic community was very protocol-conscious, and I felt a little awkward at first. I finally joined a group listening to a fashionably dressed Indian gentleman heap abuse on America's efforts to aid India. "If the Americans give us ten million dollars, how much do you think reaches the poor? Less than half!" He glared around as if it was *our* fault.

I cleared my throat. "What if the U.S. took over handing out the money? Then the poor would get all of it, right?"

I thought it was a fair question, but his nose got all pinched-looking as he said, "India does not need rich Americans meddling in her internal affairs."

"So you don't want to do anything about the problems, just complain about them?" That really pissed him off, and his face began to quiver like water starting to boil.

"Are you insinuating that I would conspire with those who steal from the poor?" he demanded.

I had my answer ready, but somebody whispered that the ambassador wanted to see me. I walked over to the guy, and he was very nice, but in the middle of being nice, he suggested that it really was time we got back to the hotel. "Can't have people blaming me for keeping you out too late, and we want to do well at our meet, don't we?"

Coach Olsen, who'd been having a good time, growled at me as we left, "Why in hell did you have to open your big mouth?"

I shot back, "Because he was acting like an aristocratic asshole, a typical product of a caste system." It didn't occur to me until years later that I probably was too.

We all enjoyed visiting India, but Josh Culbreath fell in love with the place. After serving in the U.S. Marines, he would return to direct the Indian National Track and Field Program. During that time the guy lived in a small castle, married, and named his three boys Maliq, Kaliq, and

Jahan.

Josh was also the next victim of amoebic dysentery, becoming deathly ill by the time we reached Colombo, Ceylon, now Sri Lanka. Our rooms were exotic and beautiful, with openings at the top of all the walls. This helped air to circulate better, making the humid days and nights more bearable. But you heard every sound from adjoining rooms. I still recall Josh going through hell, sitting on the john with his head in a bucket, vomiting his guts out. He became extremely weak, so we sent for a doctor. He gave the patient paregoric to stop the dangerous dehydration, but Josh continued to lose weight, not good since he barely weighed 150 before he got sick.

Coach had learned his lesson about forcing sick athletes to compete, so he let Josh off with giving lectures for a few days. Weak as he was, he showed up at the pole vaulting pit one day to coach me. I hadn't thought it would be difficult to put on a good show. How high could the pole vaulting record in Ceylon be? Then somebody told me 14'6", and I nearly fainted. Globe-trotting Bob Richards had gotten there before me. But I figured I could beat his record, and was even gloating about it.

I worked my way up and tied the record height, but I heard a rising murmur from the crowd. I looked up and saw a black cloud heading my way, flying low, skimming the field. It was a migratory flock of giant fox bats, big suckers with nasty pointed teeth, like we used to carve on pumpkins. I started to follow everybody else dashing for cover, but Josh grabbed my arm. "Now wait a minute, Tarzan. You don't think a few little bats would chase off the King of the Jungle, do you?" The words were just out of his mouth when a huge bat swooped down, seemingly intent on roosting in his hair. Josh took off, with me right behind him, brandishing my pole over my head to deter the damn things. Nobody in the place remembered that I was trying for a record: I didn't even care. The undisputed champions that day were the bats.

The tour was almost over, and we were all worn out, but one of the runners, who'd already earned a rep for wild ideas, had another brainstorm. He inveigled fellow runner George King and me to accompany him to a jewelry store in the sleaziest part of downtown Colombo. He pointed out some exquisite cats-eye opals, about three carats each. "Take a look at those! I've got an idea that can make us all rich." He called over the manager, and confirmed that the price per carat was about five dollars.

Our would-be entrepreneur was almost foaming at the mouth. "Look, I can wire home for $10,000. Do you know how much two thousand carats of opals will bring at U.S. prices?"

I didn't much care, but I thought I saw a flaw in his scheme. Whenever we came home after a tour, the customs people usually asked where we'd been and marked our bags for approval. They always opened a few bags at random, though, and I told him so.

"Yeah," he said, "That's where I thought you could help. Tell me about your pole. Is it hollow or what?"

When I told him it was hollow, but capped on both ends, his eyes took on an avaricious gleam. "Then we're home free," he said. "How 'bout it?"

It didn't take me long to weigh possible financial gain against hard time in a federal pen, so I said no. The guy continued to bug me about it, telling me it was a deal I couldn't refuse, but I wouldn't budge.

The New York customs officers greeted us by name and approved all of our luggage without opening a single bag. Our hot shot opal dealer hissed in my ear, "You dumb ass, we could have made a bundle."

Someone else had a few choice words for my other ear, however. One of the officers came up to me as I started to leave the customs area. "Hi, Don, remember me? I'm from Villanova."

I'd never laid eyes on the guy, but I said, "Good to see you again. How ya doin'?"

He leaned a little closer and whispered, "The Department has its sources, and we've been watching you guys closely ever since you left that jewelry store. You made a wise decision."

I felt like running after Mr. Opals and yelling, "Nyah, nyah, who's the dumb ass now?"

———————

Upon returning to Penns Grove, my first order of business was to decide what to do with my life, but Uncle Sam took the decision out of my hand. I was drafted into the U.S. Army.

PART FIVE

TARZAN'S TREK

Not for the old, but the newborn few
who venture forth with their spirit anew.

-- from "Baptism" by Don Bragg

Chapter Fourteen

Warrior-Athlete

I reported to Fort Dix, New Jersey, in June of 1958. If I had to serve, I was grateful that I'd only be fifty miles from home and Theresa. Besides, I knew that the Army had sports teams, and I had hopes I could continue vaulting. As I was getting processed into Dix, I ran into Rosie Grier who was just being mustered out. That seemed like a good omen.

Wrong!

Before I even unpacked, two grim-faced West Point cadets on their summer tour came to see me.

"Private Bragg, as a college graduate you're eligible for OCS."

But that was a three-year deal. "I don't think I'd be interested."

"You're passing up an opportunity to become an officer?"

Serve an extra year and I too could make life miserable for the Army's working stiffs? No way in hell! "Thanks, but no thanks."

The cadets' faces suggested they'd just gotten a whiff of an open sewer, and I was sure I'd never fit into the Army mold.

Then three weeks into basic training I was called into some general's office. I didn't even have my salute down pat, and I'm in the general's office, sure I was about to be shot. He introduced me to a man in civvies. "This is Judge Fusco. I want you to teach his son to vault. You can do it on weekends."

Dumb me, I had to open my mouth and point out to the general that I wasn't permitted to do that. His face turned scarlet, and he informed me that *he* was in charge on this base. If he wanted me to spend weekends teaching or sweeping the sun off the roof, I would, by God, do it.

The joke was on the general, though. I received a terrific bonus when a warm friendship grew between Judge Fusco and me. He took me under his wing and taught me a lot about how to get along in the world.

The lessons he gave me weren't easy. "I can't do this, Judge. It's ass-kissing."

"No, it's getting along in society. It's a game, Don. Play it well and *you'll* do well."

So weekends Judge Fusco taught me about being a gentleman, and I taught his son about being a pole vaulter. He was a nice kid, and he became a fair vaulter. Even the general was pleased, so I had him off my back.

Problem was, the platoon sergeant and the company commander weren't happy. Using words even I'd never heard before, they told me just how unhappy. Who did I think I was, receiving special treatment and having exceptions made to rules? Bad recruit!

They took special pleasure in telling me I was soon to be shipped off to finance school in Indiana, a place I had no desire to experience. I'd heard about those midwestern blizzards, and besides, I'd never get home. In desperation I asked a fellow jock, Frank Nappi, how in hell I could keep my butt out of finance school. He got a conspiratorial gleam in his eye. "Can you play football? If you're any good, they'll keep you here forever."

I tried out for the team and caught balls with my arms, my hands, my fingernails, my eyelids. This impressed the brass sufficiently to have orders cut to keep me at Fort Dix. Once on the team, however, I realized that the other players were taking out their frustration at being in the service by beating the hell out of the guy with the ball: me. Toward the end of the football season I decided to get off the team before a career-ending injury took me out. It was simple. I just let a pass glide right by me during a game. This enraged the coach, who was pretty sure the miss was intentional. But by that time it was too late to send me away to Indiana. Off the Hoosier hook, I could tend to an even more important development.

———————

Brett Marrett had appeared with a new pole for me, the Gill Vault Master. Like his previous pole, it would accommodate an extra ten pounds over the old cut-off weight of 195. But most important, it eliminated the shoulder shock I'd been experiencing. This new pole motivated me to drop at least twenty-five pounds, essential since I'd beefed up to 225 on the football team. The '59 indoor season was just a couple of months away, and I was only half-way in shape.

Once I got back into training, I began to receive invitations to meets again. I was up at Madison Square Garden, and I happened to beat out some Marines vaulting for Quantico. The UP release read, "Army's Don Bragg beats Quantico."

The Marines absolutely hated that, and they sent a colonel to see me. "We'd like you to switch to the Marines, Bragg," he said.

Officers. You just had to love 'em. The stuff they could dream up!

The colonel went on to promise me the choicest facilities, unlimited practice time, the moon.

I though he'd lost his mind. But I didn't want to be hasty. My old vaulting rival, Bob Gutowski was jumping for Quantico, so I looked him up.

"Bob," I said, "they're offering me all this stuff. Is it on the level?"

The two of us had never been friends, but he wouldn't let a fellow vaulter get screwed. "Practice time? They don't even let you take a leak in peace. We're lucky if we get two hours a day."

Thanks to Bob, I continued to vault for the Army. With the exception of the Collegiate Championships, it was just about the same circuit of meets I'd attended at VU, plus service meets, like the Quantico Relays.

There was a difference, though. Because of the Marines' interest in me, I'd become a precious commodity to Army brass. Although I was only supposed to practice two hours a day, they gave me permission to work out at Lawrenceville Academy, a prep school right outside Princeton that had a magnificent indoor board track. Unlike Villanova's celebrated indoor track, this one really was inside a building, and having a chance to use it was a great motivation for me.

By 1959, thanks to the quality practice time, I was doing well at the meets, and the word on the circuit was that I'd probably make the 1960 Olympic team. To me it sounded like that very familiar kiss of death. Of course the Army loved the prestige of having an Olympic hopeful in its clutches, and saw to it that I made all the big meets under the protective umbrella of TDY: Temporary Duty Assignment.

I was in good shape for the Inquirer Games at the Convention Center in February, and a good thing it was. I'd be playing to the home crowd. I didn't mind young guys coming down from Villanova, despite the wild expectations they'd have for a VU grad. Even the fact that I was unsuccessfully fending off the flu wasn't so bad. What turned the Convention Center into a pressure cooker was the presence of my close friends and family, especially my dad. And with Bob Gutowski also competing, a win was far from a done deal. I also seemed to have hit a barrier in my jumping. Photographs of my jumps indicated that I was getting the height, but just the same I kept bringing the bar down with me.

The night before we left for Philadelphia I was determined to get some rest, but I fell asleep dissecting every aspect of my vaulting style. I hadn't expected any clear answer, then just before I was fully awake everything snapped into place. It was as if I'd found an island of analytical clarity floating in the pleasant fog of drowsy awakening. The problem was obvious: the position of the standards wasn't permitting me to apex above the crossbar, but rather in front of it. So I didn't have to change my technique, only pull the standards in a little. The answer was absurdly simple. Why hadn't I seen it before?

Despite the revelation, I wasn't out of the woods. I entered the arena on the thirteenth of February with a temperature of 102. In case it had missed my attention, friends also took pains to remind me that Friday the thirteenth was bad luck. I blew it off, saying it was bad luck for everybody jumping against me. They thought that was hilarious and laughed all the way back to their seats.

I wasn't laughing.

Bob's fiberglass pole easily flung him over 15'3". With the Gill Vault Master I cleared it and the next height of 15'5". Bob wasn't so lucky, and couldn't make that height. Maybe it was the fever, but I felt euphoric, and decided not to settle for an easy win. I asked the officials to raise the bar to 15'9½", which would be a new indoor world's record. It would be nearly an inch over the 1942 record set by Dutch Warmerdam, the seventeen-year-old record that had eluded both Bob Richards and me throughout our careers.

It took me a moment to dismiss the tension I felt building, knowing how much was riding on the jump, wanting to make Dad proud here on our own turf. But once I was heading down the runway, the doubts seemed to melt away. In fact, the lift off, the swing up to the bar, the pivot, everything was perfect. I winced as I fell into two meager feet of packed sawdust, but the pain paled in importance when the arena erupted into a thunderous roar.

Dad, Georgie, and Theresa jumped out of their seats, ran across the floor, and swarmed all over me. They were the only ones in the place who realized what my victory represented. Little more than a year before I'd been seriously contemplating retiring. I'd battled through physical pain, through the lowest points of my life all the way back to a world's record. By the time the arena settled down, I was a little dizzy, but what the hell! I told them to raise the bar to 16'1". This trip down the runway was very different from the last. My legs felt wobbly and it was hell to keep even half-way focussed. I put all I had left into the jump, but hit the crossbar on the way down. All that my tremendous effort produced was an impact that sent me flying out of the pit onto the concrete arena floor. I was one of the few vaulters ever to bounce out of a pit before they began to fill them with foam rubber.

There was no time for me to rest on my laurels because the next day I had to leave for the Los Angeles Times Meet in the Coliseum. I looked on every meet as an opportunity to pull a little ahead in the financial department by collecting the twelve dollar per diem, then squeaking by for as little as possible, pocketing the difference for a rainy day. Despite the long trip, I was happy to do the LA Times meet because they'd made me an offer I couldn't refuse. Former football great Glenn Davis was the meet director, and he'd promised to cover Theresa's plane ticket as well as my own.

The money for her ticket wasn't forthcoming, however, though plenty of logical explanations were. Ah yes! California rules again. I marched into the stadium, warmed up a little, took one jump at 15'1" and cleared it, thereby winning the meet. I packed up my pole and was on my way out, when Glenn trotted alongside. "Aren't you going to try for the world's record like you did last night in Philadelphia?"

I looked him in the eye. "What about Theresa's plane fare, like you promised?"

His face kind of closed up. "Maybe we can work something out."

Maybe? "Too late! See ya, Glenn," I said, and headed out of the arena. I yelled back over my shoulder. "I gotta go have supper with a couple of movie execs at Chassen's." I made that up for Glenn's benefit, but it was too good an exit line to pass up.

––––––––––

Wrapping up the indoor season were three big meets in the Midwest: Milwaukee, Cleveland, and Chicago. Nobody could afford to miss these. The deal was this: we'd collect first-class round-trip tickets for each destination, plus the five days' per diem for each meet. Then we'd buy the cheapest plane tickets we could find, stay in a cheap hotel, and live on cheese sandwiches during the meets. If you jumped well, there was a chance for some bonus money in addition. If you could persuade meet sponsors to provide an additional ticket for your girlfriend or wife, you could save even more money for the lean months ahead. Freddy Dwyer, a former miler from Villanova, lived in Milwaukee, and kindly let me use his home as a base of operations, so most years I didn't have to invest much in hotel rooms at all.

The Milwaukee promoters had promised me a nice bonus if I broke either the meet or world record. Finnish vaulter Eeles Landström was studying at Michigan, I believe, and he was my main competition. I beat him with a 15'¾" jump which also broke the meet record, but failed to better my 15'9½" jump in Philadelphia, so I felt a little down. The meet director brushed away my apologies as he handed me my first place prize of a watch. I slipped the watch on my wrist, admired it, and started to toss the box.

With an agonized moan, the director grabbed my hand. "Why don't you go down to the locker room by yourself and open the box carefully?"

I was puzzled, but did as he suggested. When I opened the box, hundred-dollar bills tumbled out. Not a bad week's work for an amateur athlete.

I had to take off almost immediately for a European meet in Paris, where I also took first place with a vault of 15'5". The French press went kind of nuts for the Tarzan thing, and I had a lot of fun with it. But then it was back to Cleveland. I'd tried to watch what I ate in Paris, but clearly not closely enough. I came charging down the board track, and my foot crashed right through the damn thing. Landström took that meet, but I had my revenge the next week in Chicago where I once again took first place.

Chapter Fifteen

Tarzan Goes Home

As soon as I got back to Fort Dix, I had to pack again. Tarzan was going to Africa. In the fifties, the USSR had been flooding the emerging African nations with anti-American propaganda about race relations in the US. Our State Department was determined to refute this, so they decided to send a racially-mixed team of American athletes on a tour from Ghana to South Africa. They would train African athletes in track and field as part of a two-pronged counter-offensive. Not only would the U.S. win points for getting Africans to the Olympics, but we'd show, by our camaraderie and cooperation, that white and black American athletes got along very well together. That much wasn't mere propaganda. At least in athletics, inter-racial harmony was business as usual.

Our group was first-rate: Josh Culbreath, 400-meter hurdles and the quarter-mile sprint relay, versatile Ira Davis for sprinting plus triple and broad jump; Parry O'Brien, who threw shot and discus; Bob Gardner, javelin and high jump; and one Penns Grove farm boy, pole vaulter and sometime shot or discus thrower. Parry and I could also thunder down a track if needed for the relays. The idea was for us to go around each host country for ten days, giving demonstrations, clinics, and lectures. Then there'd be a meet, with the five of us covering all events between us as we took on the host country's best track and field athletes. It sounded like an exciting and challenging opportunity for all of us.

The flight to Accra was long, but I didn't mind, despite my usual bout of airsickness. I wasn't just going on some junket for the government. I'd completely identified with Tarzan growing up, and now I was on my way to the real Tarzanville.

My first sight of the African continent was a line of surf foaming onto the sandy edge of grasslands, but in the distance were immense patches of green. The hairs stood up on the back of my neck when I realized that I was looking at the outer margins of Africa's great jungles.

As we stepped off the boarding ramp we were hit with a blast of hot wind heavy with exotic smells of flowers and spices I couldn't identify. Josh was right beside me, and he was all excited. I knew he felt he was coming home.

The people at the airport were friendly and seemed genuinely glad we'd come. We were overjoyed at the welcome, since the State Department guy'd scared the hell out of us with his warnings about the Mau Mau uprising in Kenya. Yeah, Kenya was over in East Africa, but still too close for comfort.

We were supposed to meet President Kwame Nkrumah at an official luncheon, but he never showed up. The other Ghanian officials just shrugged off his unexplained absence, and I decided I liked Ghana's laid-back take on life. Anyway, we were tired from our flight, so we were happy to go kick back at the Overland Hotel.

Then somebody told us we had to dress for dinner. I was trying to be on my best behavior, so I meekly put on a dress shirt, tie and jacket. It didn't do any good. The upper-crust English tourists sitting around our table still eyed us reproachfully, as if wondering how vulgarians like us could be sharing these superb accommodations. Also, we'd been expecting that the dining room would be air conditioned, and it was -- to about eighty-eight degrees. All of us jocks sat there yanking on our collars to get a little air inside those damned dress shirts. I figured that after a month of such festive evenings, the U.S. sports delegation would have sweated down to a collective weight of ninety-eight pounds.

Next morning we wandered out to an immense outdoor farmers' market with stalls full of fruit, squawking chickens, freshly butchered meat, and bins of fresh vegetables. We also saw a long table covered by rolls of beautiful African fabric. Parry fingered the material and said, "This stuff would make fantastic Tahitian pareus." He explained that those were the skirt-like garments Polynesian men wore. They sounded comfortable as hell, so we had a bunch made up for next to no money. That night we showed up in the hot crowded dining room with the obligatory dress shirts, ties, and jackets topping our new pareus and sandals.

Now none of us had felt that underwear added much to our native dress, so we'd dispensed with it. Our waiter, rolling his eyes and oozing condescension, commented how cool we looked. I propped one foot up on an empty chair to reveal our secret. After that, for some reason, both the waiter and the blue-nosed Brits left considerable space around our table, convincing us that pareus should be our dress uniform for the remainder of our stay at the hotel.

There wasn't much going on that night, so O'Brien asked me if I used any special exercises. I didn't have a rope swing handy, so I did a dozen hand-stand push ups. Parry tried about five, then fell over, but he was having fun. "Keep going," he said. "Let's see how many we can do!"

By the time I'd done a hundred, in sets of tens, he'd completed fifty, and we were both dead beat on the floor, our arm muscles knotted from our insane workout.

O'Brien's head wobbled up. "Try one more."

I tried, but fell over on my nose, which started bleeding.

He grinned triumphantly, shoved me out of the way, and did one more repetition, crowing, "I win."

I disputed this vehemently, and we were about to start swinging, when Josh stuck his head in the door and told us there were better games to play. He said they were promoting an upcoming fashion show downstairs, and that there were models running all over the mezzanine. Our squabble was forgotten as Parry and I tried to beat Ira, Bob, and Josh to the elevator.

Next morning, I jumped out of bed and my arms fell on the floor. They hurt so much I could hardly brush my teeth. And here I was supposed to go show people the intricacies of my sport. Thank God the competition was very brief since neither Parry nor I were worth diddly-squat. The African athletes stared open-mouthed as O'Brien heaved the shot with a mounting screech of pain, clenching his teeth afterwards as he cradled his arm. I too had a memorable day: so as not to aggravate my torn-up muscles I charged down the runway carrying the pole sideways. As I fell into the pit, I'd roar in pain every time I rolled onto the throbbing shoulder. Together, Parry and I gave the world's first sports clinic on pissing and moaning. We were lucky they didn't throw things at us.

———————

We went to a party at the American Ambassador's house that night, and I really enjoyed myself. Some of the social graces I'd been taught by Judge Fusco and Dr. Bellieu had started kicking in. For one thing, I realized I couldn't just stand around being a jock, but had to be up on some neutral subjects that normal people could relate to. The history and philosophy books I'd begun to enjoy provided a common ground, and made talking to people a helluva lot easier.

However.

There was a group of Armenian business men there, all immaculately tailored, standing off in a corner by themselves. They didn't seem to want to have anything to do with Americans. Josh was light-skinned, and looked more like an Arab than a member of the American team, so he went over and started talking to them.

I was getting thirsty, so when a pretty girl asked if I'd like something to drink, I told her I'd love a Coke. She went into the kitchen, but when she reappeared with my drink, one of these Armenian guys pulled her aside. He might have been hustling her, but that wasn't my problem. The point was, neither she nor my Coke was moving, so I went over, reached for the Coke, and said, "Excuse me, just let me have this Coke, okay?" The next thing I knew, one of them knocked the Coke out of my hand.

Now Josh was still talking to these jerks, and Parry O'Brien had been playing pool a few feet away with somebody from the embassy, so they both saw what had happened. I said, "I'm going to knock this guy into next week."

O'Brien gave me a heads up, holding his pool cue at the ready. Of course all the expensive suits were glaring at me, and there was Josh, glaring right along with them. Without changing the expression on his face, he lifted his hand a couple of inches to show me he had a wine bottle by the neck, ready to cream the bastards if push came to shove.

I was ready to wade in, when the ambassador appeared, on a pace to beat the two-minute mile, talking a blue streak, getting everybody separated and civilized. I felt sorry for the guy, having to live in fear that somebody might start saying what they really think.

The heat was brutal the next day. We remembered the wave action we'd noticed flying into Accra, so we asked where we could body-surf. Parry, Josh, and I headed out to the beach. There were trees right up to the sand, and we could see the grass huts of a village a little way off. We passed close to one mother heating Coke for her infant. I was surprised that she'd give that to her baby, especially since the little one seemed sick. Evidently the local people believed Coca-Cola still contained cocaine, so they used it as a medicine.

There were a few fishing boats out in the water, but we had the gorgeous beach all to ourselves. We thought this was a little peculiar, but that didn't stop Parry and me from charging into the water. The waves were enormous: once you caught a good one, it flung you at the beach with amazing force. We weren't too happy with the vicious undertow, but hey, you can't have everything. Josh was a little hesitant to join us in the towering surf, but eventually he started riding the waves closer to shore. Parry and I went out to the second line of waves, but after about a half hour, the surf became noticeably rougher. We came in to check on Josh, who wasn't the greatest swimmer. We passed him on a huge curling wave as he paddled like hell to keep afloat in a somewhat less monstrous swell.

We waited for him on the beach until the wave dumped him on the sand, coughing and choking. "Okay, I didn't come to Africa to drown," said the sensible Josh. "If you have a brain in your heads you'll get out of the water too."

But the crests of the waves had become even more magnificent as the wind picked up, so Parry and I headed out again. After a while we noticed Josh showing off with wild-looking jumping jacks, and pretty soon a large crowd gathered. Josh now seemed to be practicing a peculiar style of lay-up shot, but his audience was all looking out to sea. Of course we assumed they were fascinated by our expert maneuvering on the waves. When we finally waded in to the beach, Josh ran out and dragged us out of the water.

"Didn't you see me waving you in?" he demanded.

"Is that what you were doing? We thought you were doing exercises. Is there a problem?"

"I'll say." Josh glowered at us. "Last week a couple of people from Pan Am were swimming right here, and they disappeared. Vanished without a trace, understand? Nobody knows whether the undertow got 'em or a great white shark had them for dinner."

Somehow, Josh's indignant mother duck act cracked up Parry and me, and we walked back up the beach laughing. Josh followed, shaking his head, trailed by most of the village.

At that moment, the fishing boats from the village began to pull toward shore with the day's catch. We joined the villagers, grabbing ropes and hauling in the boats to the exhilarating rhythm of the African chants.

It was hard to say goodbye to these friendly people, but it was getting late, and we had to start back to the hotel. As we walked to the road for a taxi, Josh said simply, but with pride, "My people."

As we returned to the hotel, we heard music playing and went to investigate. People were dancing to a five-piece combo on a little square, and the music was something they called the High Life. It was like a combination of African rhythms with a Jamaican twist, and the dancers swayed side to side, slow and sensual. I could have listened and watched all night.

The next morning we headed for a village about fifty miles away. Our exhibition was going to be packed with local dignitaries, and the paramount chief of the district had promised to honor the occasion by giving a speech. Our African driver didn't want us to be late, so he took the twisting, one-track dirt roads at about ninety miles an hour. We sat on the edge of the seats, expecting a truck to sail around a curve at us and take us out at any minute. We were already a little jittery from reading a newspaper account of yet another Mau Mau attack in Tanganyika.

Suddenly, out in the middle of a desolate stretch, the driver glanced back at us and slammed on the brakes. We tumbled forward onto the floor as the car spun around and slid sideways down the road. We'd barely come to a shuddering halt when he lunged at us, waving some kind of weapon. Arms and legs and heads were flying all over the place as we scrabbled for the door lock, trying to avoid the rain of blows. Of the five superbly conditioned athletes, not one had the coordination to open the damned door and get the hell out of there. It was like a wannabe clown act at the circus.

Eventually we realized the African was whaling away at the back of the seat, not at us, and with a newspaper, not a machete. A moment later he proudly displayed his kill. "Tsetse fly," he explained. "Him bite, you sleep."

Sheepishly, we brave Americans crawled back into our seats. A few minutes later we made a dignified entrance into the village and pulled up in front of the stadium. It was surrounded by rolling grassland dotted with kinds of trees I'd never seen before.

None of the dignitaries had arrived yet, so to kill a little time, I ventured out to have a look around. After only a short walk I came across the most fantastic looking tree, with roots that extended far above ground, all the way up to the branches. It looked like the tree was on stilts, though some roots hung free like swinging vines. I just had to climb it.

About forty feet up, the tree forked out in three directions. A large snail was sitting right in the crotch of the tree, which it had covered with its slimy filament. I stepped around the ugly creature and climbed until I was at about seventy feet. The jungle rolled away endlessly before me, while a breeze surrounded me with the rich, intensely alive fragrance of the forest. The magic of the moment was enormously enhanced by my love of trees and the freedom and beauty they represented for me when I was growing up. For a time I was floating above reality, moored only by a high-flung umbilical of roots to the solidity of the earth below.

Back toward the village I spotted the stadium field about a quarter-mile away. I could hear snatches of somebody making a speech over the loudspeaker, so I figured I wouldn't be missed for a while yet. I wanted to grab a vine and swing off into the jungle so bad, but that would have been suicidal. So I did the next best thing. I indulged in a tremendous Tarzan call that echoed through the jungle, causing flocks of birds to take flight in alarm. But it was time to return, so after one longing glance back at the jungle I started down the tree. The snail hadn't moved, so once more I stepped around the critter and his puddle of slime.

I was halfway back to the field when our British coordinator came running up. I figured he was upset, since I'd never seen a Brit foam at the mouth before. "I thought we'd lost you," he sputtered. "Didn't we tell you this place is thick with black mambas? Those are snakes, you crazy Yank, and they love to lie near the paths just to bite silly people who wander off by themselves."

"I take it they're poisonous?"

"*Poisonous?*" he squawked. "You might say so! One of the natives was bitten just last week, and he lay down and died on the spot!"

"Well, I didn't see any snakes, just one huge snail up in a tree."

The guy turned pale. "Look here, you didn't actually touch the creature, did you? No? Well, you're one lucky chap. They secrete a poison that reacts like acid on the skin, don't you know."

He told me I was more trouble than the bloody Mau Maus, and made me walk in front of him back to the stadium. I think he wanted to keep an eye on me.

Josh met us half way there. "Boy, are you in hot water! That Tarzan yell of yours ruined the paramount chief's speech. Coach says you have to walk back to the hotel."

Coach didn't make good on his threat. Maybe it occurred to him that turning me loose in Africa wasn't the brightest idea he'd ever had.

———————

The next day, we left for a series of lectures and clinics on the Ivory Coast, just northwest of Ghana. We ran into one problem. Parry O'Brien was going to run a leg of the relays, but he'd left his spikes behind. Not only was Parry surprisingly fast for a shot-putter, he also had very small hands and feet. He could fit into Josh's shoes, in fact, so those were the ones he borrowed. Thing was, he weighed about 250 pounds. My clearest memory of Ivory Coast was Josh staring in awe at his shoes after Parry was done with them. The spikes had been flattened forward against the sole!

The Ivory Coast athletes were especially attentive, and when we finished the competition we felt like we'd accomplished something lasting. Their paramount chief expressed his gratitude by inviting us to a luncheon at his large, elegant home. One of the elders told us not to speak to the king directly, but rather to an interpreter, as was the local custom.

I'd heard plenty of pidgin English in the towns, and after lunch as we were leaving, I decided to give it a try. The chief, sitting on an intricately carved ebony throne, listened attentively as I said, "We go now, okay? Good we meet chief."

We were stunned when the chief responded directly, "And it's been a pleasure having met you chaps as well. Do stop in again!"

When we got outside, we busted out laughing, but Josh just stood there with his hands on his hips. "God Almighty, Don! The man has his doctorate from Oxford University. You sure embarrassed yourself talking like an ignoramus."

Chapter Sixteen

Jim Crow Again

O ur next stop was Lagos, Nigeria. As we registered at the hotel desk, we noticed Bob Gardner still standing by the door engaged in deep conversation with an earnest-looking Nigerian. When he rejoined us, Bob was grinning ear to ear, tremendously proud of himself. "God, I love these people. They just love to barter, and I made one helluva deal." He showed us an odd-looking wrist watch. "I just swapped my Bulova for this Omega. Look at the workmanship on this baby."

Josh's eyebrows shot up, and I reached out and tapped the motionless minute hand. It bounced off the "G" in Omega, which miraculously turned into a "C". Bob had managed to snare a prize all right: an Omeca watch with a free-swinging minute hand. The guy'd been hustled by a pro, and none of us was surprised when Bob's frantic search didn't turn up the enterprising salesman.

We were wondering what to do that night when somebody said they were showing a Tarzan movie nearby. I dragged Josh to the theater, an open-air amphitheater under the starry African night sky, but the picture was disappointing. They only let Tarzan do one or two yells, which disgusted me. I glanced over at Josh, and he was giving me a dirty look. According to him, I started to quiver all over.

"Don't you do it," he said.

"Sorry. I gotta." I let loose with a really good Tarzan yell, and the place exploded. Enthusiastic Africans crowded around, and I introduced myself. "Me Tarzan, King of Jungle," I said. I put one arm around Josh's shoulder. "And this is Boy!" That absolutely delighted the African nationals, and did more for America's image on the continent than fifty years of diplomatic shell games.

From then on, Josh and I'd clown around with a Tarzan-Boy routine. Whenever I got myself into deep shit, however, Boy had a way of disappearing. He'd be back in a hurry if Tarzan happened to attract some pretty girls. That guy collected so many phone numbers from lovely women, his little black book weighed forty pounds by the time we went home.

Though the country looked much the same as Ghana, we noticed some differences right away. The people in Ghana had plumper faces, while the Nigerians' features were pulled more tightly over their facial bones. Ghana put an incredible emphasis on education and building schools, while the Nigerians seemed to be proudest of their new police academy and their ability to keep order. There was more of a military atmosphere in Lagos as opposed to easy-going Ghana.

Two things were identical, though, the temperature and humidity, and they were beginning to wear on us. We were able to do little more than get through our scheduled clinics and competitions because of the heat. Our tour coordinators also warned us constantly not to go off by ourselves lest we disappear off the face of the earth. That sure took the fun out of exploring Africa on our own, though I suppose they were just trying to keep us from churning up any international incidents.

One evening I received the biggest scare of my life. I had a volume of Nietzsche on the floor, and I was hanging over the side of the bed, reading it. All of a sudden I happened to catch a swift movement out of the corner of my eye. I looked up and yelled in terror. Mild-mannered Bob Gardner was charging at me with his javelin, and I figured I'd been hanging out with the only white Mau Mau on the planet. The javelin whizzed by my head and pinned down a five-inch-long squirmy insect just as it marched across my book. The great Bwana hunter made us all admire his trophy, which inspired everybody to start peering under pillows and behind curtains before we went to bed. I never read Nietzsche again without thinking of Bob, our Warrior-Entomologist and his revolting bug.

The main reason we were in Africa was to conduct meets and clinics in outlying villages. The locals didn't have the money to throw us fancy parties, so we were on our own most nights. Between the heat and the threat of ambushes by Mau Maus or black mambas, we did very little. The inactivity began to get to Parry O'Brien when we were still in Ghana. He'd spend his evenings stalking from one room to the other, muttering, tossing the shot from hand to hand. When the coach brought him a telegram requesting him to come home because of sickness in the family, he was packed in seventeen seconds. To this day we all believe he'd set up the scenario to bail himself out of the tour. All we could do was congratulate him on his creativity, though he missed some of the best parts of the trip.

We continued south to a stopover at the Leopoldville Airport in the

Belgian Congo. Since we'd be there nearly seven hours, we all wanted to go into the city and take a quick look around. No dice. The white Belgian chief of police himself gave us the news, saying there was too much unrest in the area. To make certain we didn't sneak out, he sat with us the entire time we were there, glaring at Josh and Ira. He was joined by one of our embassy people, a white guy from Mississippi, who was absolutely clueless about what was really going on in the country. He intimated that the colonial authorities would soon have the few rabble rousers in custody. However, he agreed that we wouldn't be safe if we went into the city.

While we were sitting around we noticed an artist selling some striking paintings in what you'd call a modern primitive style, I guess. Most of them featured little stick figures and had tremendous vitality. Josh and I each bought some as souvenirs. A couple of months later, when the Congo tore free from her Belgian masters, we were shocked to learn that our artist was among those murdered.

On the flight south, I was airsick, as usual, and spent most of the flight curled up in my seat. We'd been over desert the last time I'd checked, so I was astonished to see a sprawling metropolis right below. I'd learned a great deal about Africa, but I'd no idea a city of that size existed on the continent. Josh pointed downward. "That's Johannesburg, the diamond capital of the world."

The diamond capital of the world lost a lot of its luster pretty damn quick. After the long, tense stopover in the Belgian Congo, we were exhausted. We straggled toward the immigration desk, grateful to have arrived in one piece. Ira happened to get there first. He was just pulling out his passport when a furious official popped out of nowhere, screaming that blacks had to go to the end of the line. Ira just stood there in shock, staring at this gibbering apparition, but the rest of us were incensed.

To hell with this! Josh and I advanced on the guy at the desk, but guards pushed us back. Bob Gardner, the coach, and our USIA guy had joined us by this time, and we all started arguing with the official. Nobody listened: all we heard was, "Blacks to the end of the line!"

Guards hustled Josh and Ira away from the desk. I started to boil over, but I managed to hang on to my temper, almost. "No way! We're all guests of the government. They're not going to the end of any damn line!"

But guess what? I wasn't in Kansas any more. I experienced a thrilling new sensation as the black guard shoved what looked like a Thompson sub-machine gun into my stomach under orders from his white superior. And I thought I was being so good! I'd only been in Johannesburg three minutes, and they were already preparing to shoot me.

I was barely aware of Josh urgently tapping me on the shoulder. He said, "I know you're with us, brother, but when in Rome you do as the Romans. We're in Jo'burg, and I'm gonna go do as the Africans. Let it go."

There was more craziness to come. This guy in short pants and knee socks marched back along the line trying to place Josh and Ira's color in the pigment spectrum. He reminded me of somebody trying to match up paint samples at a hardware store. I'd never seen anything so stupid. Josh was lighter skinned, so he stuck him halfway back. Ira's skin was very dark, so he went right at the end of the line.

I took a tongue-lashing from the jackass honkey, but he finally blew himself out. Eventually we all had our passports stamped. I was really sweating by the time we got out of the airport, and it wasn't just from the heat. It hadn't taken Tarzan long to get into hot water.

———————

They threw a nice press conference for us with a lot of hoopla. Of course, every time I started to open my mouth, I was aware of a USIA aide's hot breath down my neck. For some reason, I was being treated like a troublemaker.

We had a series of meets in Lusaka, the present-day capital of Zambia in the heart of the copper belt. After the incident in the Jo'burg airport, my behavior was subdued, at least for me, but I found something to occupy my mind. I decided I had to bring a chimpanzee home for Tarzan.

No chimps were to be had in Lusaka, but one of our British guides offered to catch me a baboon. The idea of Tarzan with a blue-assed baboon as his mascot hurt to think about. I tried to explain about Cheetah's unique relationship with Tarzan, but it was all over the Brit's head. He told me that I'd have better luck if I went chimp-hunting up north along the Zambezi. Since Salisbury, the Rhodesian capital, would be our next stop, I bided my time.

I'd kind of thought we left the racial segregation behind in South Africa, but I learned differently very quickly. Ira and Josh were going along a Salisbury street when the white owner of a barber shop recognized them from publicity photos in the paper. He was a real sports nut, and invited them into his shop to sign autographs for delighted customers. One patron, however, was offended. He raised a big stink, saying Josh and Ira were trying to force the proprietor to give them haircuts in the whites-only shop. Our guys wanted to take this jackass on: dammit, they'd been invited in.

The USIA man assigned to us was firm: "Be cool about this, forget about it, and for God's sake, don't talk to the press."

Josh and Ira complied. They knew that if South African or Rhodesian police detained non-whites, they might not be heard from again.

The incident made us almost too tense to compete in Salisbury, but I continued to jump well at about 15'. It was a relief to get out of the city, though, and we all looked forward to excursions into the countryside. They took us to see the site of the proposed Kariba Dam, at that time the largest such undertaking in the world. But before the dam was in place, they had to move the animals away from the future Kariba Reservoir, It was a kick to watch a bunch of exasperated Noahs in shorts hauling aggravated and utterly uncooperative wildebeests and gazelles to safety.

While we were there I talked to some of the game people about my chimp, and they said I could obtain one easily. But I learned I'd have to spend months getting permits, having papers validated, seeing to a million inoculations, and finally waiting through two quarantine periods. Nobody but Theresa would have been worth that hassle, so I dropped the idea of Cheetah, Junior.

We also took a great trip in a motor boat out on the Zambezi, among 1,500 pound hippos and crocodiles that measured between ten and twenty feet. That was all Josh needed. "If Tarzan starts messing with crocodiles, Boy's outta here," he said, giving me a stern look. But he didn't mean it.

At last I was really in Tarzanville. I kind of got into it, waving at the tourists in their canopied launches, giving them Tarzan yells, while they laughed and waved back. I'd also brought a pocketful of pebbles with me, in case Tarzan needed them, and I began lobbing them at the crocodiles. They got all indignant and dove underwater. But I wanted them to come closer, so I started rocking the boat. This drew howls of protest from Ira and Josh, neither of whom swam too well. Apparently they didn't want to have to get a lot better at it real fast.

Finally the boat nosed into a beautiful cove, where trees dipped their branches into the almost motionless water. "This is just the kind of spot where Tarzan would take his morning swim," I announced.

Bob Gardner piped up, "Well, Tarzan, do you dare?"

Our Brit had explained that crocs like to lie on the bottom and wait for prey to stray within snapping range, but I couldn't back out of an opportunity like this. I dove, and the next thing I knew, I was pulling myself back out of the water. The guys told me they'd never seen such an almighty splashing, with my arms and legs going as if I were Johnny Weissmuller himself. The thought of those crocs sure put a jet up my rear.

———————

There was a government reception for us that evening, and we met the Rhodesian Prime Minister, Sir Roy Welensky. A pleasant man, he was not only a tremendous fan of boxing greats Dempsey and Tunney, but also seemed partial to athletes in general. When he heard we hadn't seen Victoria Falls, he put a Royal Rhodesian Air Force plane at the team's disposal for an entire day of sightseeing.

The trip was marvelous. For openers we flew over Kruger National Park and had an incredible thrill as we watched a mob of zebra and antelope tearing across the plains below. A few minutes later, a herd of elephant rumbled along right under the plane, looking just as I'd always imagined them. This was truly the heart of Africa. When we turned west to Livingston and Victoria Falls, though, I realized there were fewer animals than I'd expected, and that made me sad.

We couldn't see much of Victoria Falls from the air because of the mist and spray, but we landed and drove in for a closer look. The full force of the Zambezi plunged over a four-hundred-foot drop and thundered at our feet. Clouds of rising mist made it the most hauntingly beautiful spot I'd ever seen.

As we left the Falls, we noticed several Africans selling native ebony and rosewood carvings. I bought a mask and a perfect miniature of a giraffe. Other carvings, more elongated and streamlined in their design, barely suggested the animals. But they captured their essence or spirit, and a bit of the heart of Africa as well. Of course we all had to buy some.

Just then a troop of baboons ambled into our midst, playing with each other and begging for snacks from the tourists. Everybody whipped out cameras, but our British guide herded us back to the Land Rover. When I started to argue, Josh fixed me with a reproachful stare. I got the message. After several close calls, even Tarzan catches on.

As we climbed into our vehicle, our British friend explained. When the male baboons start to encircle a group of people it can sometimes mean trouble. The females and young ones keep the humans entertained and distracted until the bulls are ready to close in and attack. So there was more to Tarzan's tropical paradise than exotic flowers and cute animals.

———————

After Salisbury we visited the large, modern-looking city of Bulawayo in Southern Rhodesia. The African people continued to be a delight, in marked contrast to the sullen white officials, who weren't always thrilled to see us. A lot of the guys we coached were superb natural athletes, and we expected many of them to qualify for future

Olympics.

There was one kid who had the makings of a first-class vaulter. He was jumping at 8'6" when we started. After an hour's instruction, he was clearing 12' easily. He complied with every direction to the letter, and had the nerve to do it all. He was fearless. It's a scary feeling when you rock back on the pole, but he didn't give into the fear. I expected to hear great things about that youngster, but to this day, Africa hasn't sent one pole vaulter to the Olympics.

I was looking forward to driving up north toward Tanganyika in hopes of seeing more herds of animals. The day we were supposed to leave, our guide, a British Grenadier, told us the bad news. Our visit had been cancelled because of unrest in the village we'd planned to visit.

Tarzan had an announcement. "Bull! We're not afraid, and we're going. I wanna see more animals."

Josh, as usual, backed the Grenadier's good sense. "Don, this is Africa. Haven't you learned anything yet?"

The next day we learned that Mau Maus killed several people in that very village during the night. Josh turned to me and said, "Tarzan stupid, but still alive. I wonder why?" All I could do was agree with him.

We went down to the Capetown area, where the crowds were warm and hospitable, and the African athletes grateful for any help we could give them in their sports. At a meet in N'chauga, I jumped 15'4½", then tried for a world's record. I came close, yet once again, no cigar.

The thing I remember best about Capetown, however, was the government's convoluted system of controlling who went to the can where. We had to choose from "White," "Black," or "Colored" toilets, the last category for anybody who was a mixture of the first two, plus all Asians. I could just see some poor guy with the runs having to consult his family tree before he could take a crap. This kind of idiocy was one fact of South African life I wouldn't miss.

One of our last nights in Africa was the most memorable: a native festival held in Johannesburg in our honor. There were African dances, acrobatics, brilliantly colored costumes, and unforgettable music performed by the South African Black Ensemble. The lead female singer absolutely blew me away. Her name was Miriam Makeba, and she entertained us all night with songs from the bush country, including the wildly popular "Click Song." Her record album was one souvenir of Africa I intended to keep for myself.

The flight home was going to be long, so I dressed for comfort: my pareu with a loose fitting African shirt. When we started to board the plane, another flight had just landed, the presidential plane carrying

Prime Minister Verwoerd. His plane pulled up beside ours, and as a band played some kind of Entrance into Valhalla shit, this tubby guy emerged from the plane. I was about the last one up the ramp, and I decided to give the old buzzard something to remember us by.

It was one of my best Tarzan yells: even the band stopped playing what turned out to be the South African national anthem. Ira dragged me inside the plane, and we all urged the attendant, "Shut the damn door!" Ira and Josh were sure we'd get nailed somehow, so until the plane was actually off the ground they sat there looking straight ahead doing the white-knuckle bit. They had no desire to return to South Africa for an indefinite dose of Verwoerd's dubious hospitality.

Well of course we made it out okay. But if they'd stopped the plane, Verwoerd's henchmen wouldn't have found much of me to arrest. Not after my two buddies got through with me.

——————

After all our adventures, it was great to be back home in New York. I was also pleasantly surprised when flashbulbs started popping as I came down the ramp in a pareu, sporting my new goatee. I figured some of the publicity photos from the jungle had preceded me home. I thought, "Waddayaknow! I'm a star." At least that's what I thought until a reporter began calling me "Steve."

"Say what?"

"You're Steve Reeves, the guy who's playing Hercules, right?"

I was gratified he didn't report the hissing sound of my ego getting deflated, but at least I had a comeback.

"Hell no! I'm Don Bragg, and I'm Tarzan for real!"

We all had to submit to a lengthy debriefing when we arrived home, and our mission was considered a success. There was one far-reaching result of our African tour. The government realized the effectiveness of ordinary Americans sharing their expertise, one-on-one, with ordinary Africans. Thus were the first seeds sown out of which grew the Peace Corps.

PART SIX

PRELUDE TO GLORY

To struggle and confront some more
Things that I have done before.

-- from "Motivation Anew" by Don Bragg

Chapter Seventeen

Fun 'n' Sun

By mid-July it was time for the Russian-American meet in Philadelphia, an exciting event. It was the first time Russian athletes were permitted to compete in the U.S., and I was curious to see what the big bad Commie vaulters would be like. Once I met them I realized they were just ordinary nice guys who wanted to compete and have a little fun. Vladimir Bulatov and Igor Pretrenko were the top USSR vaulters, and Igor Ter-Ovanesian was one of their champion broad jumpers. Though I quickly became very good friends with them, they were constantly shadowed by the KGB guys accompanying the USSR team. I decided they had to see something of the real America, so I devised a plan.

One afternoon, the two Russian vaulters slipped out a back window of the Warwick Hotel in Philadelphia, went down the fire escape, and climbed into my waiting '52 Studebaker.

I didn't care if these guys visited Monticello or Grant's Tomb, but I was determined to give them one absolutely American experience. I rounded up Dietzie and Theresa, and all of us paid a visit to the old gravel pit. We had a great time, with Dietzie and the guys giving an acrobatic exhibition, doing complicated flips off each others' shoulders.

When the Russians were thoroughly famished, we brought them to Mama Fiore's house for a taste of the best Italian cooking this side of Naples. We washed it all down with Vicenzo Gataldi's version of Dago Red, the best wine in the world. Cenz was a chemist at Dupont and really knew what he was doing: he only used juices from California.

Sitting around the table, sipping good wine, and telling stories and laughing, we forgot about political differences. But eventually the Russians began to worry about being missed by their KGB watchdogs. During the trip back to Philly I realized I was nervous, too. Both Russians, but especially Bulatov, were terrific guys, and I hoped I hadn't put them in real jeopardy.

We decided to tell everybody we'd just gone for a walk, but as a cover story it was pretty transparent. When grim looking men started reading the Russian riot act to my friends I became alarmed. Then Bulatov looked over and winked at me. So, despite the ruckus, we'd gotten away with our AWOL afternoon.

———————

The next day's competition was a gala event, closely covered by the press and a million TV cameras. The venue made it easier: Franklin Field, my old stomping ground from the Penn Relays. Knowing that Bulatov was liable to be punished if I beat him by too much, I'd halfway decided to coast during competition. Once the competition was underway, however, I realized I wanted to win, no matter what. Too late, I remembered my rule of avoiding friendships with other vaulters. But Bulatov wasn't my toughest adversary. That honor went to the shifting wind at Franklin Field. This devil wind could be at your back as you came down the runway, but right in your face at take-off.

Pretrenko was eliminated after jumping 14'10", but Bulatov continued his duel with me until the bar went to 15'2¾". I cleared it my first try, but Bulatov missed that height twice. On his final try he hit the bar on his way over it. Unbelievably, it bounced up in the air and landed back on the uprights. The crowd roared with laughter and rewarded Bulatov for this impossible feat with a round of applause.

We raised the bar to 15'5", but neither of us made that height. I was declared the winner because I made 15'2¾" my first try, and Bulatov came in second. He was ecstatic. I figured the folks back home would be proud that he came so close to beating America's Don Bragg by jumping four inches higher than his former personal best.

Bulatov and I both got what we wanted. He received the acclaim of his people, being named Grand Master of Sport on his return, with all the perks that entailed.

Me? I won.

———————

There was barely time to catch my breath before the Pan American meet in Chicago. Since I desperately needed a new pair of dress shoes, I picked up a pair on the way to the airport. Wearing them on the flight would be a good way to start breaking them in. Bad idea. You don't realize the amount of walking you do going to and from the different gates, making your transfers, and so on. When we arrived in Chicago, I ignored the stinging sensation in my foot, continuing to walk around despite the soaring heat and humidity. That night I found two large blisters on my right heel, but I assumed that if I kicked back barefoot for a couple of days, I'd be in shape for the meet.

The next morning, however, since the heel was red and terribly swollen, I realized I'd hatched an infection. I immediately went to the trainer, who seemed miffed when I insisted that the blisters were really severe. He stuck on two Band-Aids, handed me some aspirin, and started work on somebody with a more serious injury.

Next day I couldn't walk at all, and sent out an SOS for the team doctor. He poked the scarlet balloon at the end of my leg and told me my foot was swollen. He studied it for a minute or two. "I'll bet we've got an infection in there."

He became indignant at my exasperated, "No shit, Sherlock!" But at least he sent me to the hospital. I gritted my teeth in frustration. The diagnosis had come twenty-four hours too late.

The ER doctors had me admitted, STAT, and ordered hot compresses and penicillin shots every four hours. By evening, they upped the antibiotic dosage and told me I needed minor surgery in the morning. They lanced the wound, drained it, and continued the antibiotics and hot compresses.

Meanwhile I was having a battle with my nurse, whom I suspected of being a professional sadist. She wanted to give me the elephant-sized injections in my hip, but I told her it would make the leg muscles tight. A slightly sore arm I could deal with. She finally gave in, but as she jabbed me viciously in the triceps she said, "I don't know what difference it makes. You're going to be in here for at least five days more."

"No," I said. "I'm competing tomorrow."

She gave me a horsy laugh as she sauntered out of the room. "That's what you think. No doctor in his right mind would let you out of here."

The doctor who popped in a few minutes later seemed to share her opinion. "Look, you can't even stand up, let alone run."

When I struggled to my feet the room reeled, and my foot felt like fire, but I said, "Give me a minute and I'll be okay."

"How in hell do you propose to force a shoe over that foot?"

"Easy. If I cut down the heel and tape the shoe around the instep, the pain won't be too bad. The shoe should stay on, too."

The doctor didn't have an answer. Finally he said to the nurse, "We might as well let him go since there's no stopping him. But give me a call as soon as they carry him back in here."

The morning of the meet, I gamely climbed out of bed, but waves of dizziness nearly floored me. Gradually I regained my balance and started to dress, stuffing my feet into open-backed slippers. I made it to Soldier Field, but even trying seemed like too much effort. So it was a welcome surprise to look up and see Bob Richards bounding up to say hello. I didn't have an opportunity to tell him about my situation because he was filming the meet, flying around with a million things on his mind. All the same, seeing him gave me a real lift.

When I taped on the doctored shoe, I was relieved that I was able to walk without a noticeable limp. As I loosened up, however, nausea struck again, and I was back in the locker room, vomiting as if I'd never stop. Though I felt better when my stomach calmed down, I still had to deal with intermittent dizziness.

I figured I could only allow myself one practice jump, so I set the bar at 13', a good median height. Thankfully, I turned as I cleared the bar so that I landed on my shoulder, sparing the foot some punishment. The competition started at 13', and I took my first jump at 14'. Feeling taut and uncoordinated, I cleared it, but only on my second attempt. I pulled myself together and cleared 14'6" my first try. There weren't too many more jumps left in me, so I had them raise the crossbar to 15'2". If I made that, I'd break the Pan Am record of 14'11", held by Bob Richards.

Nothing was right about the jump, but somehow I cleared the bar. I was struggling out of the pit when Bob appeared at my side and pulled me to my feet. He had this intense look on his face. "Come on," he said. "You're ready for a world's record."

He had no idea how sick I was as I stood there trying to keep from retching. "I don't feel so good, Bob. I'm ready to heave."

It was like I hadn't said anything. "You'll be all right. You're prime." He called to the officials, "Move it up to 15'5".

It'd be nice to say I made that jump, but I didn't. I went under the bar and passed out cold in the pit. I came to on a stretcher as the attendants carried me off the field. Bob was running alongside. "So, Don," he said. "Are you sure you're finished? You've got two more jumps left."

I took a swing at him and nearly fell off the stretcher. As they shoved me into the ambulance I saw Bob Richards standing there with this big old proud grin on his face. That was better than breaking any record.

Back at the hospital, my doctor had to put his two cents in. "I guess some people have to learn the hard way."

I seized his coat and croaked, "Wrong!" as somebody informed him that I'd broken the Pan Am record.

"Impossible," he blustered, grabbing his coat back.

"Impossible for anybody but me," I said to his departing back, but I wasn't mad at him. I didn't even mind it when the fiend in white gave me a blistering shot in the ass. Considering the horrendous circumstances, I'd made the greatest jump of my career, and nobody could ever take it away from me.

<hr>

About this time I started hanging out more with Al Cantello, another authentic warrior-athlete. He had a mercurial nature and an imperious streak that sometimes put a caustic edge on his zest for winning. But the two of us shared a do-you-dare-to approach to life that made us gravitate toward each other. What I especially liked about him was that he was a nut case like me, even though he'd never admit it: a closet prankster.

Once after a scary movie he put on a Frankenstein mask, tied a rope around his chest, and hung himself in the closet. He wanted to be ready when his roommate Bob Gardner came back from the store and opened the closet door. But Bob chose that night to throw his coat on a chair instead of hanging it up, so Al was stuck dangling there for an hour. Finally he began to bang and yell "Bob, it's me!" through the heavy rubber mask. All of a sudden, the closet door flew open, and there's his roomie brandishing a baseball bat, ready to beat the shit out of the intruder. We nearly lost one of our best javelin throwers that night.

———————

The Citrus Invitational was outside the regular indoor schedule, and competition definitely took a back seat to enjoying the beaches of Fort Lauderdale. Al Cantello and his girlfriend Jackie joined Theresa and me for what amounted to a vacation. We played basketball on the beach, partied at the Purple Parrot, and generally had a great time. The four of us even squeezed in a visit to Theresa's brother over in Palm Beach.

After the meet, Cantello said we had to go back to a narrow high-backed bridge we'd seen earlier. We stopped the car at the highest point of the arch, and Al jumped out. He put one foot up on the railing, and said, "Hey, Don! You chicken?"

That got me out of the car, and we both stood staring down at the water about forty feet below. A few yards away, an old black guy stopped jerking his fish pole back and forth and watched us. We asked him if the water was deep enough to dive into.

"Plenty deep," he said.

"Then it's safe to dive?"

"Didn't say that. Fella got him a good-sized shark here last week." He jerked his line again. "Hear they done took two or three the week before."

I asked with some suspicion, "Anything else?"

He said, "Big ol' jewfish down there right under the bridge. Hear he weigh five hundred pound."

"What in hell's a jewfish? Will he bite us?" we asked together.

He started chuckling. "Won't bite you none 'less you be landin' on top of him. Then he might could take a bite outta you. Hear they mainly likes to grab hold of arms and legs, and just, you know, suck on 'em some."

Al didn't like the sound of this, so it was my turn to say, "Ya chicken, Al?".

Traffic was building up behind us, now, but Al was oblivious. He'd turned kind of green, but looked grimly determined. "Let's go on three," he said.

We counted to three, but Cantello jumped the gun and dove in on two, with me right on top of him. We surfaced with the same idea: getting the hell out of these shark-infested waters. Both of us grabbed for the ladder hanging from the bridge, but neither one of us wanted to be the second man up. We kept pulling each other off the ladder, laughing, wrestling around, even though we could almost feel sharp teeth crunching into our legs. When we finally scrambled back on the bridge, Theresa was arguing with a couple of livid drivers, and a police car was just pulling up alongside. The officer said, "Get that heap off the bridge and then pull over." We were still laughing, but in that nervous way guys do when they've done something supremely stupid.

"Sorry, officer," we said. "The car stalled."

He looked at our soaking clothes. "Uh huh." He'd just started to write us up when he stopped and squinted at us. "Hey, didn't I see you in the big spread the paper did on the track meet?" When we admitted he probably had, he said with disgust, "Sorry to have troubled you. Get the hell out of here," tearing up the summons. As we stepped back into the car, Al was in good spirits again. "Guess that jewfish is laughing at us hotshot jocks. He's the only one in town who didn't think we were worth sucking up to."

The R & R we enjoyed in Florida set me up for an excellent start to the 1960 indoor season. I took first at the big East Coast and Los Angeles Times meets, as well as the Chicago, Milwaukee, and Cleveland offerings.

Long about March during a flying visit to Fort Dix, solemn officers summoned me to a meeting. My two-year hitch was almost up, and they wanted me to re-up for one more so I'd be representing the US Army in the Olympics.

Whoa! I had something the Army wanted. "I can't see another two-year hitch. No, not one year, either." I blinked innocent puppy-dog eyes at them. "Do you have anything else?"

After a ton of throat-clearing and whispered conferring they asked, "Do you have something specific in mind?"

Did I! I'd stay in the Army at the same pay through the Olympics in September, period. I'd start training in California, ASAP, but I wouldn't have to cut my hair or prance around in uniform. I had to be relieved of all official duties.

They bought it!

The Army retained the honor and glory of an olive drab Olympic contender, and I won the freedom I needed to train for the most important event of my adult life. It took every ounce of self-control I possessed not to break into a Tarzan yell, but I didn't want to piss off anybody. It was too good a deal to screw up.

The Army had stipulated that I had to keep a uniform handy in case I was needed for some public appearance, but they only called me up once. I was supposed to meet some general for a luncheon press conference at Skandia, a fantastic restaurant in Los Angeles. I had to hustle to make the meeting, and a few details might have gone awry with my uniform.

The General took one look at me and barked, "Soldier, come with me." He led me into the rest room and gave me a dressing-down. "Look at you! You're a disgrace! Here, let me fix you up." He grabbed me, muttering like a maiden aunt getting her idiot nephew ready for his First Communion. "Who in hell taught you to put your infantry insignia *there*?" I just played dumb, and tried not to disgrace my infantry insignia during lunch. And that was *it*, so far as playing soldier was concerned.

The meets in California were always a lot of fun, with the surfing and beach bunnies. The atmosphere was more like a luau than a typical East Coast meet. In fact most competitions would be preceded by a barbecue, which certainly contributed to making them friendly social gatherings. Maybe that's why track and field was more popular out there than back home. And for me at least, there was the added dazzle of Hollywood.

But that's how those wily Californians do it. They feed you barbecue, show you some bikini babes, and then, when you're all nice and mellow, they pounce.

In May, as I was leaving practice at the Southern Cal track, I ran into Parry O'Brien and Des Cook, a discus thrower who'd attended Southern Cal with Parry. To my surprise the two of them elected themselves as my guides to the real California scene. First thing, they dragged me out to Santa Monica and Sorrento Beach at the Wall to watch the incredible volleyball action by bikini-clad babes. I wondered how the girls could stay in their bikinis with all the jumping around, and the answer was, they didn't. They didn't seem to give a damn, either, which struck me as a nice wholesome attitude. Parry and Des kicked back, taking long pulls out of something in a brown bag. "Beer," they explained. "We're in training, so we have to drink a quart of beer after practice to fight dehydration."

We body-surfed for awhile, then I mentioned that it was my twenty-fifth birthday. Des looked me over a sec and asked if I liked lobster omelets.

"Hell, yes. Why?

"I'm living in a friend's pad up in Malibu Canyon. He's a director from Southern Cal, and a real nice guy. Come up to the house, and I'll fix you the best damn birthday lunch you ever ate!"

It all sounded good to me, so I squeezed myself into Parry's snazzy black Jaguar convertible, while Des went for groceries. It was a blast driving through town in the Jag, but once we started up the canyon it got more interesting. Even with my stringent dieting, I was hardly petite, but Parry's strapping muscularity put me to shame. His incredible bulk pinned me to the door, squashing my guts against the handle. Every time his sturdy arm shifted gears I felt the pressure in my sinuses change, as if something vital were about to pop out my nose. To add to the experience, Parry took every curve like he had a death wish, and only the Jag's maneuverability and heroic brakes kept us from sailing over the cliff.

The pad was a cottage nestled on the side of a sheer precipice, with spectacular views on all sides. The view in the kitchen was unique as well. A display of throwing knives and a rifle covered one wall, dirty dishes covered the counters, and black fuzzy things covered most of the plates. While he rinsed off a few dishes, Des poured rum into flagons for Parry and himself, carefully adding a splash of soda. I begged off, but the guys, who outweighed me by 300 pounds, insisted I at least have a light rum Coke. As Des prepared the lobsters and shrimp the drinks began to take effect. The guys started growling, "Arrrr, matey, bring me a wench," and so on. I joined in lest I be made to walk the plank.

We gobbled up the fantastic omelets in about three minutes flat, but the rum Cokes had already done their work. Maybe that's why I went along with the next event: two-against-one wrestling matches. Parry and I went for Des, who flopped onto the couch and kicked out violently when we tackled him. He put a foot through the TV set, which, according to California rules, meant he'd won. Next, Des and I took on Parry, each taking a leg and dragging it in opposite directions until the poor guy yelled uncle.

Then it was my turn. As the other two jumped me, we thudded out onto the deck. Though I was busy defending myself, I felt something give way under me, and then heard heavy things bouncing down the canyon. I assumed part of the house had just departed, so I tried to mention it. But Parry had his huge arms wrapped around my neck, and Des was gleefully shouting, "He'll never break loose."

Right then I kicked free, and Parry crouched into a karate stance. I organized myself into the classic Marquis of Queensberry stance, as if that would do any good. Parry bellowed, but as he charged, I side-stepped and karate-chopped the back of his neck. He spun back, thoroughly enraged. I figured he'd keep at me till he had the satisfaction of one good hit, so I dropped my arms and took it. He walloped me on the neck with such force that I saw stars.

Now *I* was mad, and I didn't care that the deck was swaying alarmingly under us. I plowed into Parry, knocking him back into the house. Des jumped in to stop the rough-housing before it reduced the house to a heap of wood shavings. To distract us, he grabbed the throwing knives and brought them out to the wobbly deck. Parry seized one. "Let's see how close we can come to each others' feet. The first one to hit a foot loses." So he threw a knife at my foot, and it stuck right between two toes.

I reached for a knife. "I'm from New Jersey. I get to lose first."

Immediately, Des asked Parry to put the knives away. Parry complied by throwing all the knives at once at the kitchen wall. I don't know how he did it, but most of them stuck. Then Parry grabbed the rifle hanging beside the knives. Des seemed alarmed, and shouted, "Parry, that's loaded," but Parry ignored him.

"See that car down in the canyon coming to the stop sign?"

Des moaned, "No, no, no!"

Parry pulled the trigger, and the stop sign splintered into pieces. The car down below was motionless for a second, then streaked down the canyon, disappearing in seconds. Des seized the gun and fled into the house with it, hiding it before any of us became a target.

Now Des couldn't wait to get rid of us. "Hey guys, it's starting to fog up. You 'd better leave before it gets dark." It had been dark for ten minutes, so I don't know who he thought he was kidding. We offered to help clean up the place, but he turned down our offer with a resounding, "No! I'm saving the mould."

The trip back down the canyon was truly exhilarating. I was woozy from the rum Cokes, and my head felt swollen, as if it were detached from my shoulders. It was my first out-of-body experience, which was just as well, because Parry's shoulder was hammering me into the door again. As our speed approached mach four, tree limbs and rocks flew at us out of the dark, so I tried shutting my eyes. That was worse, since it made me focus on the sounds of tires screeching and rocks falling into the abyss below. Meanwhile the crazed driver comforted me by wailing, "Oh shit! Oh shit!" at the top of his lungs. This was one birthday I can safely call unforgettable.

It was painful to even think about moving my neck or shoulder, and at the meet a few days later, I finished a miserable fifth. Ronnie Morris, another Southern Cal alumnus, won. To this day I wonder if my poor showing was the intended result of a nefarious Southern Cal conspiracy.

———————

The weather was beautiful, so after the meet I took off with USC's Wally Levack for some surfing at Manhattan Beach. I'd heard about a shark attack in Monterey, so I felt a little paranoid, but not enough to stay on shore like a sane person. We surfed for about an hour, then decided to call it a day. Wally'd just caught a wave, and I was by myself waiting for the next big one, when something made me look over my shoulder. Not ten yards away were two eyeballs, staring at me. The biggest, fattest, brown hammerhead I'd ever seen was sitting there, deciding where to take his first bite. I heaved myself onto the next wave and pulled for the beach, closing my eyes against the horror I was sure was pursuing me.

"What in hell are you doing?"

I opened my eyes and saw feet. The wave had retreated, and I was lying there on the beach in two inches of backwash, still swimming with all my might, much to Wally's amusement. I sat up and bellowed, "Shark!"

Everybody tore out of the surf and gathered around while the lifeguards swept the water with high-powered binoculars. Then I heard one of them make a peculiar noise. "Where are you from, anyway?" he asked.

Wally said, "He's from New Jersey. Why?"

The guy eyed me with disgust. "Will you please explain to this East-Coast dork what a seal looks like? He might want to remember that sharks don't usually wear fur coats." The beach erupted in laughter at the jackass from New Jersey, but that was okay, since I'd escaped Jaws' gnashing teeth.

We celebrated my close escape at Pancho's Bar, but Wally spent most of the time telling everybody how his asshole buddy had panicked at the sight of a seal. It got a little old. So when I went up to the California Relays in Modesto, I decided it was payback time. I collected my per diem and stayed at a friend's house as usual. But instead of burgers, I dined on steak at the sponsoring restaurants, and signed for the meals as Parry O'Brien or Wally Levack. The meet environment was such a zoo, I knew it would take the bean counters a thousand years to root out my indiscretions. I took first place in both the Modesto and Compton Relays, too, so my revenge was doubly sweet.

Chapter Eighteen

Fly or Die

The Quantico Relays were next, and I had to win. Twelve vaulters, the cream of the All-Service meets and the NCAA and AAU National Championships, would go to the Olympic Trials. I had a good idea of how my competition in Quantico would do, though, so it didn't worry me. My focus had already shifted to picking up the intensity of my training for the AAU Championships and the all-important Olympic trials at Stanford in early July, now less than a month away.

I needed to be at my absolute best at Stanford, and my preparation had to be meticulous. I don't believe it's possible to sustain optimum performance indefinitely: the muscles can't take it. So I tried to plan my conditioning and training so that my performance would peak when I returned to California. I knew how to train, and I had access to an arsenal to use against my number one enemy: over-stressed muscles.

The physical pounding pole vaulters take must be married to a regimen that takes account of muscle deterioration: the wearing, pulling, and straining. A part of that is being aware of the body even when you're not competing. If you don't pay attention to the stiff shoulder or aching back, you may pay with a performance that is inexplicably off, or even a serious injury. You pace yourself, watch yourself. You ask, is everything working? If it isn't, you fix it. Otherwise you'll have to ask what in hell can you do about it in the few seconds you have before the jump.

But the athlete's weapons can backfire. Too much rest can throw off crucial timing. Too much massage can soften muscle. So balance is essential in preparing for a major contest.

Then there's the mental attitude. Any athlete must be able to retreat behind a wall of mental toughness, that narrowing of perception which excludes everything but your own performance. While Bob Richards might be able to maintain the white-hot intensity of battle for the entire track and field season, that's too much to expect from mere mortals. I concentrated on shutting out all distractions, including fear of failure.

And that's where I ran into trouble.

It started with an insignificant muscle twinge in my leg after an easy practice jump at Quantico. Next time I landed it hurt a little more. I told myself it was nothing, but there was a cold, sick feeling in my gut as I fought the belief that it was the 1956 nightmare resurfacing.

I won at Quantico with a jump of 15'3", but the victory seemed pretty damn hollow. I knew what a doctor would say: take it easy and see how it goes, but the pain -- and the fear -- stayed with me. I'd continued to fixate on one awful idea. I was living out a replay of the 1956 Olympic Trials. My leg would give out again. I'd fail again.

Coach Kehoe was livid when I told him I wouldn't jump at the Bakersfield AAU Championships, but I called him on his threat of "or else."

"Or else what? I won at Quantico. That means I go to the Olympic Trials. Are you really gonna try to keep me off the Olympic Team because I won't jump on a bad leg?"

Of course he wasn't. But to keep him happy, I had to go down by the vaulting pit and lead the cheering section in my swell official AAU jacket. It was hard for me to stand there and watch every damn vault in the meet. I kept thinking, that's how you jump with two good legs.

When I packed for Palo Alto, I didn't know what was going to happen to me. Beside the leg pain, I was worried about jumping on Stanford's grass vaulting runway. It had been many years since I'd even run on grass, and having to deal with yet one more unknown at this crucial meet was unsettling. The idea of a Penns Grove farm boy spooked by a little grass was ludicrous, but I couldn't control the anxiety.

So when I arrived in Stanford I was carrying a whole sack of demons with me. Not only did my legs feel fragile and tight, I was torn between the desire to protect my leg and the urge to blast away at practice, to prove I could do it. I decided to baby the leg, refraining from vaulting for the entire week of practice. That nearly did me in. I hadn't put in enough tough practice to reach my top form, and I was afraid to even try for it. I was losing my edge.

Your competitive edge is like a baby. You have to coddle it, nourish it, protect it. It involves every aspect of athletics -- speed, strength, coordination -- and it's hard to maintain. But when you do, you arrive at your ultimate goal: perfect timing, the key to all athletic achievement. It's hard to stay there. Lose a little speed, lose a little power, and timing slips away from you. Without it you can't succeed.

You can compensate, though. My speed wasn't good enough, so I'd have to make it up with strength. While Morris and the others did practice vaults, I did handstand pushups and chin-ups. I worked on my running with wind sprints, then the 220. Usually I'd finish up jogging a half mile on the grass, rehearsing how I'd place my feet during the competition. Like all experienced vaulters I knew the exact number of steps before take off: I could have come down the runway blindfolded and hit the mark on the pad. If I didn't, I'd be screwed for sure. If my take-off was too far in, I could rip my grip off the pole or hit the bar going up. Too far out, the jump's too loose, and I'd risk coming down on top of the bar.

The maddening thing was, I knew I'd do well on this track if I ever got it together. Coming down the vaulting runway on nice springy grass, then taking off from a clay pad was an incredible sensation. It felt like a launching pad under my feet. No wonder Bob Gutowski broke the world's record here. That grass runway was a pole vaulter's dream, and I'd wasted so much energy being afraid of it.

Just before the meet I was wandering around the field, when I happened to run into Dave Sime. We knew each other pretty well: he was the other guy from New Jersey who'd been injured at the 1956 Trials. He too was worried about his conditioning, and said his legs felt tight. Dave had been in medical school, and hadn't been training at all, so I assumed I was in much better shape than he. Did I get a nasty surprise! When we started running wind sprints together I had to struggle to keep anywhere near him. Of course Dave was a sprinter, but I used to chase Charlie Jenkins around the track when we were at VU. I never exactly kept up with Charlie, but I didn't disgrace myself either. But no matter how I pushed, I couldn't get near Dave, and I was running harder than I had since Quantico.

When we stopped, Dave was still disgusted with his time, and went back to the locker room. I was alone again and felt like the devil. Make the Olympic pole vaulting team? Hell, I couldn't even outrun a rusty sprinter. Four years of work down the toilet. Maybe I should just retire.

I didn't snap out of it until the meet itself. My first jumps were god-awful, but then, at about 14'6", something was very different. I took a couple of steps down the runway and stopped. I repositioned myself and started again. Each step felt powerful as I raced toward the clay pad. For the first time in weeks, the vault was one flowing continuum of movement: down the runway to the take-off and up and over the crossbar into the pit. I had my timing back. Battling to catch up to Dave Sime had somehow given my speed the workout it needed.

The leg was still bothering me, but I knew I could win the Trials, even against the strong opposition of Morris, Wadsworth, Graham, Dooley, Gutowski, and a fantastic kid named Dave Clark who came out of nowhere and really pushed the rest of us. I couldn't afford to worry about the competition because I still had to concentrate on adjusting to the grass track. Since it was exceptionally fast, I had to adjust my steps and accommodate to its speed.

By 15' I'd slipped into a relaxed groove. Once things started clicking again, the confidence that had been eluding me for weeks flooded back. Even Ronnie Morris's determined charge didn't faze me. We both cleared the bar at 15'5", but Ronnie couldn't make 15'9¼" in three tries. My first jump at that height gave me the win and a new world's record. Best of all, I was on the U.S. Olympic team.

By the time I was out of the pit, the crowd was screaming. I had it in the back of my mind that this was the time to go for 16', but my heart was too full just then. I was bouncing around and yelling, and here comes Theresa right out of the stands, running up to me. I scooped her up and tossed her in the air, catching her on my shoulder and carrying her around the field in a victory lap. The crowd got a big kick out of this. After all the hoopla, I didn't have another jump in me, but carrying Theresa around that field was the sweetest moment in all my years of competition.

Dave Sime came around to congratulate me afterwards, but he was pretty happy himself. He'd qualified as an alternate, and he'd been so sure he'd come in dead last.

"And after the way I ran with you," he said. "No matter how fast I ran, you stayed just a pace or two behind me."

"I do run, you know," I said, a little defensively.

"Sure you do. But if I couldn't outrun a big galoot like you, I figured I'd had it."

It struck me funny. God took a couple of down-on-themselves guys from Jersey and had them chase each other onto the U.S. Olympic Team.

Chapter Nineteen

Escapes and Escapades

Only one thing occupied my mind in early July: the Olympic Games in Rome. But there were Olympic "tune-ups" scheduled first. Why? The AAU and the Olympic Committee were responsible for covering all the expenses in Rome, and sponsoring exhibition track and field meets starring the Olympic Team was an ideal way to collect a nice piece of change. I didn't like the idea of the meets, because I had only so much time to train for Rome, and I resented every second taken from my practice time.

There was no way in hell you could vault every day: you'd beat all the spring out of your legs. Normally, I'd jump Monday, Wednesday, and Friday, but weekend meets required resting up from Thursday on, costing me precious practice time. Of course I vaulted during a meet, but with a difference. In a meet, I'd be jumping high and hard, with extra strain on my back and shoulders. My legs would take a beating, too, because I'd be falling from higher and into a compacted pit.

Practice isn't about height. It's about enhancing every facet of the vault, especially anything that's been off. For that I'd keep the bar lower so I could up the number of vaulting reps. The thing I usually focused on was continuity in finishing off: the way I'd come off the pole. As I pivoted by rotating my hips as I went over the crossbar, my left hand came up and over my head. An extension with the right hand as I pushed off the pole gave me a little extra height. I knew if I perfected finishing off in practice, I'd have my height at the meet. If it was out of sync, there wasn't a damn thing I could do about it during competition.

Everybody went down to Pomona, and they put us up in the dorm at Pomona Poly Tech. The meet itself was at Mount San Antonio College -- Mount SAC, we called it -- but I didn't jump. The AAU people didn't like that, since customers were paying good money to see the world's record holder. My leg was starting to improve, however, and I wasn't about to put it in jeopardy for an exhibition meet.

Al Cantello was there of course, but for the most part we behaved ourselves. There was one time, though. One of the theaters announced that all Olympic athletes could go to the movies there for free. Al and I went one night, but the movie was pretty boring. Al leaned over and whispered, "You do the Tarzan yell, and I'll go up on the stage and walk on my hands."

"Right in the middle of the movie?"

"Yeah, if you do the yell first." That sounded reasonable, so I did my Tarzan yell, and Al ran up on stage and began walking around on his hands. I broke up when I saw the shadow of his upside-down legs walking around on the bottom of the screen The audience howled, but the management was not amused. Next day, they announced that not only was the free-pass policy cancelled, two particular athletes were barred from ever setting foot in their establishment again.

One night we were all down in the Commons Room watching TV, when they announced that a champion pole vaulter was dead. A moment later the full story came on: Bob Gutowski had been killed in an automobile accident near Camp Pendleton by some nitwit driving on the wrong side of the road. We'd never been friends, but Bob was a great athlete whom I certainly respected. In fact, when I was in trouble with my own vaulting, his splendid performances were the inspiration and challenge that kept me competing. The sport would miss him.

Of course Theresa saw the first announcement and just about passed out, so she missed the full story. I got a frantic call, and after talking to her for ten minutes or so, I finally convinced her I wasn't dead.

We had another exhibition in Baltimore July 24th, and since my leg was almost back to normal, I competed with everybody else. I wasn't about to strain or tear any muscles, so I coasted. My puny effort of 14'6" won the meet, so I guess none of the other vaulters were going all out, either.

The end of July saw us all in Eugene, Oregon, for the last U.S. exhibition meet, and I was consumed with managing my training program correctly. I still had an occasional twinge in the leg, so I worked on strength exercises with my chin-up bar and on even greater consistency in running. I cut my caloric intake again. I had to. I didn't intend to heft a single extra ounce on that pole. I loved to swim, but since it seemed to rob my muscles of their tenacity and snap, that was out too, except for an occasional dip. I watched myself anxiously for the first signs of fatigue and muscle stress. I wasn't a kid anymore. Overnight I'd become a cautious twenty-five-year-old.

Our host coach in Oregon was the renowned Bill Bowerman, an

experienced man who understood the pressures on Olympic-bound athletes. Rather than having us ricocheting around the dorms, he suggested we go canoeing.

Bill's son Jon dropped us and his dad's canoe off fifteen miles up the McKenzie River. He warned us about the rapids, and promised to pick us up down-river in a couple of hours.

Al, Dicky Howard, and I waved goodbye and pushed off down the fast-moving river. The whole scene, especially the way the sun reflected off the water, was perfect. Dicky Howard drove us all crazy, though. He was a black guy who claimed to be one-quarter Cherokee. He sat up in the front beating on the canoe, singing Indian chants in a truly horrible voice. Only when we threatened to throw him into the river did he shut up and start paddling.

The sun got pretty hot, so we stripped off our clothes and worked on our tans. This was the life! At least it was until we got to the rapids. Ten seconds after we hit the first rough water we were flipped into the drink, and so were our clothes and paddles. We righted the canoe, but the clothes and one paddle were gone.

Nonetheless, we continued down the McKenzie, naked and happy as jaybirds. When we came around a long bend in the river, Cantello began making little chirping noises. Then I saw it too: the Hayden Bridge spanning the river. It was a glorious bridge, and I knew what Al was thinking even before he said, "Let's climb up and dive off."

I had one reservation. "Um, Al, we're naked, and people are driving over the bridge."

Al looked at me like I'd sprouted a third head. "So?"

Up we climbed, and despite being stark naked, stood around discussing the pros and cons of a forty foot dive into unknown waters. Below us, Dicky was collapsed in the canoe, helpless with laughter, but shouting that he wasn't about to fish out the pieces. What decided me was the sound of brakes, as a flabbergasted driver caught sight of the brace of bare butts at the side of the road. I said, "Here goes Tarzan," and dove off that sucker with Cantello right behind me.

We were all still laughing when we resumed our journey. But when we began to see houses on the river banks, we realized we had a problem. I suggested we pull in and try to beg some clothes from some kind soul.

"Kind soul? Somebody sees naked guys creeping around his back yard, he'll give 'em buckshot, not a change of clothes."

In the end, I alone climbed up the bank, uprooting a couple of bushes for cover. Then I saw a man standing on his balcony, with a cocktail in his hand. He stared open-mouthed. "What in hell do we have here?"

I explained our predicament, but he wasn't about to lend his pants to some guy wearing a bush. So I tempted him with tickets to our meet. He finally said, "Oh hell, tell them to come on up."

"Please sir, could we have the pants first?" That got him laughing, and it got us the pants. He and some friends showed up at the meet, too, and I was right there to thank him again as I handed him the tickets.

———————

When I woke the next day with sore shoulders, it occurred to me that I'd been out of my mind. Maybe I was tired of being twenty-five, and for a little while I was back at the gravel pit in Penns Grove with the Gypsies. Whatever had possessed me, I'd come through unscathed, so I filed the entire experience under "cross training."

Of course, Ronnie Morris took that meet. Afterwards, when a bunch of us were walking outside the dorms, a couple of girls drove up in a convertible. All big-eyed and demure, they asked if we knew of anybody who'd like to go water-skiing. Before they even finished the question Cantello and I dove into the back seat of the convertible. The rest of the guys chased us down the driveway, trying to jump in with us, but Al and I beat them off.

I was determined to be prudent, so I let Cantello take the water-skiing honors while I watched from the boat. When he got tired of showing off, we both enjoyed a high-speed ride around the lake. Al was all proud of his water-skiing ability, and he wouldn't stop bragging. Somehow, I had to pull even, so I said, "Al, you ever jump out of a boat going fifty miles an hour?"

"No."

"Ya chicken, Al?"

"You jump first."

Well, that was okay. How hard could water be?

Damn hard. Hitting the water was like being smashed by four linebackers at once. I saw those little stars again, and my back really hurt. When the boat had circled around and picked me up, Al asked if I was all right.

"Sure," I lied, ignoring the pulsating pain in my back. "Nothing to it. Your turn."

"Okay, you watch the speedometer and tell me when we hit fifty."

As soon as we made sixty, I yelled, "Go!"

He hit the water like a rubber ball, skidding and bouncing until he sank. When we pulled him out, his eyes were glassy, and he was spacey as hell. "How was it?" I asked, all concerned and sweet.

Al knew he'd been had, but managed to gasp, "A piece of cake."

The girls thought this was great fun and suggested we do it again.

Speaking as one, Cantello and I answered, "Golly, we'd love to, but we've gotta get back to the dorms. We're late for supper."

When he recovered, Al carried on like a madman. He insisted on getting revenge, on me and anybody else who didn't run like hell when they heard him roaring. He dragged a dozen of us back to the Hayden Bridge and challenged us to jump the forty feet from the railing into the river. About half of the guys did. I dove in head first again, but Al had to do these complicated gainers. Some guys are so competitive. I had visions of the two of us climbing higher and higher on the bridge and leaping off into the water until one of us either chickened out or killed himself. Luckily, a rival javelin thrower, Bill Alley, was there for Al to harass instead, and that got me off the hot seat.

We finally dragged Cantello back into the car, and we ended the day by arguing for hours over who'd been the baddest guy on the bridge. It was hard to believe we'd been stone cold sober all day.

———

Perhaps the strain of marking time till the Olympics was getting to us. We were certainly grateful to be leaving the next day for New York, the jump-off for Berne, Switzerland. In Berne we'd have to wade through one last money-raiser, but then the waiting would be over. From Switzerland, we'd fly to Rome.

I saw Theresa in New York, and she went with me to visit my dad. He was in a kind of rest home, and not doing well. He cried when I told him I was off to Rome for the Olympics. I wished I could have taken him with me, and Theresa too, for that matter. Some guys did that kind of thing, but I couldn't see bringing pleasant distractions with me on purpose. Staying focused when I was alone was hard enough. Years later, I heard that running great Jim Ryun would be taking photographs of the '68 Olympics in Mexico for some magazine. I knew he'd either lose his race or take crappy pictures. There was no way he could do both well, and his focus should've been the race, not the camera. It was a shame Jim was loaded down with added responsibilities which, I believe, cost him the race.

PART SEVEN

A GLADIATOR IN ROME

Something monumental, an ultimate endeavor,
Never ending in its continuous climb,
A consuming search that treks through time.

-- from "Consumed" by Don Bragg

Chapter Twenty

The Weight of Waiting

The trip to Switzerland was a delight. Knowing we had to face yet one more money-raising meet in Berne was a pain, but the conditions on the plane had us in near revolt. In the first place, nobody'd calculated the combined weight and mass of equipment, muscles, feet, and luggage we had to take with us. As the plane took off we noticed it seemed to be straining, and friends later told us the plane barely cleared the end of the runway. I guess we were lucky we didn't crash.

They crammed the track and field team in with the basketball guys in coach class. Nobody had any room to stretch out and sleep, something guaranteed to screw up everybody's performance. When we landed in Berne, the attendants practically had to pry us out of our fetal positions so we could drag our cramped butts off the damn plane. I would've hunted down Mr. Brundage and complained, but he wasn't there. Olympic officials would fly first class directly to Rome on a later flight, after which they'd be whisked to their air-conditioned suites. More than one person wondered why the Olympic Committee treated us athletes like field hands if we were the heart and soul of the Olympics.

Berne, Switzerland? People warm, country cold. The mountains were pretty, but they mainly reminded me of the frost buildup in Mom's old Kelvinator fridge. Right off the bat, both legs started aching something fierce at night, but the one I'd been nursing for months also began to cramp. The meet was scheduled for the evening, and as soon as the sun went down, so did the temperature. There was no way in hell I was going to jeopardize my leg by jumping outdoors in that chilly night air just to make money for Brundage and his cronies. If the Olympics meant anything, the welfare of each athlete had to be the AOC's highest priority, but I didn't think it was. All I wanted to do was get to Rome and start to acclimate physically to the one competitive environment that counted. Word got back to me that Avery Brundage was upset when I didn't jump, which gave me a nice warm feeling.

After the Berne meet, the guys were all showing the strain of waiting. We wouldn't be leaving for Rome for a couple of days, and there was nothing to do but sit around and torment each other. Before any blood was shed, I decided to concoct a diversion to preserve the general sanity. Since this was a gathering of America's modern-day warriors, my game would have to entice the most outrageous egos on the planet. It would have to be a uniquely challenging contest, something outside of all their areas of expertise.

I told a young Swiss athlete my problem, and he smiled knowingly. "Just take a look outside.".

Far below the hotel window, I could see some kind of turbulent canal crossing the countryside. Wow! A gigantic waterslide. Not only did it meet all my criteria, it provided an unexpected bonus: the urbane members of the Olympic Committee would have a cow if they found out.

Not everybody accepted my invitation to brave the serpentine watercourse, but about thirty of us committed to the adventure.

We were making our way to a bridge, admiring the snow-tipped mountains, when I realized we were dealing with snow melt. That water would be frigid, so it made sense to scramble down the stony bank to ease into the water gradually. That's what I did, but everybody hooted with derision at my supposed cop-out. I ignored them. If I do something risky, I always try to gauge the danger first. In water this cold, cramps and shock were real possibilities, so my precautions were just sensible. The things I do only *look* crazy.

Rafer Johnson and about fifteen others, however, jumped into the racing water from a low bridge. When he surfaced, Rafer had actually turned a bright blue. He had to climb out with cramps after a few hundred yards, and most of the others soon followed his example. But Parry O'Brien, our renowned shot-putter, led the charge as he, Cantello, and I continued down the flume. I felt proud to be one of the stalwart three remaining, but prouder still that my idea had shaken us all out of the doldrums.

This blissful complacency continued until we heard a subdued roar. We came around a stand of trees and saw the giant turbines of an electric power plant smack in the middle of the damn stream. I was ready to haul out onto the canal bank, when Parry pointed to a small channel just before the turbines. "Let's see if we're strong enough to outswim the current to that runoff."

Now wait a minute. If we didn't make it, the turbines would surely suck us into their grinding blades. Glancing back at Cantello, I noticed he was staring at O'Brien, probably with the same thought I had. Was the big shot-putter bluffing? If he was – and we didn't call him on it – the three of us might foolishly goad one another into mortal danger. But the wily javelin thrower was also a master psych artist.

"Sounds great, but hey! Maybe we should do this after the Games in Rome. They're slightly more important, right?"

Parry looked crushed. "Well, if you're sure."

"We're sure!"

By the time we were out of the water, we realized we were absolutely freezing, but hell, it had been a great stunt. Not till I was alone in my room did the enormity of the risk we'd taken hit home. The knowledge that I could have jeopardized my gold medal by a dumb prank made me feel a little sick. The crazy stuff had to stop. As I fell asleep I made mighty oaths and vows that I had absolutely learned my lesson -- until the next time.

It turned out we weren't going to fly to Rome after all. Mr. Brundage and friends decided to give us a chance to compare and contrast a miserable plane trip with an appalling ride on a train. We assembled at the station in Berne, and the scene reminded me of the gathering of the clans in the highlands -- until they started herding us into the parlor cars like so many cattle. Eight men to a compartment, four abreast, shoulder to shoulder, no leg room, no air conditioning. It wasn't so bad while we were in the Alps, but as we dropped down into Italy, the heat became unbearable. Since our "express" train made a lengthy stop at every town and village, everybody started getting irritable and feisty from the heat, the cramped seats, and hours of boredom. Realizing this, Al Cantello pulled out his harmonica and began serenading us. I joined in, singing every Italian song I knew. I finally had to stop when my throat demanded something wet. We were at a station, and Cantello called over one of the vendors who'd been yelling, "Vino, vino,"

"Welcome to Italy," Al said. "Have a little wine." I didn't drink, so I waved the guy off, but Cantello couldn't believe it.

"You've been singing for half an hour. You gotta be dehydrated. You need a little wine for the throat".

"Nah, I'm fine," I said. But a few stops later, I was so desperately thirsty that we grabbed the first wine-seller and bought a few bottles. We all took a pull at the jug, and when it was my turn, I honestly only drank enough to take the edge off my thirst. After all, I wasn't a drinking man.

All of a sudden I seemed to be looking at the other guys through fun-house mirrors. Everything was grotesque and distorted, as though the sides of the parlor car were closing in. I remember thinking that one diminutive distance runner was responsible for the undulating walls and that Tarzan should make him stop. During the chaos that followed, I know I dangled the little guy out the window, while Cantello and Rafer Johnson pleaded for me to pull him back inside. I only vaguely recall squeezing my head and shoulders back into the car with the guy in my arms, and him shouting that I was crazy.

I'd no sooner hauled him inside than there was a terrific *whoosh, whoosh, whoosh* as the train whizzed past a series of poles only inches from the window. One inebriated vaulter and his innocent victim had just narrowly escaped death. From then on they kept the wine jug well away from me. I didn't miss it because I'd passed out from my exertions.

By the time I woke up it was evening, and I was unbearably hot and sticky. I also had a foul taste in my mouth. Cantello told me it was from all the flies that had flown in and died, overcome by alcoholic fumes. I sat up groggily and realized we'd arrived at Rome's Termini Station. After months of preparation we were finally in the Eternal City.

We were all stiff and sweaty, and barely had the energy to pile onto the buses that would take us to the Olympic Village. I was looking out the window, trying to stay awake, when, up ahead, I saw an immense structure shimmering with light.

It was the Coliseum.

For a moment I couldn't even breathe. I had a stunning sensation of shame and deep sadness, and it was as if I'd felt it before. I couldn't take my eyes off the ancient amphitheater as my inner anguish was transformed into a sense of victory. I turned, kneeling up on my seat as the bus drove past it.

"Hey, everybody, I win here. I've been here before," I called out. I didn't quite understand my own words or where they'd come from. I was also amazed that the bizarre sensations I was experiencing weren't frightening. I rather had a sense of a piece of a puzzle falling into place. Shouts from my teammates to sit down and shut up snapped me out of whatever had been holding me transfixed, but something was different when I slid back into my seat. For an instant I saw my life intersecting with destiny. Whatever lay ahead in Rome had been decided eons before.

Al, Dave Sime, and I were all sleep-walking by the time we stumbled into our room. The heat was stifling, and the bathroom was way down the hall, but at the moment we didn't care. All we wanted was bed. I collapsed onto mine and instantly jumped back up. The beds were only about two feet by six, and squishy soft. Dave, nearly my height, was shaking his bed to see if an extension would pop out. Big Parry

O'Brien was down the hall bellowing, so I knew we weren't the only ones with lilliputian sleeping arrangements. Al's stomach was bothering him, so he immediately curled his 5'9" frame into his bed, yawning, "I don't know what you're griping about."

Maybe we should have raised hell right then, but I didn't have any fight left in me. I folded myself back into bed and tried to get comfortable, but I kept thinking of the officials in luxurious hotel rooms. I sent Mr. Brundage best wishes for a boil the size of Cincinnati on his ass, and closed my eyes. But my last thought before sleep was of a ruined amphitheater bathed in light.

I awoke from a weird dream of being pursued by an outhouse around the fiery margins of hell. It was no dream, however. Not only was the heat already oppressive, dysentery had struck during the night, and one of my roomies hadn't made it to the john in time. Poor guy was probably disoriented, being in a strange place, I told myself smugly. I stretched, turned over, and fell off my toy bed.

When I started down the hall to the can, there was a line. Though each room had a little sink, there was only one solitary john to accommodate the bunch of us. For me it was an inconvenience, but to those afflicted with Al's malady it was a taste of hell.

A lot of the guys were excited about the opening ceremonies, and the idea of marching like a gladiator of old into a Roman arena appealed to me, too. But it was over ninety degrees out there, and the humidity was way more than we were used to. You were also expected to wear your dandy official blazer and hat while you waited for hours to go into the stadium. Together with a few athletes nursing injuries, I watched the ceremonies on TV at the Village in relative comfort. When I saw people passing out from the heat I was glad I did. Some athletes came back dehydrated and exhausted, and that shouldn't have happened.

The cafeteria at the Olympic Village was excellent. They gave us all sorts of choices, beautifully prepared: steaks, lobster, pasta with garlic and fresh Parmesan, fried shrimp, lasagne, the works. But since I didn't want my pole to break under me, I couldn't dig in. I had to see and smell all these epicurean delights, then go graze in my dinky bowl of salad.

My main thought when we went out to the practice field was to avoid over-exercising. I planned to limit myself to a little vaulting practice and a little running. I also was going to do some walking: it was the safest way to start everything working without risking an injury. But I did want to keep up my upper body strength. What I really wanted was a visit to Tarzanville, but I found something almost as good. The poles for the field telephones were joined by lengths of two-by-six timber at a height of maybe seven feet: perfect for chin-ups. I didn't want to tire my arms either, so after a few reps and some jogging, there was nothing left to do.

The waiting was lethal, so a few of us decided to do some exploring. We wandered out behind the Village, with the intrepid trio of Cantello, O'Brien, and me in the lead. We saw some buildings through the bushes, and stealthily made our approach. Behind a hedge of tall evergreens, a posh pool party was in progress. We decided to infiltrate it.

One by one, we sidled in from between the trees, smiling and nodding to the guests, until we found a lavish display of fruit and sandwiches. By the time a guard confronted us we'd consumed most of the food, but we just pretended we didn't know why he was yelling at us.

Before we could start on dessert, the guard and his buddies started a flanking operation to trap us at poolside. We flipped our apple cores and banana peels into the pool as we swarmed up to the high diving board and cannonballed into the water. Of course I capped my dive with a fierce Tarzan call, which made the ladies shriek and run in tiny circles. We swam to the far side of the pool and fled through the wall of evergreens. Whoever was chasing us got tangled up in the trees, so we crept back to Olympic Village in the clear.

The following day, guys in serious blazers demanded the names of those who assaulted the country club next door. We all voiced amazement that any Olympian would be suspected of such an uncivilized act.

One of the most welcome diversions in the Village was a young boxer of about eighteen who never stopped talking. He was full of himself, but there was no way you could be offended unless you chose to be. He was a very likeable guy who reminded a lot of us of our kid brothers back home. Now and then, the two of us would bullshit, just to pass the time, and I remember him saying, "So you wanna be Tarzan? Okay, but I wanna be champ of the world."

One time I was talking to Jack Kelly, a friend from Philadelphia who'd medaled in sculls in Melbourne. All of a sudden this kid jumped up and started talking about kicking the ass of every fighter in Rome. Then when Floyd Patterson, the current world champion, walked in, the kid got right in his face. "You better enjoy your fame while you can, because I'm coming."

I turned to Jack and said, "That Cassius Clay's really crazy."

Sitting around in the heat was both nerve-racking and boring, so Cantello and I decided to find a place to cool off. We joined forces with my Russian friends: fellow vaulters Vladimir Bulatov and Igor

Pretrenko, and high-jumper Igor Ter-Ovanesian. Journalist Dick Schaap and *Sports Illustrated* photographer Bob Reiger also decided to tag along. Dick would later find his niche as a television sports commentator, and Bob became famous for his pen-and-ink drawings, in addition to his skill with the camera.

We were just out for a cool dip in the Tiber, but I was eager for publicity. Publicity made things happen, and anything that could help solidify my claim to the role of Tarzan was welcome. The plan was to dive off one of Rome's many bridges, but the water beneath the one we found seemed a little shallow for diving. We strolled further down the Tiber looking for a better spot. When we came upon a huge three-story houseboat that jutted out into deep water, we knew we'd found it.

Bob's camera was busy as we got into it, doing crazy dives, ducking each other, when this old Italian with a shotgun materialized beside us. Luckily, Cantello spoke Italian, and convinced him we weren't trying to steal his houseboat. The old fellow and his daughter watched as we continued our show of front and back flips and gainers. European headlines made a big deal out of this supposed new US-USSR rivalry, though of course it was no such thing.

A guy from *Life* Magazine liked the idea of Tarzan in Rome. "Don, let's take a few pictures in case things go well for you."

He took me out and had a chamois loincloth made for me, then photographed me around all the Roman ruins. This nonsense received a lot of attention from the locals and helped me forget the pressures of competition for a while.

Rafer Johnson, our decathlete, had asked me for some vaulting tips, so I joined him down at the practice pits and gave him a few pointers. He tried a vault, and slammed into the ground-level pit. Finally I'd found a vaulter whose landings were as deafening as mine.

"Holy mackerel! Man, I think I broke my back," he groaned, staggering to his feet.

I checked the pit and was infuriated: they weren't using sawdust, just sand. Rafer was damn lucky he wasn't injured, but he shouldn't have had to count on luck.

I made a big stink about the condition of the pit, saying I wouldn't practice-jump until they put a good big pile of sawdust in there. The press got wind of this and reported, in great big headlines, that Bragg was refusing to jump in the Olympics. I took the heat. As long as they replaced the sand in the practice and competition pits, I was happy.

But the problem with the pit made me edgy, so when Wilma Rudolph suggested we run wind sprints together, I jumped at the chance to work off some of the tension. I'd known Skeeter, as we all called her, from the meets, but we'd never run together. Once we started, she easily matched me stride for stride. This got me stewing again about the strength of my own running, until Skeeter began winning gold medals. Hell, she left *everybody* in her dust, so I stopped worrying.

Rafer's finals were in the evening, so I took a blanket into the stands to watch. Everything hung on the 1500 meters race. C. K. Yang from Taiwan, who'd attended UCLA with Rafer, was trailing him. But if C. K. could beat Rafer by fifty yards, he'd have the points to win the event. Both guys were exhausted. Rafer began to lag behind, and I thought C. K. had him. Then C. K. began to wobble a little too, though Rafer held his own. C. K led the way across the finish line, then the two runners collapsed in each other's arms. But Rafer had the gold medal.

The morning of September fifth I learned an interesting fact. As difficult as waiting for the competition had been, with all the "what ifs" running through my mind, it wasn't as horrible as trying to compose myself while sitting in the bus that was rushing me to my moment of truth.

The practice field was right next to the stadium. Even this warm-up area was ringed with statues of Roman warriors, and we jogged around the field under their unseeing stone eyes.

We all raced over to the practice pits as soon as they let us into the stadium. You always tried to be at the head of the line because sometimes the ones at the very front get an extra warm-up vault. My friend Vladimir Bulatov reached the closest pit first, and the German Preussinger was already at the other one, so I dropped in behind Bulatov. He was looking good as he went up and over, but he crashed into the pit with a scream. Everybody ran to help him, but one look at the grotesque angle of his foot told the story. This was no sprain: Vladimir had just broken his ankle.

Over the protests of the officials, Russian coaches and trainers swarmed out on the field, but I had no problem with that. Sure, the rule said no coaches on the field, but their guy was down, and they were going to help him. They shot Bulatov's foot full of novocaine and carried him off the field on a stretcher. But how in hell had Bulatov smashed his ankle in a jump that looked so good?

The answer became evident when we examined the pits. The other pit may have contained sawdust, but the one the Russian used was 95% sand, with a cute little top-dressing of sawdust for show. It looked like they'd run out of sawdust and hadn't bothered to get more. Damn. A world-class athlete needlessly injured because the groundskeepers had been lazy.

We finished practice in the one decent pit, and I couldn't help thinking how I would've fared if I'd beaten Vladimir to the head of the line. Only by the grace of God had I escaped injury.

Chapter Twenty-One

The Day of the Warrior

E ventually they called our event, and for the first time I fully absorbed the atmosphere in the stadium. There'd been 10,000 people at Stanford's Olympic trials: there were 100,000 here. Above the rim of the stadium we could see even more people gathered on the surrounding hills. One hundred thousand voices filled the stadium with a roar, both welcoming and challenging those who dared to vie for Olympic gold. The way their shouts swirled and echoed around the stadium had an eerie, almost mystical quality that connected us to every contest the Eternal City had ever witnessed. It was both exhilarating and frightening.

Right off, the German champion Preussinger started warming up at 13 feet with one-handed vaults. Eeles Landström came over and said, "Just look at him! One-handed vaults at that height. You can see why he's the European champion."

"That's very nice. But I'm the best with two hands, and that's what this competitions's about," I said. He got all shocked, like I'd farted in church, which was fine with me, because he went away and left me in peace.

When we started vaulting I discovered another attribute of the Olympic stadium. Its massive bowl was an aerodynamic magnet for every vaulter's arch-enemy: the wind.

And it was a devious, wicked wind that would sweep in on you right when you came down the runway trying to focus on your perfect take-off point. No matter what direction it came from, the wind disrupted your measured steps, and ultimately, the entire vault. Maybe it bothered me less because I was so strong. If I got thrown off, my overall body strength usually allowed me to compensate by muscling over, which some vaulters couldn't do. Now if the wind was behind you, you could blast onto the pole a lot harder, and, with the added momentum, maybe jump a little higher. But only a fool could consider the fickle wind an ally.

It was an equalizer, though. Preussinger was having a devil of a time, and Eeles Landström came over to pick my brain about his problem. I wondered why the Finnish and German stars had become so chummy, and finally realized the Europeans were trying to double-team the Americans. Anyhow, Landström asked me why Preussinger was having so much trouble at the lower heights.

"Easy," I said. "The wind's pushing him back at the take-off point. He really needs to adjust his markers for more height over the bar."

Landström hurried over to his buddy and began whispering in his ear. Preussinger glanced at me, and accordingly adjusted his markers for the wind. He made his approach with his teeth all clenched, but while he was doing that, the wind shifted direction. I almost yelled for him to stop, but I just had to see the fun. He went straight up, crashed through the crossbar, and kept going. He got his height, but he also got eliminated.

After that, I kept seeing Landström looking at me funny. I figured he was trying to decide whether or not I'd psyched out the European champion. I had to laugh. I'd given Landström my honest opinion to a question he really had no business asking. And justice was served in the end.

My main worry, after the damned wind, was to keep from irritating my leg any further. So my trips down the runway were pretty wimpy. Without an aggressive approach, I was no match for the wind whipping around the stadium. The crowd booed and whistled when I missed, and that was hard to take.

It was almost funny: we were down there in a cyclone, about to have our shorts blown off, and the crowd's bitching because we weren't jumping high enough. I was relieved when I earned a little applause by qualifying at 14'6". Ronnie Morris never made 14'6" but an earlier jump at 14'4" put him into the finals as the last of the required twelve vaulters.

After qualifying, I took my rear back to the Olympic Village to escape the sun and heat and to rest up for the finals. It was great to have that extra day to relax before the final test, but it also gave me more time to think.

The U.S. hadn't done as well as expected. Our best sprinter, Ray Norton, hadn't performed up to his ability. Ira Davis missed the bronze in the triple jump by two centimeters, but the shocker came in the high jump. The great John Thomas only received the bronze medal, losing not only to silver medalist Valery Brumel, but also to gold medal winner Robert Shavlakadze, a guy we'd never heard of.

That loss was disquieting. I wondered about the saggy-baggy Wilson shirts that we had to wear, with heavy, thick numbers pinned on the front. Did John's sweat-soaked cotton shirt catch the bar and contribute to his loss? He went over his jumps on his stomach, like me. A dragging shirt might conceivably pull down the bar.

But I believe the main reason he lost was because this great high jumper failed to make his performance his highest priority. John had qualified in the morning, but his finals weren't until later that same day. Instead of heading back to the Village to rest and conserve himself, he stayed out in the sun watching all the other jumpers. Even before the competition started, he spent every night in the rec hall, dancing up a storm. I remember asking him, "Doesn't all the dancing kill your legs, John?"

"Nah, it keeps me nice and loose," he said. Not so, my friend!

It was disturbing to see a top competitor fall because of his errors in judgement. I began reviewing my own routine, wincing at every dumb choice that might have jeopardized my chances of victory.

———————

The Russians made a lot of Shavlakadze's victory, and banner headlines read: *Today Thomas, Tomorrow, Bragg!* I knew it was mostly propaganda, but what if something in my bad leg tore or I let pressure get to me? Those and a million other unanswerable questions were my constant companion all that long night before the finals.

I also kept thinking of my dad back home, trying to dry out, trying to put his life back together. He'd had so much misfortune lately, but he was still one helluva man. Much of my success as an athlete rested on the constant support he'd given me. I could almost see him, back when I'd lost in '56, lying in the tall grass, staring at the sky for hours. I loved and respected him so much, and I couldn't bear the idea of disappointing him again. But the hours I'd spent poring over historical books had taught me one lesson: it was appallingly easy for the blood and courage of the fathers to fail to run true in the sons. I wasn't going to let that happen to me. It was very late, but I got up and wrote him a letter.

I wanted to tell him how it had been out there. If you imagine the pressure at the core of a volcano you've got an idea of what it felt like in the Olympic stadium. The adrenaline rush nearly blew me away, and I could feel it eroding my control. Hearing the whistles of the volatile crowd when I missed a jump made me feel vulnerable. Having to fight the constant attacks of the wind made my jumps erratic.

So I wrote, "Dad, the wind was in our faces so bad, it was almost impossible to jump. Vladimir Bulatov, the Russians' best, was carried out with a smashed ankle. Everything seems uncertain, but I promise you something. Because of all the things I inherited from you, I'm going to make it. I'm going to win that gold medal. I'm going to be the king."

I sealed the envelope and went back to bed. This time I slept. When I awoke, I knew what my strategy had to be. To hell with the distractions and the pressure. I wouldn't be tearing down a runway of hard Roman clay. In my mind I'd be barrelling down the board track Dad had built for me. It was a matter of focus and discipline, and I damn well would do it.

The pressure cooker that was the Olympics had certainly taken its toll during the qualifying round. No matter how you prepare mentally, you know damn well this ain't just another track meet. Bulatov; Preussinger, the European champion; and Dave Clark, the American prodigy, were all out. Ronnie Morris only qualified by the skin of his teeth.

It was a funny thing about Morris. He was a consummate technician, and his vaulting style had unmatchable finesse and polish. But none of that had served him well when he had to react to a wild card like the intermittent blasts of wind in the stadium.

I'd taken a battering from the wind, too, but something was different when I went back to the stadium for the finals. The crowd was chanting something, and it reminded me with a jolt of Rome's gladiatorial contests. The insight that pervaded my soul as we'd driven by the Coliseum came flooding back. It was all right. I would win. As I prepared to jump, I felt that something deeply spiritual was at work, that I was being watched over.

Although I wasn't running at full bore, I cleared every jump up through 14'10". Rolando Cruz was the Puerto Rican vaulter who was heading for Villanova, and I hoped he'd outlast Landström. A U.S. medal sweep would have been neat, but Cruz fell back at 14'10", finishing in fourth place.

We'd been out there for hours. I'd brought a little jar of honey with me for energy, and every so often, I'd grab a swallow, then have some water. There was a group of U.S. Navy guys in the stands, and every time I got a drink they started waving and hollering at me. Wow! I had a cheering section courtesy of the Navy. Then I realized that they were yelling, "Bragg, you asshole! Don't drink the damn water." So much for my ego buzz.

It was evening. As the hard white stadium lights came on, my depth perception seemed to take on greater clarity. The wind had died down, and the great stadium was quiet. Landström ran out of steam at 15'1" and was eliminated. He'd take the bronze medal home with him. Here was the situation: the U.S. had the gold and silver medals no matter who won. So now it could be personal, and Ronnie Morris was my only rival left standing. The Californian. One of us was going to win the silver medal, one the gold, and I sure as hell wasn't going home with the silver.

Watching my long-time nemesis under the brilliant lights, everything became simple. Forget this humongous international festival of sport. We could have been two guys in a vacant lot, squaring off to play king of the hill. But wasn't that the true spirit of the Olympics? A contest between gladiators, a battle, not to the death, but to the gold?

The bar was still at 15'1". I'd jumped that height a hundred times. But I knew if I faltered in any way, I could kiss the gold goodbye. I told myself, this is it. Turn everything loose or you're finished. I cleared the bar my first try, breaking Bob Richard's Olympic record of 14'11¾". Ronnie made it on his second attempt.

Now the officials wanted to boost up the crossbar in one-inch increments. That sounded like a bad idea. We were both tired, and either one of us could make a fatal mistake if this contest kept on all night. To hell with a war of attrition. It was time to attack.

I said to Ronnie, "Look, it's just you and me. Let's go for my record of 15'9." Ronnie kind of gulped, so I said, "Okay, how about 15'7"? No? Then let's make it 15'5". You know you've jumped that." I knew he'd only cleared that height once before in his career. Naturally he hesitated.

I goaded him. "Come on, you cleared that 15'1" by at least six inches." This was a bald-faced lie, but it was up to Ronnie to keep track of how well he'd jumped. He looked at me, deciding. He knew what I meant was, "Hey Ronnie! Ya chicken?" We set the bar at 15'5".

Now it was my turn to deliver. If I jumped well, it would turn up the pressure on Ronnie, but I had to make the damn jump first. My entire life was on the line. I had a strained muscle, but so what? What in hell did I have to save it for except this moment? I forced myself to analyze this all-important jump. If my charge down the runway was all-out, I had to move my steps back to hit the take-off perfectly. There was no room for errors or miscalculations now.

I was shaking when I reached the head of the runway. The wind gusted a little, so I waited, straining to focus, trying to ignore the mythic atmosphere that surrounded me. My mind flicked back to Penns Grove and that board track that stuck almost into the street. I took a deep breath. "This is for Mom and Dad, Theresa, my family, my country. Now go!"

It was the hardest I'd ever pulled on the swing up. I half expected the pole to break, but it held. Then over the top, pushing off the pole, bearing down with all the strength I had in my arms. Next, disengaging, swinging my arms away from the crossbar with the grace of a maestro conducting his orchestra. I landed hard and nearly slid out of the pit.

The roar from the crowd confirmed what I already knew: the jump was perfect. It took all the control I had left, but I immediately checked my steps and pole to ready myself if I had to jump again.

Now it was the Little Technician's turn. As he measured his standards and his pole position, I said, "Come on, Ron. This is yours." He took his pole and turned toward the head of the runway. I patted him on the back as he passed me, and said, "Do this one, and then we can go for sixteen feet."

He glanced back at me, looking slightly appalled. I nodded encouragement. "You can do this!" When he was almost out of earshot, I added, "I think."

He came down the runway, not only with great form, but also with competitive fire lighting up his face. I said to myself, "Hell, he's going to make it, and we'll be here till tomorrow morning."

Ronnie went up but not quite over, hitting the bar with his hand. That seemed to take the fight out of him. His next attempt was only fair, and it failed. I watched him preparing himself, and I could see that nearly eight hours of competition were getting to the little guy. Nothing went right for him, and his last jump went under the bar.

It was over.

I rushed to Ronnie and grabbed him in a bear hug. Part of me was congratulating him for winning the silver, but mostly I was thanking him for not winning the gold.

Then I realized I had to try to go higher: that's what pole vaulters are about. I turned to the officials and said, "15'10½" This would be one inch over my world record. I'd have to come down the runway at top speed, so I made adjustments to the standards and marker accordingly. I pressed the bulky number pinned on my loose-fitting shirt close to my chest, and hoped it wouldn't snag the crossbar. The wind might still be the spoiler, but it had gentled and cooled once the sun had set. There was nothing left to do now but clear that bar.

I waited for a moment at the top of the runway, revving up my adrenaline with every pep talk I could think of. Then I began to run. I came down the runway with excellent speed, a strong, smooth swing-and-pull up, and an almost perfect finish. Almost.

I was sure I was clear of the bar, but I felt the shirt drag a little going over the top. I crashed into the pit, sending sawdust into my eyes and throat. I brushed my eyes clear and looked up at the bar. A tremor ran through it, but then it was still. The crowd that had been holding its breath exploded into a full-throated roar. I climbed to my feet and stepped out of the pit -- and the bar fell on top of me.

I was stunned. Had the boisterous shouts of the crowd dislodged it? Had I touched the bar myself and not felt it, or had the draggy shirt done me in? I'd never know. My next job was to try again.

Victory platform in Rome in 1960. Ronnie Morris, silver; Don Bragg, gold; Eeles Landström, bronze.

Halfway down the runway I knew I was exhausted. I had nothing left but the memory of a fading adrenaline rush, and that wouldn't be enough. The jump was pretty bad, but the crowd cheered anyhow. It didn't even bother me. I'd missed a new world's record, but my four-year struggle was over. The gold medal was mine.

I had to hit my honey bottle before I did anything else. I'd weighed 198 pounds going into this eight-hour ordeal: coming out I tipped the scales at 187. I didn't want to pass out right there on the victory stand.

We took our places on the medal platform with Eeles Landström, third place, Ronnie Morris, second, and Don Bragg in first. I had to grit my teeth as Avery Brundage approached us with a supercilious smirk on his face. It'd slipped my mind that the man who symbolized so many things I despised would give me my gold medal. I avoided eye contact. Then I felt the weight of the coveted prize pull against the back of my neck.

Before it sank in that I actually had it, the U.S. national anthem started playing. I hadn't expected to have tears running down my face, but run they did. What was I supposed to do, pretend I had dust in my eyes?

Then I saw Brundage's self-satisfied face, as if he'd been the one who'd accomplished something. As soon as the music stopped, I caught his eye and let out a magnificent Tarzan call. The crowd screamed and applauded for Tarzan. Brundage's startled look was immediately replaced by one of patrician disdain, but I had him, and we both knew it.

Right after the medal ceremony things were a little crazy. Some reporter asked me what I wanted to do next, and I blurted out, "Call my girlfriend Theresa and tell her we're getting married." Some news service broadcast this in the United States, and of course Theresa heard it. The thing was, I hadn't actually asked her to marry me yet. I guess I took it for granted that we'd be married as soon as I'd won the gold medal.

There were all kinds of celebrations afterward, but the one that meant the most was when Vladimir Bulatov hobbled into my room on crutches. Igor Ter-Ovanesian was right behind him, carrying a bottle of vodka.

Vladimir said, "Now we drink vodka for victory." He poured out a water glass and slammed it. Igor followed suit, then handed me a glassful.

"Hey guys, I don't drink," I said, but Cantello started egging me on. While the two Russians clapped hands and starting singing some crazy patter song, I chug-a-lugged the stuff. Instantly I felt like a dragon ready to spout flame. I didn't know anything could burn that bad. The stuff bounced, of course. So here's the world-renowned gold medal winner hanging out the upstairs window barfing.

Bulatov was delighted and started laughing. "Bragg champion for vaulting, Bulatov champion for drinking. For drinking, Bragg a baby!"

Some of my buddies did pretty well in Rome. Dave Sime had won a silver medal in the hundred meters, though he lost the gold when the U.S. 400-meter relay team fouled in passing the baton. Wilma Rudolph had her three gold medals, and Parry O'Brien won the silver in the shot-put as part of the U.S. sweep of the shot and discus. Dickie Howard, our manic canoe drummer, took a bronze as U.S. men ran away with both hurdling events.

Al Cantello hadn't fared so well. He'd done magnificently, especially considering that he'd been badly weakened by dysentery. I saw his final javelin throw. His style was so energized that he would end up flying forward almost into a handstand. His two-handed landing kicked up dirt and scuffed it over the foul line. No way did he cross it. The Italian judge hadn't been paying attention, but saw the dirt and disqualified Al. That was it. Al's gold medal went to Rudenkov. I don't think he was quite the same after that, as if he were soured on life. The incident made me feel oddly melancholy.

It was hard to believe that I had actually won myself. The night of my victory I stayed with Chico Clemente, my long-time mentor, and good friend of the Fiore family. I couldn't stay asleep, and when I'd awaken, I'd be sure I'd only dreamed I'd won. I asked Chico, "Did I really win, or was it a dream?"

He just laughed. "Yes, Sara Bootie, you won. Now go to sleep and dream of all good things."

First thing next morning I called Theresa and told her to set the date for our wedding. Without missing a beat, she said, "November twelfth." I hung up the phone a happy man. Family was something only other people seemed to have, and now I would be starting my own with the girl I loved.

Almost immediately, I received a call that seemed a segue to the next phase of my life. Sy Weintraub called me from Hollywood telling he wanted me to do a screen test, and there were telegrams from 20th-Century Fox and Warner Brothers saying they wanted to talk to me. I had to call Theresa up again to share the good news and let her know I wanted one last tour while I was on the top of the heap, and that Europe was the place to do it. Track and field was the second most popular European sport after soccer, and its stars had enviable status.

PART EIGHT

MURPHY'S LAW

The thing that bothers me
and makes me mad
Is when I've been conned
and I've been had.

-- from "Hustled" by Don Bragg

Chapter Twenty-Two

Tarzan's Realm

So for the next month or so, I vaulted in all the European meets and played the Tarzan role to the hilt. However, this tour was a little different from others I'd enjoyed: the craziness seemed to be missing. If Cantello had been around, there'd have been craziness to burn, but he'd gone home to be with his wife, Jackie. The coach-leader of our group, Jamaican runner and 1948 gold medalist Herb McKinley, had things other than fun and games on his mind. The poor guy spent most of his time breaking up fights between a couple of Jamaicans -- twin brothers, actually -- who squabbled constantly.

I was also aware of the new dimension my impending marriage had added to my life. For instance, when we stopped at Malmö, I had no desire to visit Marie-Louise. I was only aware of missing the woman who would be my partner for the rest of my life: Theresa. She was beautiful, smart, loyal -- she'd already seen me and my family through more than her share of hard times -- and most important, she wanted a family of her own as much as I did. And I did want a family. Maybe it's just ego, but I loved the idea of little Dons and Theresas running around our house. It's the closest a man comes to immortality in this life.

It was a great feeling to pick out our wedding bands in Switzerland, and when I arrived in Hamburg, Germany, I told them the prize I really wanted was a superb watch for my fiancée. After I won, they presented me with a Ulysses Nardin watch, the finest in the world, they said. Right. That was the watch for Theresa.

The competition started in Greece, where Dave Clark and George Roubanis led the pack. I didn't really mind, since I was enjoying being off my diet.

It was a different story in Germany, however, where the vaulters were the best in the world. They kept me on my toes, so I couldn't relax for a minute. Their sand pits were hell, especially in Berlin, where they felt as if they'd been filled with rocks. Yet even the unforgiving pits were forgotten in the thrill of competing in the Berlin stadium where Jesse Owens had run the goose-stepping Aryans into the dirt.

While we were in Germany, I spent a lot of my free time with Wilma Rudolph as a kind of bodyguard. Some German guy had been sending her mushy letters, calling her his "Black Angel." Wilma showed me a picture of this doofus, with his black leather collar turned up all cool. She said, "Look at this guy. What is this about?" She was afraid he might jump out and grab her during our tour, so I promised to take care of him if he did.

Maintaining my Olympic conditioning while relaxing the rigid diet gave me loads of energy. It felt like my body was grateful for the extra calories, which made sense. I'd been artificially suppressing my weight with stringent dieting for years, and the vacation from salad city felt great.

I noticed an immediate increase in muscle mass and body weight, and I began to bulk up. I only realized how much when I hopped on a scale, expecting to see, maybe, 205. The scale registered 225. Oops! I knew I'd have to bring down the weight before the next indoor season. But even before the end of our victory lap around Europe, poles started kinking under me. Luckily, I'd brought along a spare: the inflexible, shoulder-jarring pole I'd used in '58 that handled my heavier weight.

The real killer, especially at the very end of the tour, was having to mark time at airports. That's where I really munched out, boosting my weight to 242.

After forty days of touring, I flew back to the United States and to Theresa. Almost immediately I started instructions in the Catholic faith with Father O'Donnell, a close friend of Theresa's family. And to my immense relief, in mid-October I was mustered out of the Army.

And finally, on November 12, 1960, Theresa Fiore and I were married at St. James Church in Penns Grove. There was only one problem. I'd purchased our rings almost fifty pounds earlier. Theresa said, "With this ring I thee wed," but there was no way she could do it. It wouldn't go over my knuckle. I still tease her that we're not officially married.

Two days later we left for Hollywood, feeling fortunate that we had a place to stay waiting for us. Decathlete Bob Mathias had attended

Jack LaLanne giving a speech at the Van Nuys party Horace Heidt
sponsored for Don and Theresa in 1960.

Stanford with Jack Heidt, son of the famous band leader Horace Heidt.
When he learned of our California trip, Jack's dad kindly set us up in an
apartment at his Van Nuys ranch.

He also threw us a cocktail bash soon after our arrival. I wasn't
looking forward to spending an evening with total strangers. Then here
comes Rafer Johnson in the door, another gold medalist trying his luck
in Hollywood. By the time I met fitness guru Jack LaLanne, I felt more
comfortable. Several producers also seemed eager to talk to me, and a

flock of pretty girls made a fuss over me, so I figured I was well-launched on the Hollywood circuit.

It turned out to be a treadmill rather than a circuit. We visited Rafer Johnson on the set of *Pirates of Tortuga*; I played volleyball at Sorrento beach with Doug McClure, Jack LaLanne, and Jim Mitchum, Robert's son; I even played with the Hollywood All-Stars to warm up the crowd before the Lakers game. That was a lot of fun. Rafer was one of my teammates, along with Robert Conrad, Ricky and David Nelson, Gardner McKay, and a midget named Billy Barnes who used to run through the guys' legs to steal the ball. I think we played the LA Television and Radio Announcers, who weren't as bad as the name sounded.

Though I was playing basketball, the real name of the game was publicity. Towering Jeff Chandler, petite, vivacious Barbara Eden, Paul Anka, Jeffrey Hunter, Simone Signoret, and Laurence Harvey were some of the celebrities happy to pose with me for pictures, and why not? My Olympic gold medal made me the personality of the moment, and a photo with the new guy in town could be a leg up to their next picture. I was doing the same thing, of course, hoping to parlay all the publicity into a shot at playing Tarzan. There was only one thing I balked at: all the kissy-wissy stuff. Hell, I'd just gotten married, and here comes some old lady planting a wet one right on my mouth. I didn't like guys slobbering all over my bride either, and it wasn't just jealousy. Maybe you didn't pick up hideous diseases from every toilet seat, but indulging in mouth-to-mouth tonsillectomies with strangers was asking for trouble. I hoped really sincere hugs would do the trick.

Evidently they did. Somebody pointed out a female studio exec who was willing to guarantee acting lessons, parts in her studio's productions, even a snazzy apartment. All I had to do was squire her around town, and wine and dine her at Chassin's and the Coconut Grove. Theresa would have loved that! Anyway, I naively believed that acting lessons weren't necessary. Hell, I *was* Tarzan: I didn't have to act.

With the start of the indoor track season in January, I headed back to the East Coast for a round of meets, then flew west to the Land of the Rising Sun for some tournaments in Japan. When I returned to Hollywood, several producers expressed interest in using me in their pictures, which was a nice ego boost. But I was so sure of playing Tarzan that I passed up roles in several action pictures, including Richard Egan's *Five Hundred Spartans* and Tom Tryon's *Marines, Let's Go.*

I'd wondered about keeping up my training in Hollywood, but I didn't have to worry after meeting Jack LaLanne. He took a personal interest in my conditioning, and trained me within an inch of my life.

Once Theresa and I joined Jack, his wife, and daughter at Muscle Beach, for what I had thought was a swimming party. No such luck. Jack started off with a breathtaking high bar routine, clearly enjoying himself. Next, he threw me at the chin-up bar and counted out our reps till my arms felt like jelly. I thought I'd acquitted myself damn well, but Jack hadn't even broken a sweat.

We moved over to the parallel bars, where he did an unbelievable number of handstand pushups. I took my turn, and Jack kept me at it till I took a nose dive into the sand. He ignored my injured beak, but commented on how well I was doing, especially considering that I outweighed him by about fifty pounds. I wobbled away from the workout before Jack could dream up any more challenging games for us to play.

—————————

Earlier in the season my left heel started bothering me, the result, I assumed, of an overly rough trip into the pit. Right before the Los Angeles Invitational Track Meet, Meet Director Al Franken asked me how I was doing.

"Everything's working great, except for this heel bruise that just won't quit."

"Make an appointment with Dr. Danny Levinthal. He's the best."

Dr. Levinthal was terrific, but I couldn't forget I was in Hollywood. I was in the rehab room with the ultrasound and whirlpool, and when I looked over there's Randolph Scott on the next table.

When the doctor examined my foot, he simply said, "Tell me exactly *how* it hurts."

"Well, it kind of stings, almost a burning feeling."

He stood up and pinched my ear lobe. I let out a yelp.

"Uh huh," he said. "I want you to have your uric acid checked at the lab. I think you have gout."

"*Gout*?" I'd always associated gout with leprosy or bubonic plague: the really nasty stuff. I stared at my foot anxiously, half expecting it to fall off, or swell grotesquely and turn some revolting color.

When Dr. Levinthal peeled me off the ceiling, he asked, "What do you eat?"

"One meal a day: steak, salad, and tea."

He started chuckling. "Three foods, two of which are the worst things for gout. No steak, no tea, but plenty of chicken, fish, and vegetables. Understand?"

That didn't sound too bad. At least it wouldn't interfere with my playing Tarzan, which is what I'd been afraid of.

But Tarzan was out of reach for the moment. Sy Weintraub was still tied up in court with his former partner, Harvey Hyutin, each trying to acquire exclusive film rights to *Tarzan*, which belonged to the estate of Edgar Rice Burroughs. I kept smiling for the camera and making the rounds of parties, while my frustration mounted.

When my agent Reese Halsey suggested I audition for the role of a college football player having an affair with an aristocratic older woman, I jumped at it. But I'd heard about the movie, *The Chapman Report*: they were having trouble sliding the racy script past the censors. Bob Mathias had been originally offered the role, but thought it was too risqué for his All-American image. So he recommended me.

Reese sent me to meet the director, George Cukor, who'd led Katherine Hepburn through so many of her great roles. Dick Zanuck, the film's producer, pointed me to a cottage on the Warners lot, where I met the great man.

The director had me read a few lines, then do a passionate love scene with a bosomy actress who was almost inside her skimpy costume. When we were done I collapsed onto the sofa. Cukor dismissed the actress, sat down beside me, and asked me to tell him about myself.

"The boy can't act," he eventually said to an aide who was taking notes, "but he's an athlete and used to discipline. He'll learn." Then he smiled at me and put his hand on my thigh, rubbing gently. "You'll meet with me once a week so we can go over your part."

What in hell was this? And just what part of me did he intend to go over? Actually, I had a pretty good idea. The man was practically salivating, and his eyes had gotten way too glittery for my taste. He scooted closer and locked his eyes onto mine.

"You have a talent for story-telling, and that's the basis of all acting."

I jumped up and told him I had another appointment.

"That's fine," he said, "but I'll see you here next week."

My agent phoned me a little later. "You're in, Don. Cukor likes you."

"He likes me, huh? Just what does that mean?"

There was this little silence, then he said. "Look, you have an advantage here. Grab it. If you're making a big deal out of this, you shouldn't be in Hollywood. It's a rat race out here, and the rats win. Period."

Horace Heidt took Theresa and me aside for some fatherly advice. "Look, you kids don't belong in Hollywood. Why don't you just get yourselves back to New Jersey?"

I knew he was probably right, but I wasn't ready to give up on Tarzan. By this time, however, Theresa was pregnant with our first child.

She loved people and the excitement of the Hollywood whirl, but she missed her family terribly. In May she flew back to Penns Grove to prepare for the baby's birth. I started missing her before her plane was off the runway.

I gave up the apartment and stayed instead with some other tenants, the Lo Biancos, who'd become friends. One evening their son asked if I'd take him to the airport in his sports car, then drive the car back home for him. That was fine, but once we were on our way, he suggested we stop at a party. "You can probably make some valuable contacts."

The host of the party was a big guy named Hal, who shouted a greeting as we came in. He lounged at a table, one leg in a cast, while pretty girls scurried around bringing him drinks. They must have been busy, because he was already smashed when we arrived. He was arm-wrestling all the guests, and got pretty cocky after each win. He finally asked me if I'd like to try him.

"Why not?" I said. "I'm the best."

He didn't like it when I won the first time. After my third win he didn't like me. He started drinking even more heavily, and settled into an ugly mood, rude and obnoxious.

I thought we'd overstayed our welcome and went looking for my friend. I found him out by the pool draped around a redhead. He told me I could take the car on home because his brand new girlfriend would drive him to the airport. I headed for the door, but a gorgeous blonde who'd been hovering over Hal asked me if I'd drop her off.

"It's not far, and I can show you the way."

It was pretty late when I pulled into her driveway. She asked me if I'd please come in and make sure the house wasn't full of burglars. This sounded a little peculiar, but she seemed genuinely scared, so I walked her into the house. She suggested I wait while she checked the doors and windows. I was just sitting down on the couch when here she comes in this fluffy negligee thing and starts putting ice cubes into two glasses. "Bourbon or Scotch?"

"I don't drink," I said, getting up.

"That's right, you're an athlete. Let me pour you a Coke."

She'd just handed me the soda when the front door bangs open and Hal busts in, limping along on his cast. The girl shrieked, "What are you doing here?" but he just headed into the other room.

I put down my glass just as Hal hobbled back, carrying a snub-nose .38. Now the little blonde was screaming, "Stop it, Hal! Nothing was gonna happen!"

This would have been more convincing if she'd been wearing more than a quarter-ounce of silk. Even I knew that.

Hal called me a lot of names, the nicest of which was asshole. He finished with, "Get out of here or I'll kill you!"

This was an exit cue if I'd ever heard one, though I didn't like leaving the girl with this nut. My keys were lying on the coffee table, and I thought I might be able to take the gun away from him when I retrieved them. As if he read my mind, Hal pointed the gun at my chest.

"Don't move or I'll kill you." He scooped up the keys and threw them at me. "Now get out!"

When I was halfway down the front steps, I heard the first bullet ricochet into the concrete landing. I walked slowly to the car, determined not to give this maniac the satisfaction of seeing me run. Another gunshot, and something thudded into the ground between my feet. Dammit, that was enough.

I turned and faced him, ready to charge. But suddenly my heroism came up against reality, as Hal cocked the weapon. For the first time in my life I was confronting something I couldn't handle. Curses and saliva were flying from his mouth as he drew a bead on my head.

"I'm gonna kill you and roll you into Ventura Canyon where they'll never find your body, you bastard," he screamed.

Coming to my senses, I backed up to the car, groping for the door handle. I eased the door open, slid behind the wheel, and started the engine, expecting a bullet to smash into my face any second. I backed half-way down the driveway, gunned the motor, and slammed out onto the road.

The horn of an oncoming car made me swerve just in time. The driver pulled up just ahead of me, rolled down his window, and began to give me hell. I had no chance to tell him that stopping in front of this particular driveway was a really bad idea.

Then here comes Hal stumping across the lawn brandishing his gun, screaming. "I'll kill you too, you son of a bitch, if you don't get out of here!"

In a flash the other driver disappeared: only two hands remained visible, clutching the steering wheel. The car zigzagged away, weaving all over the road. Still, it wasn't bad for a guy driving blind from under his own front seat.

Then it was my turn to run the gauntlet, but the sports car didn't give me room to slump down anywhere. I passed the driveway okay, but I was horribly aware that my right temple had been a nice target for the madman's gun.

A few blocks away I stopped shaking and began to get mad. Going back for another round with Hal would have been insane, but I drove back to the party and told the guys what had happened.

"That's just Hal," they said. "He's been so depressed since he broke his leg. He plays semi-pro ball, you know. You probably ticked him off when you drove his ex-girlfriend home. He was pretty drunk, and probably high on something else as well. He usually is. He's such a character!"

My courage returned to me in a rush. "Tell Hal to keep his gun handy, because if I ever see him again, I'm gonna shove it up his ass."

Meditating on the mental processes of Californians, I drove home. I climbed into bed, very grateful to be alive.

Next morning I received a call from the District Attorney's office. The girl's neighbors had called the police as soon as they heard gunfire, and Hal had barricaded himself in the house. After the police talked him into throwing out the gun, he immediately pleaded self-defense. "I was up against Don Bragg, the Olympic champion. Have you seen the arms on that guy? I had to use a gun to defend myself."

The police wanted me to press charges, but I just wanted to forget the whole nightmare.

Wouldn't you know some reporter saw the police report? The next day newspaper headlines throughout the country read: *Olympic Champion Sprints from Girl's House as Lover Pursues with Gun.*

I called Theresa immediately and told her what had really happened. Before I could do anything else, Sy Weintraub called, all hopped up. "Don, my friend -- how are you? Fantastic publicity stunt! Just what we needed to get this project off the ground."

I caught the next flight to Philadelphia.

Chapter Twenty-Three

Now What?

The ridicule I received in my home town after the scurrilous publicity was hard to take, and I even had a few fights with some assholes. I tried to keep a low profile as I wondered how to support my family until Sy got Tarzan out of court.

The obvious answer was to continue hitting the meet circuit, but it was harder than ever to train. With a baby on the way, my focus had shifted from the vaulting pit to the nursery. Also, the chicken and fish diet made my gout happy, but I didn't seem to have quite the energy I'd had on steak and salad. But perhaps more to the point, I knew that my pole-vaulting days were numbered.

More and more guys were using the fiberglass pole: it was clear that fiberglass would soon be standard in competition. I'd already tried them, but they'd shattered even when I'd weighed less. Moreover, all the younger vaulters were already using gymnastic techniques that would largely supersede my strength-based approach. It wouldn't have bothered me so much if I were being pushed out of competition by superior athletes. That was the way of the warrior, and it happened to everybody eventually. It just seemed ignoble to be bested by improved equipment that merely passed me by.

But what the hell: life goes on! I earned a little money at arm-wrestling, but that was hardly a regular gig. In between meets I went to plenty of job interviews, but I was told the same thing. "You're overqualified, Don. This job wouldn't hold your interest."

One large corporation really played dirty. Five times they called me back, but never made me an offer. I realized that I was being called back so their people could meet an Olympic champion. They never had any intention of hiring me.

With the nice summer weather, I'd go swimming in between meets at the old gravel pit, the one place I could really relax. Penns Grove kids still played in the woods, and one day as I was drying off from a swim, a couple of them came up to me. "Can you help us with our rope swing, Don?" I climbed the tree barefoot and secured the rope.

Then I took a swing to test the knots. I touched down in thick undergrowth, felt a sharp pain in one foot, and realized that blood was spurting all over the place. I'd landed on a broken bottle, but luckily I was able to stop the bleeding. I got myself home, and Theresa drove me to the hospital. A couple of hours and sixteen stitches later, they released me on a pair of crutches. When I walked in our front door, Mamma Yolanda had some news for me. "Sy Weintraub's on the phone for you!"

This was great: I hadn't heard from Sy in awhile.

"Don, fantastic news! I have the rights to Tarzan all sewed up. We've gotta get cracking on *Tarzan Goes to India* and then *Tarzan's Three Challenges*. If we have one in the can before the end of the year, I get a nice tax break."

"The thing is, I gashed up my foot, and I'll be on crutches for awhile. Say four weeks. Six tops."

"You're kidding."

"No, I'm not."

There was dead silence on the end, and then Sy began mumbling something about Jock being free.

"What's that, Sy?"

"Just thinking out loud," he said. "Look, Don, we'll see you when we're back from India, okay? Good luck with the foot."

The next year, *Tarzan Goes to India* was released, and I had to watch Jock Mahoney in a fright wig playing the role I'd spent most of my life pursuing. I could hardly face the harsh reality. The dream was over, and my chance to parlay my Olympic victory into a livelihood that would support me and my family seemed lost forever.

Okay, fine. But I had to make a living, especially with a baby coming, and pole vaulting was what I did well. I contacted a few meet directors on the outdoor circuit, and they gave me a little extra expense money. Sometimes I jumped well, sometimes I didn't, and I didn't care all that much any more. I was mainly concerned with what would happen at the end of the season.

There was one development in track and field competition that made participating difficult. By 1961, athletic meets had become racially charged, reflecting the civil rights battle ripping through American society. Led by John Thomas and Ralph Boston, black athletes boycotted the Texas Relays in 1961 to protest segregated dorms that were definitely separate but not equal, as well as other racial inequalities in the state.

Since I'd already spent the expense money, I had no choice but to compete. I'd also invited Ed Wilson, a buddy of mine from the Tarzanville days, to join Theresa and me at the Relays. He was going to college in Louisiana, and he drove up with a friend from school who happened to be black.

I told them, just look for Theresa: that's where your seats will be. Now Theresa was in the VIP section right up front, with all these important bubbas in big hats. When my guests joined her, the press swarmed toward them, and the popping of flashbulbs around their box looked like sheet lightning. The mood of the crowd was turning ugly: Theresa told me later that she expected a riot to break out right then. When I came out to jump, it seemed to defuse the situation a little, as did the applause when I hit 15'3¾".

As soon as I finished jumping, Theresa suggested we all leave. That seemed like a good idea. Our black guest had walked into this tinderbox at our invitation, and I felt responsible for getting him -- and all of us -- out of there undamaged. We put him between us and headed for the exit. The crowd started booing: really offensive, asinine behavior. There wasn't much I could do unless I descended to their level.

So I did.

I turned around and stuck out my tongue at them. During the momentary ripple of laughter, the four of us got the hell out of there.

————

The 1961 National Championships were held at Randall's Island, New York, with the top two guys going to Russia to compete. I would have loved to take Theresa there, and have one last visit with Bulatov, Ter-Ovanesian, and the others, but I simply didn't have any good jumps left in me. I hurt all over, and my back was killing me. Right after that meet I retired: no fanfare, no dirges played on the pipes. After nearly thirteen years, my pole vaulting career had ended.

About this time, an old friend offered me a hand. Judge Fusco, whose son I'd trained in vaulting during my Army days, brought me to Trenton and found me a job. I started work as recreation director for the Green Acres Program, a bonded, funded state agency. The idea was to expand existing state forests and develop recreational facilities on some of the land. Since our son Mark had been born in January of 1962, I was grateful for the job. But I also enjoyed it, mainly because much of the work was outdoors, where I was most at home. But another big reason was Sam DeGasperis. He was a great guy, and kind of took me under his wing. We tramped all over New Jersey together, looking at land, evaluating its potential. Sam became a good friend to Theresa and me through good times and bad.

There was one parcel I absolutely loved: a beautiful forested tract with over a thousand feet of frontage on the Wading River. I walked every inch of that property, and decided it was even better than the woods around Penns Grove. As I drove off, I thought, "Somebody should put a boys' camp there."

I was with the Green Acres Project for two years. About then I also became involved in Rafer Johnson's pet project, the Special Olympics. The brainchild of Eunice Kennedy Shriver, the Special Olympics seemed like a helluva good way to help disabled kids reach their fullest possible potential. The kids were terrific, and I was happy to donate my time. Theresa was pregnant again, but she took a secretarial job anyway to help make ends meet. Her willingness to pitch in lightened my load considerably. When our daughter Renée was born toward the end of winter, the Bragg family fortunes were on the upswing.

It was good to hear from old friends, too. I'd kept in especially close touch with Charlie Jenkins and Josh Culbreath. Every so often, I'd hear from Cassius Clay as well.

In 1963 Cassius fought Doug Jones in Madison Square Garden, and I went back afterwards to congratulate him. But at the dressing room door, a guy blocked my way.

"I'm here to see Cassius."

"Nobody called Cassius here. There's just Muhammad inside."

This was crazy. "I don't know any Muhammad, I want to talk to my friend Cassius Clay."

The guy peered at me. "That you, Bragg?"

I peered back. It was Cassius's brother. "Yeah, Rudy, it's me."

"Please. I'm Rakhman now."

"Look," I said. "I've always known him as Cassius. I can't go calling him Muhammad now."

Rudy stared hard at me, then smiled and opened the door. "Just call him Champ. He likes that, too."

Frank Nappi, former middleweight champ Ike Williams, and I made plans to meet Ali in Harlem at Small's Place, which Wilt Chamberlain had recently purchased. But when he joined us, Ali clearly wasn't well. His bout with Jones was the first time he'd gone ten rounds, and he was hurting. I remember Lloyd Price was singing "Stagger Lee," when Ali excused himself. He had to go to the rest room and heave. His body was already struggling with the punishment it was getting. So I wasn't the only one who was paying a price for athletic excellence.

Eunice Kennedy Shriver and Don at the first New Jersey Special Olympics in 1963.

Whenever my work for Green Acres permitted, I also attended sports banquets and cocktail parties thrown by *Sports Illustrated* and other major corporations, speaking or socializing for a small fee. But I was after more than the money. I was keeping the name of Don Bragg out there, and making contacts for the future.

It paid off. A few people must have been paying attention when I'd been introduced at some function or other, for I began to receive attractive offers. Atlantic City was going to host the Democratic

National Convention, and one of the party leaders asked me to organize and administer a program for the wives and kids. It was the opening I'd dreamed about: getting a foot on the ladder to political success.

And 1964 was an Olympic year. ABC made some overtures for me to be a color commentator on their Olympic broadcast. Cook's proposed that Theresa and I lead an Olympic tour to Japan. The gods were smiling on me at last.

But one phone call made all those bright possibilities pale by comparison. It was from a movie producer who wanted to test me for the role of Tarzan. His name was Sandy Howard, and he'd just tested Johnny Weissmuller's son. I was next on the list: was I interested?

"Wait a sec. Doesn't Weintraub have the rights to *Tarzan*?"

"Don baby! Trust me. Six books are out of copyright now, so that's no problem. Come up to New York, so we can test you."

For an entire afternoon, I ran around Central Park, climbing trees, doing the 'yell. Even I was impressed by the way I slid into the part. So was Sandy. He hired me on the spot. I would start filming *The Jewels of Opar* immediately in Jamaica, then cross the U.S. in a promotional tour for *Opar* and the next film in Sandy's projected series, *Tarzan at the Earth's Core*.

Without thinking twice, I cancelled on the Democrats, and said good-bye to both ABC and Cook's. My Democratic contact was distraught, but this was the chance of my lifetime. Everybody at the Green Acres Project chipped in and gave me a wonderful send-off. I partied with old friends and new, all of whom remarked that they knew I was destined to play Tarzan. They just hadn't known when.

When I kissed Theresa good-bye and was actually boarding the plane, it hit me that at last I had everything I'd ever wanted, plus a working vacation on the laid-back island of Jamaica.

Ha!

Up at 4:30 A.M., grab a bite, and start shooting by sun-up. We kept at it as long as there was light, sometimes up to twelve hours a day. I'd never worked so hard in my life. I may have been the star, but the crew wasn't about to coddle me. When I cut my foot in one scene, they slapped on a bandage and continued to shoot from the knees up.

One star perk I did have was a stunt double, a guy Sandy'd found driving in the chariot races at Coney Island. He could handle himself pretty well, though he was about a head shorter than me, with nothing like my build. But he had my nose. I guess Sandy figured anything with a beak would do for the long shots. I was lucky they couldn't find a tall parrot.

This stunt man was also mighty particular about when he'd condescend to fill in for me. We shot some of the scenes at a quarry, and in one of them Tarzan had to run down a steep incline. My stunt double balked at this.

"No problem," I said. "I'll do it."

"The thing is, we need you to stop just short of that 200-foot drop." I thought that was a good idea too.

They assigned a squad of Jamaicans to stop me before I reached the edge, but I had my doubts about this primitive braking system. The charming Jamaicans were willing, yet I probably outweighed the whole bunch by twenty pounds.

Right on cue I came racing down the hill, and when I got to the bottom the Jamaicans jumped me. The crowd of us kept right on going. At the very edge of the precipice I grabbed for some saplings, which luckily took the weight. I kind of hung there for a second with three or four Jamaicans still hanging on, determined to keep Tarzan from falling. We finally scrambled to safety, but all the dumb-ass stunt man could do was dance around and say, "Better you than me!"

He backed out of a dive, too, from a tree limb thirty feet up into eight feet of water. I quickly volunteered; if I turned my body immediately, I'd be okay. Hell, I'd been rehearsing for the scene my entire life, and it was high time I showed off. "Get it on the first take," I told the director. "I'll only do this once."

The stunt went perfectly, and the crew seemed awestruck. The producer, however, was thoroughly pissed when he heard about it.

"Look, you're the star. You can't take that kind of chance. If something happens to you, we're screwed."

My back had started aching, so I took it a little easy until it was time to wrestle the alligator. The considerate producers didn't want me eaten, so they hired a local hunter to shoot one. He hauled the damned thing over to us in a truck and dumped it in the river. I'd seen Johnny Weissmuller do this a hundred times, so I sprang into the water on top of the reptile and grabbed him by his scaly shoulders. In a heartbeat I lunged back on shore.

"Damn thing's alive! He just tried to shake me off his back!"

"Come on, Don, that's just an involuntary muscle twitch."

"Twitch, my ass! Shoot that son of a bitch again, or I stay out of the water."

They pumped the gator with four more rounds, whereupon he gurgled and promptly sank. The director frowned, then brightened. "Don baby, before the current carries the carcass away, why don't you just dive down and bring him up? It'll make a great shot."

"Why don't you? Why doesn't the stunt man?"

The stunt guy wasn't having any of it either, so they hastily began to write a different scene. It was that kind of picture.

Since we needed extras for some of the river sequences, Sandy made a deal with a Rastafarian head man named Sam Goode. Sandy wanted some of Sam's people because they had the requisite scary look. When they met us on the beach outside Port Arthur, Sam's Rastas proved to be sufficiently frightening: machete-toting toughs from the slums of Kingston. They wore their hair in dreadlocks, and their eyes were glazed on ganja. Their expressions were sullen. They'd just tried to "capture" a goat, but had been interrupted by the arrival of the animal's owner with a shotgun. They hadn't gotten over it.

The deal with the scene was this: Tarzan and the great white hunter, played by Hank Madden, would pole their rafts by a group of African natives who'd start raising some hell. Our cameraman, Zoli Vidor, set himself up on a raft opposite the Rastas, who really looked their parts, all decked out in African costumes and fake bone necklaces. But they stood there like stumps.

"Hey, I'll get 'em agitated," I said. Waving my arms, I yelled, "Sam Goode Rasta man, no capture Tarzan." All the Rastas began to glare at me, and they started to chant, swaying rhythmically.

"That's great," said Sandy. "Roll 'em!"

So here I come, poling up on my raft, and I said my line to Hank, "Wasuri warriors attack only if land." Then I glanced up at Sam. He was almost in the water, quivering with rage. "I capture you, Tarzan, and cut you up in little pieces, and eat you!"

The rest of the Rastas were shouting, "Harvey Oswald hero! Capture Tarzan!" The scene was getting out of hand, but behind me I heard Sandy's gleeful cries of "Keep rolling." The next thing I hear is my great white hunter choking. I look over at the Rastas, and damned if they weren't all masturbating as they yelled, "Oswald hero! White man devil!"

Then our director started directing with a vengeance. "No! Pan to the right! Keep the jerk-offs out of the frame."

I maintained my stoic calm until I was out of camera range, then doubled up laughing and fell off the raft. I damned near drowned. My hilarity didn't help Hank, who still had to keep a straight face while the second raft floated past the camera.

Then it was over and pandemonium broke out all over the set. Zoli lifted his face from the viewfinder and asked, "Is that a take?"

"How in hell would we ever reproduce that scene?" demanded

Sandy. "It's a double-take in one."

The Rastas went back to the beach for their clothes, machetes, and drums, and continued shouting threats. I had my knife, so I wasn't too worried: I was Tarzan, wasn't I? Eventually they all straggled off somewhere, and the cast and crew relaxed.

Then the driver ran up looking embarrassed. "Small problem. The Rastas just 'captured' the truck."

Sandy jumped to his feet. "Screw that!" He ran up to the road and told Sam to get his guys the hell off our truck.

Sam buried his machete into the floorboard, his eyes flashing fire. "Rastas capture truck!"

That convinced Sandy that confrontation wasn't the way to go. "Okay, fine. The driver'll take you home, but that's all."Evidently satisfied, the Rastas started toking up, and we watched them and the truck drive off in a mighty cloud of ganja.

We doubted we'd see the truck any time soon, so we built a big fire on the beach and settled down to wait. It was fantastic, lying there on the sand in the soft Jamaican night, howling with laughter as we rehashed the day's exploits.

———————

While the crew worked out the logistics for the remainder of the location shots, the rest of us had a few days off, which I fervently hoped would ease the pain in my back. I looked up our coach from the post-Olympic tour, Jamaican running great Herb McKinley. He showed up two days late for our appointment, saying, "Take it easy, Mon. That's how you get by in Jamaica."

During our lunch at the Casa Monte Hotel, I told Herb about my increasingly severe back pain. I'd already endured horse needles from doctors and pummeling by therapists in America, but nothing had helped, not even Darvon and Percodin. Herb hurried me off to a massage therapist, who beat me up with some horrible voodoo routine called Rolfing. When I got off the table, every muscle in my body was throbbing. But next morning my back was better, and I was able to face another day's shooting. Herb told me the guy was world famous, and I could see why.

The next day we began rehearsing a carefully orchestrated fight scene. We were ready to start shooting when a big Cadillac rolled up. Two men got out, and I waved to them from the top of the cliff. We'd met on the flight from New York, and I thought they were stopping by for an autograph.

But their business was evidently with Sandy Howard, because they slapped official-looking documents into his hands. The men were attorneys representing Sy Weintraub and the Edgar Rice Borroughs estate. I felt a surge of anger that they hadn't revealed their identity on the plane. The papers forbade our use of the Tarzan name, and ordered us to cease production in Jamaica immediately. They didn't leave us one legal leg to stand on. If we'd been shooting in Puerto Rico, we'd have been under American law. We could have continued shooting while the lawyers hashed the whole matter out in court. But this was Jamaica, and under British law you were evidently guilty until proven innocent.

We returned to the hotel in stunned silence, trying to comprehend what in hell had gone wrong. Sandy figured he'd royally pissed off the head of a local production company by not using his people on *Opar*. He must've been the guy who'd ratted us out. Then Sandy started raving about how he should have shot in Puerto Rico: then we could've at least released the picture in countries that hadn't signed the Berne Convention.

Hell, none of that mattered now, not to me. In a few short weeks I'd destroyed a promising future by running after a pipe-dream. What was worse, I couldn't quite let it go. Maybe if I stayed in Jamaica a little longer, Sandy could work something out. That was crazy, but clinging to a counterfeit hope was better than going home a failure: the big blowhard that couldn't. Facing a life without any soaring challenge was almost more than I could bear. It wasn't grueling labor I dreaded, but rather the tedium of a drab and predictable life. This had been the plight of humankind since the beginning of time, but my ego didn't want to accept it as my lot too.

To save money I moved into a room at the vacant, echoing stadium dormitories in Kingston. I was completely isolated, except for the Rasta camp a few hundred yards away. There was still no news from Sandy. I considered looking for a job in Jamaica and sending for Theresa and the kids, but unemployment on the island was sky high. And I certainly had no money to invest. I began to lace my Cokes with 150 proof white rum to keep going during the day. At night I lay in bed listening to the ganja-driven chanting of the Rastas while sleep eluded me.

Of course, I finally went home. The compassion and understanding of Theresa and our families made it bearable. But we had two kids, and I had no immediate way to support them, thanks to the bridges I'd burned. I did find another job fairly quickly, selling pharmaceuticals. Yet every other client I approached seemed to be somebody I'd known from VU. I felt they had to be thinking, "What a comedown." That was hard to take, but I figured things would change before long.

They did. I awoke one lovely morning and realized I couldn't move.

Chapter Twenty-Four

Creative Survival

The doctors did a myelogram, shooting my spine full of dye: it told them nothing. When they suggested exploratory surgery, I told them to get right on it, much to their surprise. Searing pain had a way of making me real cooperative. They came back with a recommendation for full-blown surgery ASAP, and I wasn't surprised. My back had been hurting for years.

Just before the operation, who should I hear from but Sy Weintraub. "Don, my friend! How are you? Sorry about the business in Jamaica, but no hard feelings, right? So when can you leave for Brazil?"

He was shooting *Tarzan and the Imposter* and wanted me to play the damned Imposter. "It'd jump-start your movie career and get you set up for work down the road," he said.

But I'd stopped listening. The Imposter? That was insulting. Sy really didn't understand about Tarzan and me, so I said quietly, "I'm having spinal surgery day after tomorrow."

He was dumbfounded. "First a cut foot and now your spine. Talk about bad luck. It'd make a great script if it wasn't so unbelievable."

"Tell me about it." I hung up the phone and took a couple more Percodin. How many times were the gods going to beat me over the head with Tarzan? It'd been a great ride, but enough was enough.

The surgery was great fun. The extent of the damage hadn't shown up in any tests. So they ended up having to perform a laminectomy, then wire together two degenerating disks in the lumbar-sacral area. The operation not only set us back financially but left me a psychological wreck. I felt emasculated, nothing but a burden for Theresa. And I was still in pain.

A few months after the surgery I heard that Sy was now doing a Tarzan TV series, with actor Ron Ely in my part. I almost cried. It got worse when I heard this great thespian proclaim that acting was more important than athletic ability in playing Tarzan. Every time the show aired, I went around the house bellowing, "That skinny ass!" until

Theresa told me to get a grip.

It was only years later that Rafer gave me the lowdown on Sy's picture. The chimp playing Cheetah had taken a bite out of Tarzan -- football player Mike Henry -- so he walked off the picture, saying the playing field was safer than a movie set. The picture was almost finished, so Rafer suggested they use me for long shots, since my build was close to Mike's. And here was the kicker: Sy had also planned to use me in the *Tarzan* TV series before surgery put me out of commission. My loss was Ely's gain. Damn.

As I tried to get back on my feet, one of my main goals was to earn a living, but as my own boss. Being at the mercy of someone else's ego trips or stupidity was not my thing. I started a little collection agency, which kept us afloat financially as I tried to plan what to do next.

Al Cantello came by one day, and helped me toss that ball around. He thought for a minute and said, "What the two of us should really do is open a boys' camp."

Wouldn't that be something! I told my dad about Al's idea, and he thought it was wonderful. He asked a million questions about how I'd handle it, and the two of us had a great time making crazy plans for my fantasy camp. But I back-burnered the whole thing because I soon had something more pressing to think about.

On Christmas morning in 1965, when our third child, Tracey, wasn't even a year old, I went to Trenton's St. Francis Hospital with a horrendous pain in my lower chest. Omitting the standard blood tests, they shelved me for observation for twenty-four hours, until well after my appendix had ruptured. A simple blood test would have detected appendicitis instantly and spared me a bout of peritonitis complete with drainage tube hanging out my side.

That pissed me off, but there was an interesting sidelight. The doctor made a special point of telling me that I'd been an unusual case. "Ever have bad back pain? No wonder. The appendix was wrapped around your colon. Hanging on for dear life. I've never seen anything like it."

After the surgery, the pain in my back decreased dramatically. I wondered if I'd really needed all the baling wire they'd installed in my back.

It was fantastic to be able to move around without agonizing back pain, though. I could work and drive again, all the stuff I'd once taken for granted. Then my Dad sprung a get-well surprise on me that he'd been working on for months. It was a set of plans and specifications for all the buildings I'd need if I ever got around to that boys' camp.

Those plans were one of the last things Dad ever gave me. In the summer of 1966, Dad succumbed to coronary thrombosis. His death left a huge hole in my life.

Then we had a little miracle. Our second son Jeffrey was only a couple of months old, but both Theresa and I noticed a subtle change in him. It was almost as if Dad's spirit had gone into our baby son. Jeff's eyes seemed wiser, deeper, like they were saying, "Don't you see me in here?"

So Dad's tough old spirit was still with us. I also felt it powerfully every time I drove back to that property on the Wading River. I was out there looking around one grey foggy day. Suddenly I felt an urgent call to take a stab at one more dream, almost as if Dad were saying, "Go for it!" I broached the idea of a boys' camp to Al Cantello again.

"Wouldn't that be great," he said. "Think what we could accomplish. But New Jersey's out: it's too buggy. We should locate in New England."

Whenever I could, I scouted available property and talked to anybody I could find with expertise in running summer camps. I found some nice spots in Maine, but boy, did I have news for Al. The bugs in New England are just as bad as the ones in New Jersey, as my mosquito-bitten butt could bear witness.

In the end I came back to the Wading River property, and made my decision. With the Warden State Forest on three sides, it was the perfect spot for a Huck Finn summer camp for boys. Now how in hell was I going to get hold of this land? I'd need a bundle to acquire it and build the camp facilities, so I had another powwow with Cantello.

My good news was the last thing he expected to hear. "Look, I have a crack at becoming a coach at Annapolis. You know, the Naval Academy. Maybe if you get this camp off the ground, I can come aboard, but not now. Geez!"

Okay, I hadn't expected that response, but I could deal with it. I'd have to take out a loan myself. After twenty banks turned me down, I asked my friend Jack Kelly for advice. It was simple, he told me. If you want a loan, you have to produce something of value for security. Hell, if I had anything I could use for security, I wouldn't need the damn loan. Did somebody say Catch-22?

Then I started using my head. I was after forty acres at $500 each, totaling $20,000. Add another $30K for constructing the buildings, and we were talking about $50,000. I borrowed some money from Theresa's mom, Yolanda, for an option to buy, and went to the Broad Street Bank in Trenton for the rest. I told them what I needed to clear the title and put in the buildings. Bank President Ray Sateen told me he'd send down a couple of appraisers to see if their critical eyes saw the same potential as I did.

This is where I started to sweat. Suppose I drew a couple of guys fresh out of college who'd get a charge out of coming out to the Pines and kicking Olympic champion Don Bragg's financial ass? So this car pulls up and a couple of guys get out. I busted out laughing. Both of them were old friends from the Green Acres Project, and I knew I was home free.

The guys were as enthusiastic about the place as I was, and reported that the land was almost equal to the amount of the loan in an unimproved state. With addition of camp facilities, the bank's investment would be doubly protected.

They gave me the $50,000 loan, which more than covered the cost of the land, but I still had to build the facilities. Luckily, a master carpenter had already drawn up the plans for the buildings, including estimated costs for materials. There were even a few older buildings already on the property, which would do for arts and crafts and rainy-day recreation areas. We only needed to build ten shell cabins, a large bath house, and a dining hall with kitchen. Dominic Fiore, my fantastic father-in-law, brought down the Penns Grove Italian Club to pitch in on the construction.

We'd need to outfit an entire kitchen, so I located some good-quality used equipment and designed our own refrigeration box. The wells only needed to be forty feet deep, so we hand-drilled our own.

Of course we had to provide excellent recreational facilities as well. I dredged out part of the river for swimming, keeping the area closest to the beach at three feet for the youngest campers. Then I graded the bottom to an eventual depth of eight feet for the older kids. For the frosting on the cake, I constructed a Tarzanville through the cedar swamp to the river, with a network of eight swings connected by walk-ropes, logs, and platforms.

Working weekends, we managed to finish the project in only three months. All we needed now were the kids.

When I'd been scouting around New England for possible sites, I'd talked to my old Army buddy, Frank Nappi. The idea of me as a camp director tickled him. "Sounds like you're finally back home in Tarzanville," he said. "But there's a guy I think you really ought to meet."

So Frank took me to an Outward Bound camp nearby to talk to his friend Sal Comissa, from the Newark School Board.

"I'll send you the kids, Tarzan. But if you want to qualify for Title I under the Elementary and Secondary Education Act you'll have to get a sharp tutorial program in place."

"Fine. I'll hire teachers. Whatever it takes."

From then on, I volunteered to speak at every banquet and awards ceremony in Pennsylvania and New Jersey, drumming up interest in Kamp Olympik.

And people were intrigued. I collected pledges from over a hundred parents to send their kids, which I took with a grain of salt, expecting maybe ten kids at best. I was surprised when fifteen privately recruited youngsters came to the first session. Kamp Olympik was launched.

Then the ten black kids from Newark showed up. Outraged white parents yanked their kids out of the program, and there was no way this could work with only ten campers. I'd have to lay off my counselors and hope that Theresa and I could cope with running the venture all alone. All of us just sat around, utterly depressed, thinking of all the blood, sweat, and tears down the tubes. I was roused from the sulks when the telephone rang.

Sal Comissa was calling, asking how things were going. I blistered his ear answering his question. For a minute, Sal was quiet, then he said, "How many extra beds you got down there?"

"About twenty."

"I'll send you twenty kids tomorrow. That okay?"

It was. The staff was jubilant at this ninth-hour save, but Mama Fiore was ecstatic. She was Kamp Olympik's chef, and, being Italian, couldn't stand the idea of all her delicious minestrone and lasagna going to waste.

I was just plain happy to have my dream salvaged. My course was clear, too. I'd concentrate on working with Title I kids. These youngsters could spend a couple of weeks playing Huckleberry Finn while bringing their reading and math skills up to speed. It was a win-win scenario, since Federal funds were helping to pay their way. Kamp Olympik would give the kids the freedom and opportunity for individual achievement within a structured, disciplined environment.

Of everything we tried to accomplish, though, I was proudest of the way we handled our tutorial program. We put big tables out under the trees with ten kids at each one, plus one teacher and a teen-aged counselor. The teacher supervised all the work at each table and had the kids help each other, and the counselor would give a hand to the ones needing still more support. A couple of the counselors were afraid they couldn't do it, but I just said, "You mean you can't help a third-grader read or do simple multiplication?"

This system of peer and counselor tutoring freed up the teacher to concentrate on the slowest learners. No public school could offer this instructional advantage, but we could.

The kids had to do their work before they could swim or swing in

Tarzanville. That was a powerful incentive. They worked hard and played hard: we all did, studying, swimming, swinging through Tarzanville.

Their favorite game was Hare and Hounds. The counselors and I all had flags, like in flag football, and the kids were supposed to nail us before we made it back to home base on the basketball court. The kids, or hounds, were motivated: any captured flags were good for extra Popsicles or lollipops afterward. Us hares had twenty seconds head start to disappear into the forest. Then the kids came thundering after us, determined to hunt us down.

They never captured Tarzan. Once I was lying in the swamp, all covered with mud, and I could hear the kids' feet pounding around just a few yards away. I looked up and here comes a snake, heading right for me. I didn't want to give myself away, so I lay there, gritting my teeth to keep from yelling. The snake was almost in my face, when it stopped and peered at me. I did what we Braggs always do in such situations: I started spitting. I hit it right between its beady eyes. The varmint kind of jerked its head and took off in another direction, as if to say, "There goes the neighborhood."

Chapter Twenty-Five

The Greatest

By 1967, I knew Kamp Olympik would succeed. But a friend of mine was having some rough times. After the Olympics, when his professional boxing career began to heat up, Muhammad Ali, accompanied by a black friend, went to finish negotiating a contract with some white associates at a restaurant in Louisville. He and his friend were asked to leave, but the white folks continued discussing the contract without Ali, as if nothing had happened. That told Ali just what his Olympic gold medal was worth, so he tossed it into a river.

I remember him in Rome with his medal: he never took it off. It dangled in his soup when he ate dinner, and he wore it in the shower. Late one night I charged into the john with an urgent need, and there was Ali, sitting on the throne, wearing that medal. He just grinned at me and tapped it significantly. God, he was proud of it. That he would throw it into some Southern river showed just how betrayed he felt.

When he was called up to serve in Vietnam, Ali couldn't see killing these little yellow guys that hadn't done him any harm. He refused to be drafted, so boxing officials stripped him of his title and barred him from the ring. When I heard he was staying at a friend's house not far from Villanova, I went up and visited him several times. We'd talk for hours. The brash, jive-talking Olympian had grown. Ali hadn't had much formal education, but I was impressed by the depth of his intellect. The courage with which he backed up his convictions was also pretty phenomenal. We discussed Islam and our philosophies of life, and for once in my life I did most of the listening. It was then that we became close friends. When things got better for him, Theresa and I used to visit Ali and Belinda out in Cherry Hill. We've stayed close to the Champ ever since.

It was always a trip when he dropped by Kamp Olympik. We'd put up a makeshift ring on the basketball court, and he'd grab a kid to spar with. Here's the kid beating up on the air with these roundhouse punches while Ali's dancing around him, doing his ego rap routine, bopping the kid on the bean now and then. And the kid'd yell, "Hey, no fair."

Ali would stop dead. "How you gonna stop me?"

The kid would giggle and start swinging at nothing again, while the other campers laughed themselves sick. When a youngster stepped out of that ring, he looked like he felt ten feet tall: he'd just touched gloves with the Champ! Like the song says, Ali did believe in the children, and nobody knew it better than the kids.

Eventually, Ali would start roaring, "Gimme Tarzan. I wanna beat up Tarzan!"

One time, when I was clearly insane, I asked, "Hey, Champ. Is it okay if I really hit you?"

"In your dreams, sucker."

So we put on the gloves and climbed into the ring. Ali started in on me, tapping me with leisurely punches, all the while proclaiming that he was gonna stomp the King of the Jungle.

Now I'd been studying Ali. I knew that after a series of punches, he'd back up, and lower his hands just a little. In that second he might be vulnerable, especially to a southpaw like me. I waited until he threw a couple of jabs and backed up. Immediately, I hopped forward on my weight-bearing leg and threw a right to his nose. Hot damn! I'd actually landed a punch on Mohammed Ali. Then I noticed the blood around his nose, and I was frozen in horror, the way a skinny eight-year old feels when he's just lobbed a snowball down the neck of his school's hulking fullback.

Ali was all over me, demonstrating the lightning speed of a champion. Up, down, and sideways, the punches rained down on me, but they were feather-light. Though he could have stung like a bee, his opened gloves landed like butterflies, and Theresa did not become a widow.

Ali was at Kamp Olympik when we received a frantic call from Philly. His wife, Belinda, had just gone into labor, and he had to get to the hospital, pronto. Since I'd picked him up at his house, he didn't have wheels, but I couldn't drop everything and drive him. So Ali drove off in our brand new Bonneville station wagon with Theresa, who went along to bring the car back later.

As soon as they hit the open highway, Ali stomped on the gas. Theresa got the Hail Marys going, which, according to her, was the only reason they survived. Being a good Muslim, Ali was praying too, calling on Allah for help. But this only alarmed my wife, for, sweet sheltered Catholic girl that she was, Theresa had no idea what he was doing. It would have comforted her considerably if she had.

Ali and Don sparring at Kamp Olympik in 1969.

Ali didn't seem to notice the speedometer until it hit about 100. Theresa reported that he'd get this horror-stricken look on his face and slam on the brakes, arching his back with the effort. She was sure at least one of his feet would go through the floorboard. Then he'd speed up and start the cycle all over again.

Theresa almost relaxed when they turned off the Schuylkill Expressway, but almost immediately the traffic backed up. Not to worry! With two wheels on the sidewalk, Ali maneuvered the Bonneville past the traffic jam and the red-faced, whistle-blowing policeman who'd been directing traffic. He blitzed through the few remaining blocks, and pulled up in front of the hospital. Without even bothering to kill the engine, Ali shot out of the car, with my determined wife racing along behind him.

They arrived at Maternity, where Ali's one thought was to be with

Belinda. Theresa said it was so cute: this huge guy, the boxing champion of the world, completely absorbed in his wife and the impending birth.

Theresa looked frazzled but happy when she drove the Bonneville back to Kamp Olympik. She announced that Belinda and Ali were the parents of twins, and that Mom and babies were fine. All the kids went wild, screaming and cheering for their buddy Ali, his wife, and their new babies.

I cheered too, until the smell of something burning nearly knocked me over. "Who the hell is pouring tar?" I demanded. Then I realized the fumes were coming from my brand new station wagon. Praying the vehicle wouldn't blow up, I drove it back to the Pontiac dealer.

The service manager just stood there staring in disbelief.

"The brakes are history! What in hell happened?"

I shrugged my shoulders. "Beats me. We only made one trip to the hospital in the damn car."

———————

Ali wasn't the only athlete who visited with the Kamp Olympik kids. Wally Jones of the 76ers, the Eagles' Jim Ringo, and the then current Mr. America, Val Vasloff, also generously gave of their time. In addition, we had a great Board of Directors who'd work with the kids: Al Cantello, Josh Culbreath, Frank Nappi, and Theresa's Dad, Dominic Fiore. It would've been rough to manage without them.

When we first started out I didn't know if I'd survive the counselors, but as we worked together we grew closer, like family. We'd do crazy things like playing night tag on the tree swings of Tarzanville, our laughter punctuated by the howls of people crashing into trees.

———————

During the winter, I was surprised by how much I missed those kids. I missed living right in the Pines, too. By February, I'd be thinking how great it would be to wake up in my own corner of Eden, hearing the wind in the swamp cedars and the birds piping out on the river. That's when it occurred to me that other people might also be drawn to those same things. Why not acquire more land somewhere in the Pines and make a little piece of Paradise available to others? Theresa and I began to squirrel away every spare cent toward the day when we'd find the right piece of land. I also started plotting to lay hands on a better job.

As spring rolled around, I had a brainstorm, and asked Theresa to pack a picnic. We headed for the grassy field beside the State House in Trenton, where some of Governor Hughes' staff liked to play touch football after work. While my wife and kids had their picnic, I jogged around and waited for an incomplete pass. My patience was rewarded when one bounced right in front of me. I lobbed it back, and before long I too was playing. I especially hit it off with the quarterback, Steve

Farber.

One thing led to another, and before long, Steve wangled me a position in Governor Hughes' office as Special Assistant in Charge of Youth Affairs and Recreation. In addition to establishing low-cost sports programs in the public schools, I stumped the circuit, drumming up support for "Vote 19", which lowered the voting age. Though the initiative failed, it passed the next time around, and I believe our spade work helped do the trick.

There was one goal I failed to reach. My friend Ali was still unable to obtain a boxing license, so I tried to help get him one for a fight in New Jersey. But no soap. Ironically, Ali was finally granted one by a man who'd made a name for himself wielding an axe handle in the cause of racism -- before he became the Governor of Georgia. When Ali fought Jerry Quarry in his comeback fight, I was in Atlanta to cheer him on. I hoped Hughes' people were kicking themselves for letting the opportunity to host that historic fight slip away.

So there were many frustrations involved in dealing with the whole political circus, not to mention the fervent ass-kissing demanded by higher-ups. Though having a sociable drink at official functions made it a little easier, I hated the kissing up that came with the territory. So when the Republicans pushed Governor Hughes out of office, I wasn't all broken up.

We missed the income, though, especially since we'd finally found the land we wanted. We'd been investing every cent we had in a magnificent wooded tract in Bass River Township, just outside of New Gretna. To save money, we moved into one of the uninsulated cabins at Kamp Olympik, after I replaced the screen door with a solid one and added a Franklin stove with a blower for the kids' room.

At night, while the kids slept, Theresa and I would plan our dream home that we'd someday build in the Pines. From the way Kamp Olympik had been received, I didn't think it would take too long to achieve this goal. After we survived those first rigorous months in the cabin, I dipped into our savings and took the family on a well-deserved vacation to Florida.

At least it was supposed to be a vacation. I was heading for the beach one morning when I received a call from William Simon, later to be Secretary of the Treasury. He was in charge of American Airlines' Olympic Golf Classic being given at Florida's Doral Country Club, but the guy running it wasn't up to the job. Would Theresa and I consider lending a hand?

We instantly agreed. Theresa, in her element, quickly organized a fashion show at the Fontainebleau for the wives of the tournament players. I arranged exhibitions by both a champion female archer, and world-class weight lifter Joe Dubbe, as well as an Olympic diver and a swimming exhibition for poolside entertainment.

As organizers of the tournament, Theresa and I were greeting Johnny Mathis, Bobby Goldsboro, and a laid-back newcomer, Alan Thicke, when somebody said, "Hey, Sara Bootie!" I turned and got my arm pumped by an old acquaintance from Penns Grove, Wally Hoiser, who'd showed up to play golf. Wally was the original wild and crazy guy, but we'd shared some good times back home.

The highest point of the weekend was seeing Johnny Weissmuller again. The years had not been kind to Johnny, but luckily, a gentleman named Nick Tweel had taken him under his wing. Nick was an elegant gentleman and an impeccable dresser. He seemed genuinely fond of Johnny, so I was very glad for my old friend.

The bunch of us, Wally, Johnny, Nick, Theresa, and I found a poolside table for cocktails at the clubhouse, but before my martini arrived Nick asked me to accompany him to the lobby telephone. Mystified, I followed him. In the lobby, he said, "Would you mind running interference for me while I make a call? Just keep people away from the phone for a few minutes."

Keeping an eye out for trespassers, I overheard fascinating tidbits of the conversation. Nick listened for a moment, then demanded, "Then somebody go get Fitz *off* the damn golf course."

After he hung up, we chatted amiably until the phone rang again, and I went back into my watchdog act, shooing people away as diplomatically as possible. The only people that seemed to care were a couple of guys in broad-shouldered suits standing across the lobby and giving me dirty looks. As Nick continued to talk, I realized he was conversing with Frank Fitzsimmons, the head of the Teamsters. A little shiver went down my spine. Back then, when you heard the word Teamsters, you thought of Al Capone before you thought of fair labor practices.

When he was done with Fitz, Nick slapped me on the shoulder and said, "Good job, Don. Now let's have that drink."

When we rejoined our party, my martini was waiting for me. It seemed to effervesce slightly, but I fished out the olive and downed the drink. Almost immediately I felt a little dizzy, but I attributed the sensation to drinking on an empty stomach.

I've never been more mistaken.

When our party piled into two cars and took off for the cocktail party and dinner at the Fontainebleau, I felt weird, like my own motor was racing, and I was breathing fast. I floored the gas pedal and tore off, passing everything on the road, including the Jaguar XKE Wally was riding in. I slammed out of the car in front of the hotel, and shouted for them to park it, startling the hell out of the young attendant.

"But sir, you can't -- "

I threw the keys at the poor kid. "Shut the hell up and park it."

Things got worse when Theresa and I went inside for the cocktail party. I saw old friend Jesse Owens, and burst into tears. "Why can't the whites and the blacks respect each other?" I asked, sobbing. Jesse put his arm around me and motioned Theresa over.

"Take care of him, Theresa," he said, shielding me from curious eyes as my wife led me out of the room.

Upstairs, I couldn't stop crying. Theresa kept saying, "What's wrong, honey?" but I didn't know. She made me drink some water. "We've worked so hard on this banquet and show, Don. We can't just not show up."

She was right, but I didn't know how I'd get through the evening. I took an ice-cold shower and stayed there for half an hour, till I was shivering violently. Then I lay under all our blankets, hoping I'd stop shaking. Theresa helped me get dressed, and we made our way to the banquet.

I sat at the head table, dazed and silent. Johnny noticed my demeanor and was concerned. "What's wrong with him? He's way too quiet."

Theresa forced a laugh and claimed I was fine. Everybody bought it, thank God, and the banquet, like the entire weekend, was a smashing success.

The next morning I was my old self, and I couldn't figure out what in hell had happened. I mean, I'd only had one drink. Bill Simon thanked us for creating a stellar weekend, but when we were saying goodbye something clicked. I remembered hearing that the Teamsters Union had originally offered to sponsor the tournament. Wanting to maintain the squeaky-clean image of the Olympics, the Tournament Committee rejected the Teamsters' bid, opting for American Airlines instead. I thought of the two guys glaring at me across the lobby as I stood guard over a call to Teamster head Frank Fitzsimmons. And then there was the drink that wasn't quite right.

"God almighty, Theresa! The Teamsters are after me!"

Did I get paranoid? You bet your butt. I checked out ice buckets and jars of olives for explosive devices, and leaped behind bushes and potted plants, expecting to nab an assassin. And people had thought I'd been acting peculiar the night before!

All this came to an end when a guy who'd driven to the dinner with good ol' Wally said, "Hey, Don. You're lookin' better than you did last night. Hell, even before you went by the Jag like a bat out of hell, Wally was saying it was a pity you wouldn't make the party."

Oh did he, now?

My brother George, now a professional hippy and disciple of Timothy Leary, informed me that somebody'd probably slipped a little acid into my martini. I swore that if I could lay hands on that Jersey swamp rat, I'd stick my big old boot right up his sorry ass. Theresa and I fled back to our chilly cabin, grateful we'd survived our venture into the balmy south.

About this time, my former quarterbacking pal Steve Farber surprised me with a phone call from Harvard. A friend of his was helping to get a new state college off the ground in Pomona, New Jersey, and he needed a line on some good local people for various positions. "Fine," I told him. "Glad to help."

So it wasn't long before Steve's friend and I were going over his wish-list. When he came to the position of Athletic Director, I said, "Wait a minute. I'd like a crack at that one."

"Are you sure?" he asked. "It's just a small school, and the salary won't be what you're worth."

"Not a problem. I really like the creativity of developing sports programs from the ground up. That's what I was doing on all those tours in Asia and Africa."

My only proviso was that I could work a four-day week in the summer, to leave me time for Kamp Olympik. The folks at Stockton State College eagerly agreed to this, so in 1971 I became their first Director of Athletics.

PART NINE

BLOWOUT

Should we float with the stream of thought,
enveloped and absorbed in dreams it's brought,
continuously exciting one's own imagination,
reaping the joys from their creation?

-- from "Fantasies" by Don Bragg

Chapter Twenty-Six

Temperature Rising

My highest priority at Stockton was clear: get the most bang for each buck in my limited athletic budget. Organizing intramural sports -- flag football, softball, basketball -- would involve a lot of students in the sports program right away. Inter-collegiate sports we could develop over time.

In those early days, Stockton had a rep as the Berkeley of the East Coast, and attracted all manner of free spirits. The cafeteria was where they mostly hung out: young women in granny dresses, some nursing babies, guys with long hair, with lots of denim and bare feet everywhere. In those final years of the Vietnam War the campus atmosphere was volatile and exciting, and the kids were all wrapped up in it.

I remember the day I went into the cafeteria to make my first pitch to these characters. I stood in the middle of the room and I announced in a dignified voice, "Everyone is invited to softball today at four-thirty."

Nothing. Not one kid looked up. Okay, so they weren't buying dignified. I jumped up on a table and bellowed, "Listen up, people. Anybody wants to play softball, I got a full keg of beer." Now every eye was glued to the weird guy on the table. "Four-thirty at the field. Be there."

Out of my own pocket I bought the keg, figuring, if you buy the beer, they will come. They did, too, by the hundreds, and my intermural program was launched. Eventually we had about thirty flag football teams and about the same in softball. In time we also established three intercollegiate teams for men and three for women.

Of course none of it would have been possible without my fantastic staff. Rick Cheung was my indispensable right arm as head of the intramural program. Nick Werkman, All-American basketball player, coached basketball and showed his boss how it's done.

To coach track I hired Larry James. Larry was a quiet unassuming guy who'd attended VU and had been working at Pace College when I hired him. He won gold and silver medals in the '68 Olympics, and was one of the finest indoor quarter-milers the sport had ever seen.

With people like this on my team, I couldn't miss.

To help keep fit, I worked out with the basketball team in addition to my regular weight-lifting routine, so I was probably in the best shape ever. Fortunately there were people who wouldn't let me get too impressed with myself. One time I was judging the Battle of the Cheerleaders in Atlantic City, and was kind of strutting around. Then I saw my friend Bill Cosby and announcer Tom Brookshire watching me and laughing.

Tom told me that he'd asked Bill how he'd take me in a fight. Bill thought a minute and said. "You see those great big swollen veins in his leg? I'd haul off and kick him good right in his varicose veins. That'd fix him."

That was one of the great things about Cosby. He never let you take yourself too seriously.

I also received tremendous support from Dr. Richard Bjork, Stockton's president, a great administrator. During his tenure, student body activists would call strikes at the drop of a hat. I admired the way he kept the place on an even keel without coming down too hard on youthful enthusiasm. I was a big part of that balance. My job was to help the kids burn off their excess energy before they used it to take over the Dean's office. Nowadays, I use the same technique on my grandkids. When they're all bouncing around the house shrieking, I jump up from my lounge chair, drop the remote, and bellow, "Who wants to go to the park?"

———————

While things were getting started at the college, I took stock of the property we'd bought. It was absolutely beautiful. The cedars weren't quite so tall as in some sections, since they were growing back after two previous harvests. First, they'd been culled by the British for their merchant ships. A couple hundred years later, our side cleared the forest again to stoke our fledgling iron industry: George Washington was hollering for more cannon balls. But now the regrowth was sturdy enough to support a large wildlife population: deer, raccoon, beaver, and fox. If you had quick eyes, you'd see them all over the property.

Years earlier they'd dammed up a stream to flood the area for a cranberry bog. But because of the cranberry-cancer scare in the early sixties, flood controls had never been inaugurated. That left us with a nice lake filled with pickerel and catfish. Osprey and an occasional bald eagle joined the usual waterfowl for the fantastic fishing. I loved to watch them, and decided the place for the Bragg home was just east of the lake, so Theresa and I could watch sunsets across the water. That was where I wanted to live out my life.

There was a lot more land in my parcel than I needed to develop my forested lots, so when a millionaire-environmentalist offered to buy a piece, I gladly closed the deal. I knew he'd respect the land: he just wanted to watch the ducks and swans on the water.

Just before the '72 Olympics, destiny breezed into town in the shape of decathlete Russ Hodge. He'd torn a leg muscle, and wouldn't be competing. However, since he'd already rented a villa outside Munich, he was going to attend as a spectator and invited us to be his guests. Great! What better way for a harried camp and athletic director to recharge his batteries than by attending the Olympics? Despite my distrust of Olympic officialdom, the Games themselves were still the pinnacle of pure athleticism, so far as I was concerned. So when we completed our last session at Kamp Olympik, we headed for Munich.

For a while it was as if we'd turned back the clock. With a little inspired skullduggery, which included my stealing a press pass, Russ, Theresa, and I gained access to the Olympic Village. The only hard part was remembering our cover: the color team for an Italian film crew.

Mixing with the athletes, watching the young lions prepare for their moment of truth, and visiting old friends really brought me back twelve years. On September 5, Russ wanted to stop by the Israeli dorms to say hi to some buddies. I ran into Isaac Berger, a Jewish-American weight lifter with whom I'd briefly toured Israel ten years earlier. Though we didn't take the time to chat right then, we figured we'd get together later at the party the Mosler Safe people always threw during the Games.

On the way home, I was looking out the window, thinking, when Russ said, "Did you hear that?" He turned up the radio and we both heard the devastating news that a group of terrorists had crept into the Village and taken some Israeli athletes hostage from the exact spot Russ and I had just left.

We couldn't believe it. Hard news was impossible to find since all the reports were charged with speculation. We attended the Mosler reception that night, hoping for good news. There wasn't any. We wandered around feeling numb, barely noticing the magnificent ice carvings and lavish trays of hors d'oeuvres. Russ and I finally followed the crowd to the bar for the drink we thought would blot out the feeling of dread. But next morning, nothing could soften the fact that eleven Israeli athletes had been brutally murdered.

Like all those around me, I was a wreck, stunned by grief and disbelief. Then I heard that they were thinking of closing down the Games, and I experienced another emotion: blazing anger.

"No! That means those bastards win!"

Wait a minute. What was wrong with me? Was I so utterly lacking in compassion that only competition mattered?

Then I realized I simply didn't want to betray those murdered athletes. They were Olympians, schooled in the discipline of the ancient Greeks. From the tiniest gymnast to the most powerful shot-putter, every athlete at Munich was first and last a warrior. They'd battled pain, exhaustion, disappointment, and fear to earn a berth on an Olympic team, and they hadn't come to Munich to succumb to terrorism. They could only wrest victory from the hands of a few cowardly fanatics by playing out the Games to their conclusion. Then even the slain would have a victory, for they would have a share in every medal won by their Olympian brothers and sisters.

The Games did continue, bittersweet and perhaps fragile, but triumphant.

Then it was back to business as usual at Stockton College. First thing, Larry James, now my Assistant Athletic Director, said he wanted to take some time off from his coaching duties. The organizers of a newly-formed pro indoor track league had invited him to take part. In his prime as a quarter-miler, sports writers had called Larry the mighty burner with the magnificent fluid stride. But Larry hadn't made the '72 Olympic team. and now his once-flowing strides felt constricted and awkward. He needed a lot of work to make it in this new track league.

"I have a deal for you," I said. "For ninety days, I'll take over your coaching duties, and train you my way. How 'bout it?"

So that's what we did. I'd been working out fairly strenuously with weights, and could bench press 460 pounds. During this time I'd formulated some theories concerning correlating muscular strength to reflexive sports. I'd also picked up a few tips from Russ Hodge about weight training and sprinting.

"The indoor track's a little tricky," I told Larry. "You need more power, so we'll build up strength in your legs. Then we work on controlling your speed. If you run flat out, you'll be airborne on those banked turns."

We worked with weights, relying heavily on squats for the quads and hamstring curls for the back of the legs. I'd seen it so many times, a guy with immensely powerful quads starts running hard and tears a hamstring because he only developed the front part of his leg.

It was also important to cut way down on the distance running, which tends to elongate the calf muscles. When you go up on your toes to sprint, the calf muscles need to bunch up tight. The best way to pull all this together was to run the 220 at varying tempos. In some, we'd go all out in the beginning, or we'd start at a medium pace and pick it up, say, halfway. The point was to let Larry gear down smoothly during a race as part of his overall strategy, then let the afterburners kick in again once he'd passed the killer turns.

"Larry, I said, "if you can average 21.4 seconds in three 220s with only a couple minutes rest in between, you'll be on pace to break the world's record."

Seventy-five days into the program, Larry came to me discouraged, saying his running was labored.

"We've got fifteen days left. Hang in there," I told him.

But even after ninety days, his muscles were still tight. I made the mistake of telling Jumbo Elliot about my training system at a pro track meet. Jumbo laughed and made a point of belittling me in front of the other runners. It was almost as if he couldn't accept the idea that I'd kept growing since I'd left VU. That was a damned painful moment, and when Larry did poorly in his first two races, everybody ridiculed me.

Then Larry began winning, and winning big. In the 600 meters at Pocatello he came in second to Lee Evans, the '72 Olympic Gold medal winner. But both of them were under the world's record. The following year at Salt Lake City, his mark of 53.9 seconds was a new record in the 500 yards. Damn, I was proud of him. Now the very people who'd treated me like a fool crowded around saying, "What was your system again?"

"Sorry, I'm outta time, guys. See ya."

The upshot of all this was that Larry earned a little money in the short-lived International Track Association, and he decided to come in with me on the purchase of 120 wooded acres in the Pines. Land seemed to be the best and safest form of investment. It was close to Atlantic City, and perfect for future development.

My original parcel outside of New Gretna was still larger than my needs, so when a black attorney named Gipson was interested in some lakefront property, I was happy to accept his down payment. My attention at the time was being consumed by a new project: building our dream house.

We decided to set our tri-level with cathedral ceilings forty feet from the lake. After the cabin we didn't want to live in a box, so not having any square rooms would be another priority. An architect smoothed out the details, but the design was mine. Four steps led down into the twelve-sided living room that was the heart of the house. I put in three ten-by-ten-foot windows facing the lake and a hand-laid stone fireplace of about the same size. Outside, a deck wrapped around the living room and the rest of the house, guaranteeing year-round enjoyment of the lake and woods. The first time I sat in my lounge chair and watched the sun slip behind the cedars across the lake, I was a contented man.

But house? It was more like a bee hive, with its non-stop activity. Theresa was in her element. She loved people, and she loved parties, and now she had the perfect house for round-the-clock festivities. The kids had their friends in for basketball, tennis, and swimming parties. Theresa and I entertained people we'd known in Trenton, friends from the college, athletes, government staffers, congressmen, governors, you name it. Ali and Joe Frazier would come by sometimes. Everybody was welcome.

We had people from New Gretna in, too. Our spacious home was the prototype for the houses we'd eventually build on our property, and we wanted to put the locals at ease about our plans. It was kind of funny, though. They came to our house, but never seemed to accept us as part of the community. We won some friends, of course, but with most there was a chilly reserve. We talked to other recent arrivals, and they experienced the same thing. One nasty facet of this attitude was that if newcomers survived the deep freeze for ten years or so, they in turn would snub more recent arrivals, like us. It didn't matter that they themselves still weren't accepted by the old guard, just as long as they got to cold-shoulder somebody else. We had plenty of other friends, so we tried to ignore the small-mindedness.

The level of spite that some people harbored towards us was brought home to me rather painfully when we decided to sell Kamp Olympik. We'd had ten great years with the kids, but both Theresa and I were tired and badly needed a time-out. Moreover, a child had nearly drowned. Because of our fantastic staff and rigorous safety procedures he was saved, but I was haunted by the accident. I was delighted when a retired state policeman wanted to create a camp so licensed motorcyclists could use the innumerable trails in the nearby state forests.

We'd just started talking about a possible sale when everybody was up in arms because Bragg was trying to sell his place to the Hell's Angels. What do you do with people who like to spread that kind of shit around? I wondered what kind of folks were living down here, anyway.

Maybe the kind who'd set fire to a cabin. One of the older buildings we'd been using for storage burned to the ground one night, and we suspected arson. We were grateful nobody was hurt, but the stuff inside was destroyed. That included almost everything from the pole vaulting days: photographs, mementos, press clippings, letters from friends, the works. The only things that didn't go up were the gold medal itself, which I had in the house, and my red metal pole, which was under it. We found some footprints in the mud by the lake, and supposed whoever'd set the fire had come by boat. I told myself the culprit was some kid who didn't know what he was doing. I fervently hoped I was right.

But the prevailing attitude in the town was getting to Mr. Gipson, who'd put a down payment on some of my lakefront property. I'd signed the papers giving him the right to pursue his own subdivision before the city council, but he felt he was being given the run-around.

"It's like dealing with a bunch of crazy hillbillies way back in the Ozarks or someplace," he said with real regret. "They act like I'm after their stills!"

As soon as I had the property back, I took a good look at it. It was a shame Gipson had been forced out by City Hall's bullshit, but his plans for the lakefront weren't half bad. With a few changes I thought I could really make this work. Instead of one-acre lots, I decided to put the houses on two-acre parcels all along the water. If I let the land lie fallow until real estate prices increased, my family and I would be set financially.

Then some real ugliness started to surface. My friends reported that they'd heard I was in cahoots with Muhammad Ali to create an all-black development, with Mr. Gipson playing the go-between. A couple of guys said they'd even been shown a paper that proved it.

"What paper?"

"Just some paper. But the guy said it proved it."

So how do you wrestle with smoke? You don't. You just keep your eyes open and get on with your life. I made the first overtures to the City Council and the Planning Committee applying for a variance: two-acre lots instead of five, with the remainder of each five acres being set aside for environmental and recreational use. Talk about the royal run-around. They kept telling me that new regulations might be coming in place later.

"That's fine, but I'm applying today. So *now* where do I have to take these papers?"

There were rough patches at the college, too. When they'd designed the pool area they included a nice little sauna next door. It was an incredibly popular place. The kids liked to strip off their bathing suits and bake in the intense dry heat. Since it was situated between the men's and women's changing areas, a red light would go on in the men's side if anyone opened the door from the women's area, and the men couldn't use the sauna. If a guy opened the door to the sauna first, the women would see the red light and similarly be barred from the room.

This didn't make sense to me. One guy could keep sixteen women out of the sauna or vice versa, so I issued the logical directive. Everybody wears a bathing suit, and it's first come first served. The kids were comfortable with the solution, and enjoyed the coed socializing without the hassle of red lights. Then a few hippy love-children decided that the bathing suit rule was infringing on their right to be twerps, and paraded into the sauna in the nude. Of course the papers got hold of this, and reported that Bragg was conducting orgies.

I received a call from President Bjork. "About these orgies, Don?" He listened to my side of things and started chuckling. "Just find a way to monitor the situation."

Rick Cheung drew the short straw and took up permanent residence in the sauna. You wouldn't believe the weight the poor guy lost. The nature brigade snuck in now and then, but the novelty of sauna-streaking wore off, and the problem faded away.

Another thing I caught some flack over, but would not eliminate, were my staff meetings at Pitney's Tavern. We'd all have some wine and a good meal, and in a relaxed, friendly atmosphere we'd talk about any problems in the sports program. These convivial lunches were in sharp contrast to the kind of meetings I hated: stiffly formal deliberations that were closer to an inquisition than a meeting of colleagues. If something was going haywire, we'd brainstorm until we came up with a viable solution. During these meetings, the entire staff developed a sense of ownership for the sports program as a whole, which sent morale sky-high. With results like these, I didn't mind paying the tab out of my pocket, despite innuendoes that Bragg made his people hang out in cheap bars.

If there was one virtue I could have used more of as athletic director, it was patience. I never had the ability that, say, Bill Cosby had for listening attentively while people with nothing to say blew themselves out. And people were after him constantly. Guys who'd dated somebody who'd been in his cousin's biology class would strike up conversations with Bill as if he were an old friend.

I remember once at some banquet, Bill came up to me with his plate and a hunted look. "Don, sit down here beside me and pretend to talk to me so I can eat my plate of food." He'd taken about two bites when this guy comes up.

"Hey Cos! I'm a real good friend of your brother, and I thought I should say hello since I'm a real good friend of your brother."

Bill sat there chewing and nodding. "When did you see my brother last?"

"Last week. He looked great."

Down went the fork. "I'm glad to hear that. Where was this?"

"Right here in Philly."

So there's Cosby, eating his coleslaw and nodding while this guy is talking his arm off. Finally the guy moves away.

"Say hello to my brother for me," says Bill, and by this time he was chuckling. He turned to me and said, "My brother's been living in California for the last ten years, but people keep running into him around the old neighborhood."

"Why didn't you call that bozo on his fib?"

"Right in front of everybody? That's no way to do. Pass me the pepper, will you?"

That was the quality I knew I'd never possess.

Don Bragg and Patricia Doherty

Chapter Twenty-Seven

Connections

Viewed from the outside, my life was tumultuous, but I was pretty happy. My family seemed settled and secure, and I had a job I truly loved. In addition, the means for assuring our financial well-being for the future also appeared to be within my grasp. It was time to open another front.

Years before when I'd started traveling overseas, I'd experienced a sense of affinity for certain places, and it was more than mere enjoyment of the local cuisine or scenery. Scandinavia had seemed particularly familiar. I told myself that was because Georgie and I had played Vikings versus Monks when we were kids, though it didn't explain away my sense of homecoming. Anyhow, the Braggs weren't of Viking stock but of Scots-Irish lineage.

Then I experienced the same sense of recognition in the British Isles, especially in Scotland, where I heard many a tale of Viking marauders who'd made their homes in the stony glens. So maybe there *was* a Viking connection in my past.

Now and then I'd sense a bond between me and those old warriors. My mother's people were McCoys, the Irish version of Scotland's MacKay clan, and the MacKays' bravery was legendary. They were the famed gallow glassers, whose battlefield task was to tear into the enemy's line with their fearsome axes. Sometimes I'd be aware of something like waking dreams flashing through my mind, especially scenes of battles. I'd thought that the warrior identity I'd assumed over the years flowed from athletic competition. Now I began to question that.

It wasn't until I saw the Coliseum in Rome that these vague sensations coalesced into a shattering experience. I knew without a doubt that I'd been there once before and that I'd undergone excruciating suffering before dying. It was as if winning at the Games had freed me from centuries of captivity. The gold medal was token and symbol of my salvation.

During that same period, I'd been delving into philosophy and the study of religion, reading, comparing, wondering. I'd ceased to believe in the divinity of Christ, though I could revere him as a great teacher and codifier of belief. It seemed to me that much of Christianity was contained in the writings of Chinese philosophers who antedated Jesus by hundreds of years.

———————

In the intervening years since the Olympics, I'd been caught up in a battle just to keep my family afloat. I'd had little chance for introspection, or for putting all my observations together. But on the unconscious level things were percolating. Then Theresa and I started looking at property in the Pine Barrens of New Jersey. Again, I felt a tremendous connection with the land itself, completely apart from the beauty and peace of the Pines. When Theresa discovered some Bragg headstones in an ancient cemetery, that connection was confirmed, but I needed to know more. I had to find the roots of my warrior identity.

There was an experimental group dealing with regressive hypnosis that met near Stockton College, so I made an appointment with its leader, a professor from Temple University. Several sessions with him left me utterly frustrated, for I never felt hypnotized. He told me my athletic experiences might have established a superficial sense of hypnosis already, though I couldn't see how. One thing was interesting. I described the battle scenes I was aware of, and he said the locale might have been Scotland.

The following day, I had Scotland on the brain, and I asked my secretary to raid the library for books on Scotland, especially those that dealt specifically with battles.

Toward the end of the day, I opened a volume and started reading about the Battle of Culloden. Incredibly, I felt my body stiffen involuntarily as I expelled all the air from my lungs in a harsh grunt. I felt a surge of excitement: this was the door to that other plane of experience of which I'd only had tantalizing glimpses until this moment.

Larry James was in the next room, and I called him in.

"Do me a favor, will you? Watch what happens when I start reading this book." I began to read, experiencing the same jerking reaction of my body. I heard Larry's voice.

"You're going into a trance, man. Hey, cut it out!"

I blinked, clearing my mind, and snapped the book shut. "Tonight after work, I'm going home and experiment."

Larry shook his head. "Don't do this." But he knew me well enough to know my mind was already made up.

That evening I told Theresa my plan. "Stay with me while I try this, and make sure you get the whole thing on tape."

"You really think you can hypnotize yourself when that professor couldn't?" A little skeptical, she carried the tape recorder into the bedroom while I stretched out on our bed and began to read. Almost immediately, I began to stiffen, with my back arching until only the back of my head and my heels were touching the bed.

Then I began to talk about the wind, the bitter wind and rain, and the sleet slashing against the faces of the men. "How can they sustain this exhausting march through the night, then fight at first light?"

I started to perspire profusely, and I felt Theresa tugging on my arm. "Come back, Don. Forget this crazy stuff."

"No, I'm still in control." I couldn't let go now, not when I was so close to understanding.

Then the scene changed. I was hanging upside down, my legs splayed apart and tied at the ankles. My body was covered with wounds, and I was wearing rough fur garments. I was fighting something inexorable, and I recognized my opponent. It was death. Then the fight went out of me, and I knew it was time to embrace what I feared. It was a blissful sensation, close to what I'd felt more than twenty years before in the tree by the dam. Then I'd let go of a slender branch and had dived out of my fear and into courage. But now my desire for release warred with a sense of despair, and not only because I'd failed my clan. I knew for certain that we'd all been betrayed.

My very soul was being consumed, and I felt I was losing my moorings to present reality. I wrenched myself away from that place, and I was lying on our bed again, gasping for breath. My chest was covered with phlegm and the bed was soaked with sweat. Theresa was wiping my face and chest with a cool cloth. Speech was painful, but I managed to say, "Theresa, I was dying."

She took my face between her hands and said, "Never mind about that. If you ever do this again, I'll kill you myself."

Well, I did venture into that fascinating world several more times, but the intensity paled after the first session. Also, I was aware of becoming less the receiver and more the instigator of the scenes that passed through my mind. I really couldn't explain what had happened, but the Battle of Culloden was definitely the trigger.

To this day, I believe my life as a warrior has meaning far beyond the athletic stadium. Will the quest go on? Or have I finally earned peace in some Valhalla where heroes go to receive crowns of undying laurel leaves? Damned if I know.

Afterwards I experienced a connection with feelings that was completely new and somewhat unnerving, and I didn't know how to deal with it. How I ended up coping with it surprised me: I started writing poetry. Words started to pour out of me, and I jotted them down, trying to form them into a disciplined pattern. I didn't know about style or the current trends in the poetry business, but I did know I had to express these thoughts or lose my mind.

When I had accumulated enough verse to fill a slim volume, I approached a publisher, many publishers. Maybe they expected the richly scatological scribbling of a typical jock. But they didn't like my poetry, saying the meter didn't scan properly and even worse, that it rhymed. Damn straight. Poems are supposed to. But okay, I had the bread, so I published them myself. I was eager for affirmation of what I was trying to express. Some people understood what I'd written: most didn't, but I didn't care. I'd done what I had to do.

When I surfaced from my writing, I realized there was definitely something funny going on with the people who were running New Gretna. I'd won my variance, and I'd sunk thousands of dollars into architectural, legal, and engineering fees, to say nothing of things like perk tests for the septic systems. Yet it was taking forever to secure final approval. I was struggling to get the various boards off the dime with regard to my property, but nobody would budge. The stonewalling began to get me agitated, and then it hit me what was going on.

Back then, some people were just realizing that we had to take care of the environment before we ruined it forever. There was a tidal wave of support for anything with an environmental label. So when the Feds talked about targeting the entire Pinelands area as a future National Reserve, people were for it. Privately owned property, like ours, located between the two existing state forests, was painted as a threat to the local ecology.

One particular politician was determined to surf this uninformed environmentalism into higher office. He started running around playing Mother Nature's Favorite Son at the expense of anyone who owned property around New Gretna. According to him all property owners were maniacs who wanted to clear cut the Pines and put up chicken-coop houses on tiny lots. This was crazy, but it sounded logical to people who weren't thinking. A few property owners went to State-sponsored meetings and voiced concerns, but no officials really listened.

The cranberry and blueberry farmers had good lobbyists in Washington, so they made out okay. So did the tough birds down in the south Jersey swamps, where the Feds had proposed severe restrictions on muskratting. Irate farmers roared into the meetings mad as hell, with shotguns handy in their pickups. They'd been muskratting the swamps for generations, and weren't about to pay a fee to trap on their own land. The response from the government was a real treat: the sound of bureaucrats furiously backpedaling.

I figured we wouldn't be sucked under if we banded together, so I approached other area landowners. The answers were uniformly dumb.

"None of this concerns me, I'm just a little guy with seven acres. Anyway, nobody knows we're out here in the sticks."

I really loved what one smallholder said. "I'm against development out in the Pines. I want it unchanged so my son and daughter-in-law can enjoy it too!"

Hell, if you really want to restrict development, keep lot size uniformly at five acres. No developer could make enough money to justify the outlay on infra-structure, and the environment would be safe.

Finally, I made an impassioned plea to the entire Planning Board. We were all for preserving the woodsy character of the Pines: the plans we'd submitted proved that. Dammit, we lived there ourselves, why would we want to foul the nest?

Then Mr. Environment stood up, and the room was a-twitter with sighs from his smitten supporters. The guy had a real way with women, and he used it to get what he wanted. He stood there, waiting for the room to quiet, then whipped out a sheet of paper. He stuck it under my nose. "Do you recognize this paper?" he crooned. Then he glared at me and snarled, "You ought to. You signed it."

"What document is that?" I asked.

He was still waving the paper. "It's your partnership agreement with Mr. Gipson, the developer from Newark. Why don't you admit it?"

"I'm not in partnership with Mr. Gipson. He'd put a down payment on the land, but he pulled out. That paper only gave him the right to apply for a variance, but that was years ago. Where'd you get that, anyway? It has nothing to do with *my* plans for the property."

"But you signed this paper, didn't you?"

It went downhill from there. The guy was determined to sell a lie and his enthralled audience was buying. My project was tabled, and the next thing I knew a moratorium was declared on all building in the Pines.

"It's only for a year, Don," my friends said, trying to calm me down. "Everybody will take a deep breath, then you can go ahead with your project."

Uh huh. But while normal folks marked time during this moratorium, the politicians were cooking up more craziness. The moratorium was lifted, but only lots of at least 49 acres would be sold. Then they decided Pinelands lots could only be used by immediate family members. Hell, if they'd required that all building be done on February 29th in odd-numbered years, it wouldn't have been more outrageous. And this was the kicker: you weren't permitted to trim or cut any tree of more than six inches diameter without special permits. This was on your own property. At the same time, right down the road, New Jersey was selling state forest cedar lumbering rights to the highest bidder. What's wrong with this picture?

I got the message. Eventually I sold everything back to the state for less than I paid for it ten years earlier. By the stroke of a pen they'd wiped out twenty years of my life's work. I still call it confiscation through legislation. Hey, if these people wanted my land, they should have bought it at fair market price.

Then the guy with seven acres, the one who didn't want development in the Pines, came boohooing to me because he couldn't build a house for his son and daughter-in-law.

"Good!" I said. "It serves you right for not getting off your butt when you had a butt to get off of!"

Damn, I was mad. So much for the American Dream. Even when you play by the rules you end up screwed. And smeared. All my life I'd been an outdoorsman, loved nature and wildlife, but especially trees. They were damned near friends, symbolizing both refuge and freedom for me. I cared for the wild environment as much as any person on the planet. But since I failed their self-serving litmus test, so-called environmentalists had stripped me of rights and property and reputation, as if I'd been poised to destroy the land I loved.

For a while I hated nature itself, loathing trees and all four-footed wild things. A few years later we lost the house, too. Sure, I built us another on one of the lots I still had. But a stranger was sitting in my magnificent living room, watching the sun dip behind the cedars as ospreys and eagles skimmed the water for fish.

PART TEN

EBBTIDE

At night, that which moves is still,
Till the still begins to move
through the darkened eyes of night.
It begins to be, to live within its flight,
Till morning brings the dawn.

-- from "Night Moves" by Don Bragg

Chapter Twenty-Eight

Out to Pasture

F eeling personally devastated, I threw myself into my work at Stockton College. I don't know when I'd ever felt lower, not even after the '56 Olympic Trials. The way I handled it was to put on an arrogant exterior, what I like to call my malepause. Hell, I was an Olympic champion, and I'd made a lot of money on my own, right? So I had something coming to me. Drinking helped, and I took refuge in it. My attitude was that I was a big enough deal to take what I wanted in life. If anybody said different, screw 'em!

And that's what I did. Despite my commitment to my family, I started cheating on Theresa. I jeopardized the foundation of everything I cared about, and didn't have the sense to stop.

Then I received what I thought was an oddball confirmation that I was still Somebody. *Sports Illustrated* called wanting to do a story about me.

Whoa! Twenty years after my triumph at Rome, there was still some interest in what Don Bragg was up to. That was pretty gratifying. My good friend Dr. Bjork had retired as college president, but his successor, Peter Mitchell, was all for the article. Unbeknownst to me, he began telling Board members that *SI* would be doing a humongous spread on Stockton State College, and wasn't it fabulous, as if he'd had a hand in engineering the article. Why in hell would *Sports Illustrated* want to write up Stockton State over any of the hundreds of other small state colleges? In fewer than ten years we'd developed a well-established intramural program and a fledgling intercollegiate program, but that wasn't *SI*'s beat. This was to be a where-are-they-now kind of article, and where I was happened to be Stockton State College.

SI sent down a writer named Doug Looney, and like a fool I started talking.

The whole thing was my own fault, really. I didn't do my homework on the guy. If I had, I'd have known that he specialized in neat character assassinations, and one of his latest targets had been Bobby Knight of

Indiana. But I hadn't a clue when Looney Tunes came by my office. We talked about everything, what I'd been up to since Rome; the program I'd build up at the college; he even read my poetry. He appeared interested, but kind of passive. The one thing I didn't want to come out of the interview was a boring article, about some poor gold medalist now consigned to refereeing volleyball games. So I decided to pull out all the stops.

A shot similar to the 1980 *Sports Illustrated* photo, but enhanced with maturity and sophistication. 2002.

In between giving him the facts he was after, I rode the scooter and blew smoke at the camera, said outrageous things. When Looney's photographer said he had one shot left on the roll of film, I made a silly face and shoved my cigar up my nose. Why the hell not? I'd honed my PR teeth in Hollywood, after all, and I thought I knew what the ground rules were. I even let my hair down about the raw deal in the Pinelands. I welcomed controversy. And while I didn't expect my every utterance to be quoted, I did expect a professional writer to present a balanced picture of what I had in fact said.

Then the article came out.

It wasn't that Looney completely ignored what I'd said. Hell, he pounced on some of my ideas. Then he yanked them out of context, without making reference to any of the moderating or thoughtful things I'd had to say. If he'd told the whole story, I could have lived with that.

But after selectively twisting my words, he couched them in a barrage of slanted sarcasm, or took them completely out of context. For example, Looney quoted the first line from one of my poems, "All women I do despise," but neglects to mention the poem ends with idea that I prefer the company of some women, though friendship with them is difficult for me.

The person the article absolutely devastated was Theresa. She'd welcomed Looney into our home, fed him our food, trusted him, and the guy'd stabbed us both in the back.

There was no point in beating a dead, ugly horse, however, so I tried to shrug off the article. Since I received a lot of fan mail congratulating me on still enjoying life, I thought the article thing was yesterday's news.

Then I heard from the Stockton Board of Trustees. They'd been expecting an article extolling the college, not one showing Stockton's Athletic Director in the worst possible light. I suspect that, to save face, President Mitchell convinced himself and the Board that I'd hijacked the article that rightfully belonged to Stockton College. I was informed that my contract would not be renewed. So ten years of progress toward tenure were down the drain.

With one stroke of the pen.

From that point I was like a man teetering on a cliff, scrabbling for any hold. I bought a tavern in Margate that didn't fly. The environmental land-grab even engulfed the land Larry James and I had bought. Perhaps foolishly, I let everybody out of their contract and took the loss myself. But I couldn't kid myself into thinking it didn't matter. My life was pretty well shot.

Theresa came to the rescue. She got a job with one of the casinos and kept us going financially. For a long while I stopped even trying. If we lived off our modest savings, so what?

If depression is a sense of utter loss, of sinking so far down that nothing good can reach you, then I was depressed. When I thought of Theresa and the kids, I was overwhelmed with the feeling that they'd be better off without me: the loser. I obsessed on what might have been, second-guessing myself. Twenty years off the Olympic medal platform, and what had I accomplished? Nothing.

Sometimes, when I'd start grinding at fate, I'd get angry. Then I'd drink. I always hoped the booze would lift me out of the pit, but it never worked well enough or long enough. Drunk or sober, the realization of the depths of my failure clung to me. I'd done real well for an Olympic champion. Oh, I forgot. Ex-Olympic champion.

I was driving home from Atlantic City one night, late. The rain was coming down hard, big slanting drops getting cut off by the wiper blades, splashing, misting up the window so you could hardly see. I felt like hell. When I'd dealt with failure before -- and I had, plenty -- there'd always been someplace to find a foothold. Not this time. I'd even turned away from my wife for a few months of sexual distraction. That had been an empty dead end, but it had been my choice. Now I was at the end of a noose, kicking at nothing, all my options choked off.

The wet road was a ghostly ribbon heading toward the Mullica River Bridge that I used to jump off, horsing around with the guys from the college. If I turned the wheel, just a little on this straightaway, the car would go through the inadequate railing and headfirst into the water. That would be the end of failure. That's how a real warrior would end this mess, regardless of what the faint-hearted say.

But what if I wasn't enough of a warrior to end it? Purely out of habit, I might fight just hard enough to squirm out of the car and make it to the river bank.

With my luck that's just what I'd do.

I'd lie there all night, unable to call for help, with blue crabs crawling up my pants, biting my feet and legs and whatever else was hanging around. The rats would be by later on, just to piss on my head. Then I'd be home, all paralyzed and drooling in my wheelchair, and my lovely Theresa would come in with a bunch of her friends. She'd say, "We're going to lunch now, Hon, and Nannie's in the next room. You'll be all right, won't you?" And I'd kind of grunt back at her and she'd kiss me on the cheek, blissfully unaware that I was trying to yell, "All right, my ass!"

That little fantasy didn't snap me out of my pity party, but it put an end to the suicide crapola. I drove straight down the road, home to my family. This was my safe haven, and I knew it.

As if in confirmation of this basic truth, my grandkids had the good sense to start showing up about then, a timely kick in the pants about priorities. The weird thing was that with every new grandchild, it was like I sprouted another heart, open to incredible joy and laughter, but also unimaginably vulnerable. If they were sick or hurt -- man! It really got to me.

This was something I hadn't expected. I sort of believed that I'd reach a comfortable plateau when I'd completed my life's work, a place of plenty and peace. But life doesn't stop, so new joys and frustrations show up every day. Problem is, being older makes it all harder to cope with.

About 1991 I started a kayak rental business, which was the best thing in the world for me. It got me up off my butt and ratified the peace I'd finally made with Mother Nature. It was real therapy to be out in the woods, in touch with the wild environment again. But I was also in touch with a few ticks, and shortly came down with Lyme disease. The early, achy symptoms are kind of like the flu, and I just ignored them. But when the joints became so painful that I could hardly move, I took my butt into the doctor's office. They crapped around with oral antibiotics for years, but the symptoms persisted.

Nevertheless, some good things were happening in my life. At the National Drug-Free Weight-Lifting Association, I bench-pressed 402 pounds, not bad for a sixty-year-old geezer. For the sake of my grandkids, I agreed to be one of the Olympic torch bearers, as the fire from Mt. Olympus wended its way toward Atlanta. I also received the honor of being inducted into the National Track and Field Hall of Fame, and both Theresa and I enjoyed visiting San Francisco again. An added bonus was that we both had a chance to visit Renée who lived just outside of San Francisco. We were shocked to discover that she was having serious health problems. My wife and I had always loved California, so Theresa said, "Let's see if I can't find a job so we can stay out here near Renée." And damned if she didn't, as catering and sales director of a country club.

We moved to the West Coast in 1997, and I flew back for the summer kayaking season. The Lyme disease had never let up, so I went to a new doctor in New Jersey who got aggressive with the problem. He shoved a PICC line up my arm and into my chest to flood me with an anti-parasitic, antibiotic brew, knocking out the spirochetes and their fellow travelers that were raising hell with me.

My relief at putting the Lyme disease behind me was eclipsed when I underwent a sextuple by-pass. People ask me, "What brought on the surgery, Don?"

"I'd say mainly the two heart attacks."

What they did was to pry me open like an oyster so they could fit the roto-rooter in, and it still hurts like hell sometimes. Yeah, and there's the arthritis, the effects of the spinal repair, the gout, the Lyme disease, and the carpal tunnel surgery. Damn, some days I think I should hire a flunkie to follow me around and pick up any bits that happen to fall off.

That's something I'd warn you athletes about. Every hit you take, you pay for later. Not that you should shun the physicality of your sport, but just know what the price may well be, and be ready for it. Don't be all surprised when some sports-related disability hits. Don't let it blindside you.

Have another string on the bow and be sure you have a way to support yourself financially. They tell you that if you keep your nose to the grindstone, all good things will come to you. In reality, the joy of competition, the pride in a job well done, and whatever accolades you receive along the way are the only rewards an amateur athlete can count on, even after years of hard work and dedication. So be ready for it. Looking back over my life, my childhood and all, I can't help thinking, "Wow! I did all that? Then why aren't I happier than I am?" Maybe I just expected ending up with my own field of clover like a retired race horse, or some such thing.

And the last word to the wise? Beware of your emotions. If you don't keep them in strict control, they'll control you, and you won't make it. Hell, you can't go from home up to the supermarket without seeing a dozen gut-wrenching things, let alone reading about the horrors in Somalia or Chechnya. Left unchecked, emotions can wreck you.

Just be sure you're a survivor, like me. Maybe I'm not in the best shape right now, but I'm working on it. I work out at the gym right on schedule -- everything gets shot to hell if I don't. It's still my religion. Since the carpal tunnel thing, I have to wrap my wrists up tight, but I've been lifting weights, real light, only five or ten pounds. Hell, my arms were down to about fifteen inches, and my ego needs my arms, like Thor or Samson. Or Tarzan. I've pumped 'em back to twenty inches, so that's working well.

At least a dozen times a year I still have my flying dream, and it's still great. There's also a crazy fantasy that's stayed with me. It's that they've finally created a fiberglass pole that can hold me and give me the phenomenal height that metal poles never could. Then I could go back in and jump again. Wouldn't it be great, as big and heavy and old as I am, if I could go into a meet and jump something fairly good? Damn, that would be fun!

With the grandkids I keep pretty busy, but I still love ideas and learning, and make time to immerse myself in ancient history. Oddly enough, I don't watch as much sports on TV these days. I'll watch the Olympics, of course, but the Games have changed so much. They've become a streamer-waving, bridge-playing culture fest. Bridge! I still don't believe it, and neither would the founding Greeks. To me the true spirit of the Olympics is embodied in the motto of the Games: "*Citius, altius, fortius.*" Faster, higher, stronger, the cry of the warrior-athlete. Nowadays the Games seem to want to make everybody feel special. That's crazy. Add the kick-backs and the shameless politics of some of the administrators and judges, and there's the reason that the Olympics have become more of an exhibition than a competition. The Games are a lot like the Super Bowl. You have to cut through so much crap just to see the athletes perform.

There's a practical problem, too. Of necessity there are an enormous number of trials and heats to accommodate the number of competitors. By the time an athlete reaches the upper level of competition, fatigue may have set in. Even the winners won't do their best, so Olympic records tend to be overshadowed by world records made under more favorable conditions. At least that's this curmudgeon's view.

Sometimes I like to go to a bar and rustle up some good conversation along with the Captain Morgan's rum. Maybe I drink too much, and if anybody ever punches me in the nose, I'll probably deserve it. But at least I'm not some recluse sitting home in his closet, polishing a forty-year-old medal. So maybe this Olympic champion is a little worse for the wear, but he ain't yelling "Uncle" yet.

Back in '82 I went to my thirtieth high school reunion, and I went running up to kids I'd played with at the gravel pit, shouting, "Sara Bootie, how the hell are you?"

And I'd hear, "Why, hello, Don. It's wonderful to see you again. I hope Theresa's well?"

They'd turned into a bunch of conformists. One guy I know for a fact barely made it out of high school, and he's parading around with a pair of glasses hanging on his chest, looking down his nose like some Oxford don. I felt a Tarzan yell coming on until I spotted Billy Brockenbaugh, Ray Minor, and the other black guys. I sat down at their table and started in talking to them, and it was like old times. Billy just shook his head, and said, "Don, you crazy man, you haven't changed one bit." I took that as a compliment, since running against the grain is what I do best.

But I'm not alone, since I have a lifetime of friends for company, especially Charlie Jenkins, my great friend from Villanova; and Josh Culbreath, who's like a brother to me. I'm still in touch with Larry James, Bob Richards, Steve Smith – fiberglass vaulter and skateboarding friend -- and countless others. Then there are the great competitors that pushed me to my limit, and ultimately to my medal, people like Bob Gutowski and Ronnie Morris.

Bob Richards is still the King of Competitors, so far as I'm concerned. Theresa and I visited him and his wife at his Texas ranch a few years ago. Our first evening there we enjoyed an extended wine tasting and didn't get to bed until 3:00 AM. At six o'clock in the morning I was catapulted out of bed by the sound of a bulldozer. I lurched out to tell whoever it was to knock it off, and discovered the maniac to be Bob himself.

"Don! Glad you're up. I could use some help with the swimming pool. Can you bring me the mortar while I lay the blocks?"

"No breakfast?" I asked tremulously.

He glanced at his watch. "Well, I've already put in a couple of good hours, so I guess it's okay to take a break."

Next to this guy, I'm disgustingly normal.

We talk on the phone now and again, arguing over who jumped the highest. Bob still maintains that he's the best, and can beat all comers. The fact that we're still talking like kids playing King of the Hill cracks me up. His knees are gone, and I've got more patches than a ten-year-old inner tube. But Bob's already planning a tournament for after we're dead.

"On the other side, Don. You and me, *mano a mano*." Unlike MacArthur's old soldier, Bob has no plans to fade away, even though, for us, the sun has already set. Bob Richards simply will not accept the darkness.

———————

And I'd have to include Bill Cosby in the cast of outstanding characters I've met. The tenacity and stamina that fueled his athletic career helped propel him to the top of the entertainment world. But he's remained a down-to-earth guy with his hilarious take on the everyday stuff most of us blow off.

When I was inducted into the Penn Relays' Wall of Fame in 1998 I knew I'd be seeing Bill, since the Relays are so close to his heart. Without his generous support, they'd probably have long since closed down.

He hadn't arrived for the Friday night banquet, and during my speech, I took the opportunity to razz him a little about his high jumping record of only 6'5".

"Six foot five he jumped. Not bad for a TV star. Not good for an athlete, but not bad for a TV star."

I knew word of my heresy would get back to Bill the next day at the stadium: all I had to do was wait.

Next day I'm heading for the famous Wall of Fame for pictures with my son and grandson, and here's Josh and Bill Cosby waving me over. Josh was cracking up, but Bill was sitting up on the awards dais looking like a dejected basset hound. He gave me this reproachful look and said, "You've been telling stories on me. You come up here with me, Tarzan, and let the real King of the Jungle tell you how it is." He closed his eyes, like he was meditating, and I'm already laughing. He gave me a stern look. "There you go, embarrassing yourself again. Now for a little truth in certain matters. If I weren't such an honest man, the record would show me jumping six-ten."

"The comedian is making a joke," I answered.

A tight little grin, quickly controlled, broke through Bill's deadpan expression. "Hush up now and listen. At that meet in Baltimore, the biggest deal -- no, it was *not* the pole vault -- was seeing who'd win the mile. The official down at our pit was watching the race start when I was going for 6'10", after clearing 6'8". So he didn't see my leg give out or me sliding under the bar into the pit. Then he decided to pay attention again, and there I was in the pit with the bar up on the standards.

"'Cosby, good at 6'10",' this guy says. 'Next jumper.'"

Bill got this rippling little smirk on his face and began wobbling his head back and forth. "Being the gentleman that I am," he said, silencing our laughter with another stony glare, "and with some persuasion from the other jumpers, I approached the official and revealed what had happened. He congratulated me on my honesty, at which point, for some reason, the other jumpers were rolling around on the floor laughing. I got the biggest laugh of my life without telling one joke." He looked around at us with a self-satisfied grin. "And now that I've set you straight, I'm sure you will refrain from maligning me in the future."

That's Cos: a little riff on nothing at all that has you in stitches. No one's ever done it better.

Jack LaLanne is another one who's cut from that same bolt of cloth. He's a guy that puts his all into every second of life.

One time I was meeting Jack for a swim at Muscle Beach, and ran into his daughter up on the boardwalk, where she was scarfing a hamburger. You'd think I'd caught her downing LSD with a heroin chaser. "Please don't tell Dad about this," she begged. "He'd have a cow."

When I reached the beach, Jack was ready for our swim, and mortified me beyond belief by putting on a bathing cap. I joined him in the water and started to surf. Jack looked at me with disapproval. "I thought you came here to *swim*." He shrugged his shoulders, and swam off in the direction of Hawaii. Nearly an hour later the sun was going down, and no Jack. I was about to alert the Coast Guard to start dragging the bottom, when here he comes, swimming out of the sunset, not even breathing hard.

Before we all had dinner, I mentioned enjoying pre-dinner cocktails. Wrong thing to say. Despite my argument that God put those busy little enzymes in the wine for the sole purpose of helping us digest our food, Jack delivered a sermon on the evils of alcohol till my eyes crossed.

After dinner, he sang "I Believe," while his wife Elaine gave him vocal coaching. By the second verse he was in great voice, and proved it by doing a handstand on the arms of a chair for the remainder of the song, never missing a note. Maybe he's Bob Richard's long-lost twin brother.

Then there's Johnny Weissmuller, my idol who became my friend. He was the greatest Tarzan the movies ever had, yet he treated me, his possible replacement, with unfailing generosity. Early in our friendship Johnny did his Tarzan yell at some function or other, and somebody commented that my yell was better. Johnny cocked an eyebrow at me and grinned wickedly. "Wait a few years, after a few drinks and a few pounds around the middle. Then let's see how this kid stacks up against the old master."

Was he the old master? On one of the *Tarzan* sets, the chimp playing Cheetah had only one passion in life: biting people. The cast and crew were terrified of the animal, but he left Johnny strictly alone. I asked him about this. Did the King of the Jungle work some magic on the wayward chimp?

"Oh, the chimp bit me, all right. Once."

"And?" I asked, ready to take notes.

Johnny did that wonderful big grin of his. "Hell, I just bit him back. He was a pussycat after that."

Nobody will ever fill Johnny's shoes.

But the best of the best has to be Muhammad Ali. He was the consummate boxer: an invincible fighting machine who would gentle his strength to make a struggling child feel like a hero. That was the Ali I knew and loved. Theresa and I watched in tears when he stepped from the shadows to take the torch during the Atlanta Olympic Games. Finally he was receiving the acclaim he so richly deserved. God bless that gentle warrior.

But even with all these, where would I have been without my family? Although every ship needs but one captain, it must also have a keel to keep it from capsizing: thus Theresa. She's been my partner and companion for nearly forty years. Her courage, patience, and forgiveness still keep me going. Our children are working out their own lives in their own way, but they know we're here for them.

Don, Ali, and LeRoy Niemans at the artist's exhibit in an Atlantic City casino
in 1996.

Now about those grandkids. There's Janelle, fleet-footed but struggling to find herself at seventeen. I see a lot of myself in the two oldest boys. Nick is strong-willed and shy, while Sean, an excellent athlete, bemoans his slender build: exactly my physique at that age. To my delight, Lindsay's announced that maybe she wants to be a pole vaulter, and Lauren is the one who sees the humor in life. Whenever we get together, we laugh for hours. Effervescent Kendra is already confident. Nicole is the precocious one, always testing, questioning everything. Jeffrey, completely at home in his own fantasy world, is Batman this month. I think he plans to be a Power Ranger when he grows up. Zachary? He constantly drowns out the TV with the whooshing sounds he makes playing Superman. Usually he's locked in mortal combat with his Power Ranger cousin, Paul Thomas, a year older. Then there's Remy. Even at only one year old, she' was already displaying her dad's innate sense of balance. She'll be on skis before long.

Watching them, with all their abilities and potential, it's easy to see that my torch has been passed. But I take my grandfathering very seriously. I scrutinize them like a papa eagle, vigilant for anything that could hurt their chances to excel at their life choices. If I spot something, down I come like a load of bricks. Since nobody's poisoned me yet, I must be doing okay. In fact, looking at my life through the prism of family, I'd have to say it's been a fantastic success.

———————

So here I am sitting in our living room on this drowsy late summer afternoon with the sun dropping above the treetops, flickering against the curtains. My mind's not even in gear, and bang, I'm thinking about all the scrappy little kids bragging about how they can beat up anybody on their block. And about the one youngster in a zillion that boosts the bragging onto another psychological plane, the one that makes it a dream. When I say dream, I'm referring to that willful yearning that permits him to transfer himself from the reality of his existence into the playground of his very being. The longer he stays there the more it affects him, spiritually, physically, giving the dream a chance of becoming reality. And I remember the kid who bragged that he could whup anybody who climbed into the ring with him, until he started becoming the dream, started becoming the greatest: Muhammed Ali. And I think that's what happened to me in my own life, to a lesser degree. The dream that took hold of me at those Saturday afternoon matinees dragged me, drove me, until I became the Lord of the High Flyers.

The Bragg clan at a 2001 family outing in California with rope swings for future Tarzans.

And now that a movie studio is contemplating a film called *Son of Tarzan*, I'm the leading candidate to play Tarzan the Patriarch: my final opportunity to realize my boyhood dream. They're even planning to shoot it in Jamaica – talk about the icing on the banana!

So I've got work to do. Gotta cut out the booze and get rid of this pouch of mine that could only look good on a kangaroo. I need to get my mind limbered up so I can memorize all those lines. I'm primed for one last hurrah, to finally connect as the King of the Jungle, even though the vociferous chattering of the monkeys tells me the sun's getting low in the sky.

Low in the sky? Snap out of it, Don. The sun's just about gone, and you're still carrying on about Jamaica and one more chance to play the King of the Jungle. You're running away from reality.

Or am I? The long rays of the setting sun dance on the curtains and set something glimmering across the room -- a golden medal hanging on the wall. That's no illusion, it's both my dream and my reality. Hell, I'm still a pole vaulter at heart. Even now, if I were to hear a distant trumpet calling me to battle, I'd be ready.

And why not? If the wind's at my back and there's a clear road ahead, I'll know I've been given another chance to dare.